THE END OF ART

THE END OF ART

Readings in a Rumor after Hegel

Eva Geulen

Translated by James McFarland

STANFORD UNIVERSITY PRESS

STANFORD, CALIFORNIA 2006

Stanford University Press
Stanford, California

The End of Art was published in German in 2002 under the title Das Ende der Kunst: Lesarten eines Gerüchts nach Hegel © 2002, © Suhrkamp Verlag Frankfurt am Main.

Printed in the United States of America on acid-free, archival-quality paper

Library of Congress Cataloging-in-Publication Data

Geulen, Eva.
    [Ende der Kunst. English]
    The end of art : readings in a rumor after Hegel / Eva Geulen ; translated by James McFarland.
        p.   cm.
    Includes bibliographical references and index.
    ISBN-10: 0-8047-4423-8 (cloth : alk. paper)
    ISBN-10: 0-8047-4424-6 (pbk. : alk. paper)
    ISBN-13: 978-0-8047-4423-2 (cloth : alk. paper)
    ISBN-13: 978-0-8047-4424-9 (pbk. : alk. paper)
    1. Aesthetics—Philosophy.   2. Art—Philosophy.   I. Title.   II. Series.

BH39.G4913 2006
111'.85--dc22

                                                            2006006598

Contents

Acknowledgments

Part of Chapter 4 (the sections on Benjamin's artwork essay) has appeared in an English translation by Eric Baker in the volume *Benjamin's Ghosts: Interventions in Contemporary Cultural and Literary Theory*, edited by Gerhard Richter (Stanford University Press, 2005); and part of it also appeared in German in *MLN*. An earlier, much shorter version of Chapter 5 appeared under the title of "Reconstructing Adorno's 'End of Art'" in *New German Critique*, special issue on the *Dialectic of Enlightenment*, 81 (Fall 2000): 153–68.

THE END OF ART

CHAPTER I

The End in the Meantime

I invented in it all, in the hope it would console me, help me to go on, allow me to think of myself as somewhere on a road, moving, between a beginning and an end, gaining ground, losing ground, getting lost, but somehow in the long run making headway. All lies.

—S. BECKETT

I

The end of art is a rumor. As long as one speaks of an end, the relation of speech to its object remains untimely; speech is either precipitous or belated. In this respect, the end of art is fated to self-contradiction in the manner of similar claims regarding, for example, the end of nature, the world, metaphysics, or history. For either the end has already occurred or it is still to come. In the meantime, which the end displaces either forward or backward, the notorious talk of the end circulates: "Come, let's talk together, who talks is not dead."[1] Although untimely, the end of art is always up to the moment, for at every point it can be near or can already have taken place. Whatever else the end of art may be, it is also always presumption. That the end of art, whether fortunately or regrettably, has so far always turned out to be a matter of speech and rhetoric, a topos in any case, and perhaps even a discourse, does not mitigate its urgency in any given scenario.

Few topoi have enjoyed such lasting life. Beginning with the "Querelle des Anciens et des Modernes" at the end of the seventeenth century, the end of art no longer refers to the end of *one* particular artistic practice or epoch, but in an ever more radical way, with ever more finality, so to speak, it signifies an end of art as such. Consequently, it became entangled ever more thoroughly in its contradictions and exposed ever more pressingly to the growing arbitrariness of its different meanings.[2] Whether art ends in its philosophical reflection or as a political program, culminates in the spectacular *Gesamtkunstwerk*, or is memorialized in a melancholy recollection of past artistic periods, whether art is said to dissolve into everyday life, the total state, or the media age, the details of its passing mean little in comparison with the constancy and omnipresence of this figure of thought. The growing devaluation of the end's potential meanings between the extremes of teleological fulfillment on the one hand and sheer mortality on the other appears as the quasi-autonomous dynamic of the end of art. This devaluation and neutralization of the different meanings of an end of art has unfolded, accelerated, and radicalized over the course of the last two hundred years. In the time that has passed since Hegel gave the topos its definitive philosophical shape with his "thesis on the end of art," its frequent actualizations—pathetic and melancholy, reactionary and revolutionary, philosophical and aesthetic—suggest that whatever art has been until now is inconceivable without talk of the end of art. The end of art—a founding myth of art, a privileged self-description of the art system.[3]

Certainly, one cannot reproach modern self-understanding for having ignored this dilemma, of having naively proclaimed again and again a new end. Quite the contrary—the aporias of deploying this particular topos have long been known. What Marx said of the dilemma of revolution also holds for art and its revolutions under the rubric of an end: "And just when they seem engaged in revolutionizing themselves and things, in creating something that has never yet existed, precisely in such periods of revolutionary crisis they anxiously conjure up the spirits of the past to their service and borrow from them names, battle-cries, and costumes in order to present the new scene of world history in this time-honored disguise and this borrowed language."[4] The dysfunctional logic of the drama of the end of art—that we, as Bruno Latour[5] put it, have not yet become modern and certainly fail the test of modernity when we invoke the end of art—this was already old news for many members of the avant-garde that fought for an end of art. "This modernity, that behaves so rebelliously, at bottom works in a reactionary way, and is the late heir of idealism," Carl

Einstein wrote.[6] Perhaps the most convincing expression of this paradoxical understanding of the multiplicity of an end that must lay claim to essential singularity can be found in the fact that Marcel Duchamp, whose readymades brought the imbrication of the modern logic of innovation and the end of art to its extreme, later produced sample boxes with miniature reproductions of them.[7]

In the theoretical realm, the most pointed attempt to determine the function of the end of art on behalf of the survival of modernity is found in Paul de Man. The "temptation to move outside art"[8] results from the recognition that the self-securing of all modernity has become structurally aporetic. "When they assert their own modernity, they are bound to discover their dependence on similar assertions made by their literary predecessors, their claim to being a new beginning turns out to be the repetition of a claim that has always already been made."[9] The end of art as an escape strategy and core concept of modernity thrives on the very contradictions in which it is caught: "The continuous appeal of modernity, the desire to break out of literature toward the reality of the moment, prevails, and in its turn, folding back upon itself, engenders the repetition and continuation of literature. Thus modernity, which is fundamentally a falling away from literature and a rejection of history, also acts as the principle that gives literature duration and historical existence."[10]

In the more recent time of our day and age, however, obsessive recourse to an ever new end of art has brought this figure of thought to a peculiar sort of end in sheer exhaustion. With the banalization and trivialization of this figure, one of the most successful crisis discourses of modernity is itself threatened with crisis. The end of art has become such a cliché that even to raise the question seems superficial. As the 1960s repeated the avant-garde, Octavio Paz could understand the deficient originality of the movement yet again as the end of the idea of modern art.[11] Nowadays it is de rigeur to debunk the end of art as a white elephant of modernity.[12] From the lonely heights of philosophical speculation in Hegel, the end of art has meandered into the swampy lowlands of platitude. The rumor has turned into mere gossip. An example from this sphere can demonstrate why this is so, and why even this exhaustion does not amount to the end of the end of art.

Asked by *Der Spiegel* on the occasion of Documenta X to comment on the state of contemporary art, the French philosopher Jean Baudrillard failed to resist the temptation to speculate on the end of art in the age of digital media: "A collaboration began between the real world and the world of art. Through simulation the whole banality of the world has been carried into art."[13] The historical avant-garde's utopian goal of suspending the distinction between art and life[14] has been technically realized at the end of the twentieth century, and thereby profaned. The heroic topos itself, however, survives, as Baudrillard deploys it once more, despite the fact that the emergence of a media age—to the extent that it really is unprecedented—is at odds with the time-honored motif. The end of art proves to be immune to the banal indifference that has rendered meaningless all differences between art and other realities. According to Baudrillard, everything has succumbed to banality, total simulation has annihilated the boundaries between all differences and levels, the mystery and adventure of art have been disenchanted by mediation, but the end of art still has not lost its authenticity. Banalization does not threaten the topos but is currently the dominant way to actualize end of art.[15]

Diagnosing the figure of thought as suffering from triviality does not escape the discursive orbit of the end of art. The lament that art has come to an end because its choices have been rendered arbitrary dates back to Hegel, who claimed in his *Aesthetics: Lectures on Fine Art* that art had now become "a free instrument," and that nothing "stands in and for itself above this relativity"[16] any longer. What Baudrillard calls simulation, Hegel termed "dramatization."[17] Despite his appeal to the "new holy of holies," *Humanism*,[18] there can be no doubt about the essential vacancy and the merely dramaturgically staged effects of all postromantic artistic projects: "Therefore the artist's attitude to his topic is on the whole much the same as the dramatist's who brings on the scene and delineates different characters who are strangers to him."[19] In contradistinction to Hegel, who asserted firmly that "no Dante, Ariostro, or Shakespeare can appear in our day,"[20] Baudrillard believes he can still squeeze some dialectical surplus value from the end. At the close of his interview, he manages to get from the absolute end of art to the rebirth of the adventure of art out of the spirit of total technology: "Perhaps a product of pure simulation might manage to become a seduction, a confrontation with the other, an illusion."[21] Once more, the end of art is returned to a dialectical harness that requires the foundation, defense, or modification of just the sphere of autonomous art that appeared in Baumgarten's *Aesthetics* and the "Querelle"—and which has always returned modernity, in its desire to rebut Hegel's conclusion, to the topos of the end of art.[22] But the critical reduction of and engagement with idealistic aesthetics—as long as it is formulated in terms of the end of art, and so far no other formula has been found—validates this tradition to the very degree that it insists upon its end.

For this reason, the question of the end of art must necessarily involve the question of the end of the particular aesthetics that has left us with the end of art. That is the aesthetics of Hegel, whose famous end of art repealed modernity before it had even begun, thus *simultaneously* ensuring that the end of art would have to be repeatedly invoked. Today's common antiaesthetic affect remains a discourse in and of the end of art, which cannot evade the suspicion of dialectics and must always face the question of whether the new foundation of a transaesthetic concept of art remains to the extent that it involves the end of art, a mere variation of Hegelian aesthetics.

Endeavors to found a new concept of art beyond the premises of the idealist-aesthetic tradition are legion.[23] The antiaesthetic impulse that drives them constitutes a rare consensus of recent theory in the wake of de Man, Derrida, and others. Among the most subtle of these postaesthetic art theories are those that seek to shake off the Hegelian specter of the end by emphasizing the formlessness of the end, for instance by radically temporalizing the end. The dictum Hegel arrogantly decreed can be played off against the unending end presumably operative in works of art. As Baudrillard puts it with significant pathos: "Literature sets off for itself, for its most individual essence, which consists in its disappearance."[24] In another vein, the end of art is interpreted antiaesthetically, as interruption or rupture.[25] Perhaps the fascinated rediscovery of the sublime following Lyotard in the 1980s can be understood as the effort to locate an antiaesthetic moment deep within the aesthetic tradition. With the limit category of the sublime, the end reveals itself as a specifically antiaesthetic counterlogic of art.[26] In the context of such strategies, the end of art tends to be called a "departure."[27]

With polemical brevity, one could call these attempts to radicalize the end. They are preferable to the finalizations, the attempts to issue an end to the end of art.[28] But even radicalizations that try to trump Hegel's dictum remain in the double bind of merely repeating the (Hegelian) end of art in the very gesture of wanting to gain a foothold outside the aesthetic tradition.[29] One could argue that radicalizations also only take up possibilities that Hegel's end of art had made available; what appears to be a radical development is, to a certain extent, always only a movement of return and reenactment. In this sense, Rodolphe Gasché writes: "Rather than radically breaking with aesthetics, might all the (evidently necessary) attempts to reach beyond traditional aesthetics be elaborations of limit-possibilities that open up within the traditional discipline itself?" And he adds, "art speaks of itself in the aftermath of Hegel's own categorization of the forms of art after art, in ways that remain more often than not tributary to these categorizations."[30] One of these categories, and perhaps the central one, is the end of art.

In the meantime, however, an alternative to all those attempts to escape the trap of aesthetics by radicalizing its end of art seems to be taking shape. A programmatic rehabilitation of aesthetics and even of the beautiful seems imminent: art instead of the end. Should this countertendency to radicalization actually establish itself, then this late inversion would lend ironic evidence to the thesis that aesthetics and antiaesthetics remain interdependent. At the end of the end of art, at the end of its radicalization, the fine arts appear once again.[31] It is not the purpose of this study to demonstrate or defend this potential rehabilitation of aesthetics. Rather, on this side of the radicalization of the end of art on the one hand and the rehabilitation of artistic beauty and aesthetics on the other, we are concerned with the reconstruction of certain decisive stations in this figure of thought after Hegel, in the meantime and in a preliminary way.

It is thus not a matter of the end of art as an end among others, but of the end of art since Hegel, in a multifarious but specific enough sense that further references to the enormous mass of reflections on the end in modernity are hardly necessary. We are not concerned with a typology of ends,[32] or with the end as an anthropological constant of significance.[33] Not the end of art as a function of secularization or a vestige of apocalyptic tradition; not the actualization, radicalization, or finalization of the end is here at issue. Rather: an analysis of the conditions that have made such a plurality of actualizations repeatedly possible and perhaps even necessary. Particularly after the end, announced by Lyotard, of the so-called great narratives, the question arises whether stories of the end (of art) can be told. That it is impossible would be paradoxical, for since Aristotle, the end has been a function of narration, and the end of narration as well.[34] Perhaps only from the perspective of narrating from beginning to end do the different modi of ending, including mortality, appear at all. We don't narrate because we must die, rather because we can narrate, something is conceivable as an end.[35] In this context, the end of art perhaps enjoys a privilege over other final propositions. If, in all the determinations of an end, it is primarily a question of form, then the end of art constitutes a privileged site for exploring problems of the end. For art, aesthetics, including the question of their transcendence, overcoming, or obsolescence, is the domain in which questions of the possibility or impossibility of unity and closure, end and beginning, success and failure, are handled as *questions of form*, and this nowhere more thoroughly than in Hegel,[36] who started the rumor of the end of art.

The purpose of treating the end of art as a rumor in the sense of a story, a claim, a speech act, and questioning its deployment in terms of its narrative, rhetorical techniques, is not to unmask its pretensions or to denounce its truth content. Just because only rumors can circulate about the end of art, we cannot exclude the possibility that there actually is, was, or could be something like the end of art. But an interpretation that itself neither wants to settle the paradox of the end, nor to stage or to deny the end of art is left with only the provisional goal of providing a formal doctrine for this rumor. With the end of art, it seems immediately obvious that the unity and identity of this object cannot be found in it itself, but only in the claims about it. What Foucault rather laboriously showed through the example of madness,[37] that the unity of an object of knowledge is owed to the interplay of rules that make possible the appearance of objects, is clear enough in the case of the end of art. Thus the following interpretations are prolegomena toward a phenomenology of the end of art as rumor.

Because the announcement of the end of art presents us with a speech act that cannot invoke a governing instance, every end of art is a quasi-sovereign act of drawing or positing a boundary.[38] To draw boundaries and make judgments without a sovereign instance has been the business of aesthetics since Kant. But the central question has changed in the meantime.

In modern art the question is no longer "is it beautiful?" but "is it art?"[39] The end of art could advance to such a central motif in the self-conception of modernity because art itself, and no longer beauty, has been put on the witness stand. Modern art stands and falls with the end of art. What counts as art depends essentially on what is not yet or no longer art.[40] But—and this is an ironic premise to the end of art in modernity—this end of art was already formulated by the archenemy of that same modernity, by Hegel, the last theoretician of the beautiful at the end of Idealism. This fact can be understood in various ways: either Hegel, whose discourse on the end of art delegitimized modernity, is himself already modern, or one argues conversely that modernity in its radical anti-idealist impulse is still a scion of idealism. Here we are not offering a decision between these alternatives, but rather looking for answers to the question of how such alternatives can arise in the orbit of discourse on the end of art.

Like all rumors, the rumor of the end of art is a nonauthorized discourse.[41] That exposes an investigation to the dilemma of having more or less arbitrarily to assign it a beginning and tie it to an authorial voice. If Hegel serves here as the initiator of the rumor, this is not because he was the first to formulate it.[42] But Hegel delimits the multiplicity of interpretive possibilities together with its diffuse rumored character. This will be shown in a cursory way in the following section. Before and after Hegel, the rumor of the end of art circulates, but he articulates it *as* a rumor, and with extensive consequences. Beginning with Hegel is obviously also a heuristic maneuver, which will have to demonstrate its own validity in the course of the study. At the end of the book, it will be necessary to explore with Hölderlin an alternative beginning.

2

The end of art could develop its remarkably durable effectiveness— little of the Hegelian corpus has remained so continuously relevant—because already in Hegel it is so densely surrounded by contradictions and inconsistencies that no consensus has yet been reached on whether there even *is* a Hegelian end of art.[43] The lectures on aesthetics begin, indeed, with a threnody on art, which is "for us a thing of the past."[44] But by the end of the same introduction, Hegel voices the hope that for the time being, no end of art is to be feared. "Now, therefore, what the particular arts realize in individual works of art is, according to the Concept of art, only the universal forms of the self-unfolding Idea of beauty. It is as the external actualization of this Idea that the wide Pantheon of art is rising. Its architect and builder is the self-comprehending spirit of beauty, but to complete it will need the history of the world in its development through thousands of years" (1:90). Elsewhere, Hegel writes that after antiquity "nothing can be or become more beautiful" (1:517). But at the end of the systematic section of the treatise, just prior to the transition to the system of the individual arts, Goethe's poem "Wiederfinden" (Reencounter) from the *West-Östlicher Divan* testifies to the opposite.[45] Such contradictions are part of the resistance Hegel's *Aesthetics* poses to a conclusive interpretation. The text's philological unreliability certainly did not improve its generally poor reputation.[46] The text has come down to us as Hotho's transcriptions of Hegel's lectures; even in an editorial sense, Hegel's end of art is mere rumor.

The discussion as to whether or not Hegel announced an end of art is harmless in comparison to the debate that attends its evaluation and interpretation. Assuming Hegel's *Aesthetics* does proclaim the end of art, would that be a loss to lament, an emancipation to celebrate, or a welcome relief of art from its responsibility for philosophical truth claims? Because the text of the *Aesthetics* makes each of these positions possible and none necessary, an interpretational vortex results that is best resisted by starting before semantics and before the evaluation of ending with the word and name of the thing. The formulation "end of art" does not appear either in the lectures on aesthetics, or in Hegel's other major statements on art in the *Encyclopedia* and the *Phenomenology of Spirit*. Hegel writes that something is "past," "lost," "over"; that art has transcended itself (1:607). He claims as well that there is a completion to art (1:55) and that it has a "final end" (1:55). Still, how was it possible, and why would it be necessary to preempt these differences by speaking in an abbreviated way of Hegel's "thesis" of an end of art? So entrenched has this expression become that even those who know better, and who add that it is more correct to speak of a past-tense character to art, hang on to the formula, which has long become a standard turn of phrase.

It happens every day, of course, that a name, this "infinite abbreviation for natural existents" (1:167), grows autonomous, and Hegel himself generously subsumes his lectures on the philosophy of fine art under the concept that they intend to dispense with: "We will therefore let the word 'Aesthetics' stand; as a mere name it is a matter of indifference to us, and besides it has meanwhile passed over into common speech" (1:1). A similar fate has befallen Hegel's "thesis of the end of art," Heine's almost contemporaneous enunciation of the end of the artistic period on the occasion of Goethe's death cannot sufficiently account for this terminology. Yet Hegel's almost laconic observation—art is and remains for us a thing of the past—has persistently been understood, defended, or contested as a thesis. This abbreviating nomenclature is all the more striking, because Hegel himself provides a series of justifications of his dictum in his introduction, though so casually that it makes the search for reasons appear idle.[47]

The oft-quoted sentence—"in all these respects art, considered in its highest vocation, is and remains for us a thing of the past" (1:11)—is preceded by several longer passages that explore various argumentative strategies. Hegel claims initially that "only one sphere and stage of truth is capable of being represented in the element of art" (1:9). Greek culture's natural affinity to art is contrasted with the Christian understanding of truth, "which is no longer so akin and friendly to sense" (1:10). This historically relativizing justification is followed by another, related argument, with more reception-aesthetic accents: "The peculiar nature of artistic production and of works of art no longer fills our highest need. We have got beyond venerating works of art as divine and worshipping them. The impression they make is of a more reflective kind, and what they arouse in us needs a higher touchstone and a different test. Thought and reflection have spread their wings above fine art" (1:10). Among Hegel's interpreters, the first strategy corresponds to attempts to mitigate the end of art by limiting it to classical art, or the artistic religion of antiquity, while the reception-aesthetic argument serves to reveal the end of art as an immanent function of the Hegelian system. In the passage in question, both aspects initially appear side by side, unrelated but of equal weight, before Hegel adds a third aspect to them. "Those who delight in lamenting and blaming may regard this phenomenon as a corruption and ascribe it to the predominance of passions and selfish interests which scare away the seriousness of art as well as its cheerfulness; or they may accuse the distress of the present time, the complicated state of civil and political life" (1:10). We find here an anticipation of the possibility of instrumentalizing the end of art in the long tradition of cultural pessimism down to Botho Strauss's *Goat-Song Crescendo (Anschwellender Bocksgesang)*. But the tone of the next section renders these different motivational and justificatory strategies irrelevant. "However all this may be, it is certainly the case that art no longer affords that satisfaction of spiritual needs which earlier ages and nations sought in it, and found in it alone" (1:10).

The following observation raises new confusions, however, for Hegel now claims that there has been no end to art, rather a change in criteria and a shift in interest. It is "a need of ours [. . .] to cling to general considerations and to regulate the particular by them" (1:10); not for art, but for the interest in art, "we demand in general rather a quality of life in which the universal is not present in the form of law and maxim" (1:10). Art is not dead, but our contemporary preferences tend toward what, from the perspective of living art, is something dead: "Consequently the conditions of our present time are not favorable to art" (1:10).

Although one could develop from these passages a relatively complete typology of the modes of justification of the end of art in modernity, these individual moments are not finally separable, and for Hegel they are certainly interconnected. The summarizing formula finally concludes, "*in all these respects* art, considered in its highest vocation, is and remains for us a thing of the past" (emphasis added). Although the gesture toward "its highest vocation" seems to limit the verdict and allow for a continuation of art (admittedly insignificant in terms of truth and Hegel's system), this contrasts sharply with the categorical gesture "in all these respects." What sort of an end of art outside of all these relations is conceivable? None—at least none yet, and at least not "for us." And that is what matters. For it is not the case that a discourse on Hegel's "thesis" of the end of art has moved beyond Hegel and illegitimately reduced his complex justifications. Rather, the opposite is true: There *must* be a "thesis" on the end of art, for this is the only way to obscure the fact that Hegel levels heterogeneous interpretive possibilities and their differences. The obligatory addition "thesis" is justified, because only thus can a *conflict* over the end of art appear possible and necessary. The addition of "thesis" is the reaction to a superfluity of interpretations; art has not been thought or brought to its end here, but the end of art has been exhausted and, in certain respects, thought to its end in Hegel.[48] The reason why one speaks of the end of art and debates is not to be found in the assumptions of the thesis, but rather in the fact that Hegel delimits the possible applications of the topos. Hegel opens the horizon of the end of art, but simultaneously closes it off, to the extent that beyond this horizon, no end of art can be conceived.

If it is really the case that the end of art has today become so much a banality that semantic differences between, for instance, cultural-pessimistic melancholy and emancipatory triumph have been caught up in this inflation, then this is the condition Hegel had already recognized, and that the incessant debates on "Hegel's thesis on the end of art" are constantly trying to suspend and ignore. If the end of art in Hegel is seen to be a discourse in this sense—that is, a discourse that organizes talk about the end of art beyond the possible positions one might want to assume—then Hegel is not the first postmodern, but quite the contrary: only ex post facto, now, is Hegel's position as the founder of this discourse legible.[49] Hegel is not the prophet of a reality that has been fulfilled as postmodernity,[50] for if the founder of the discourse of the end of art simultaneously delineates its end, then this finalization does not lie before us as task, but behind us as something given up, given over—a relic or, if one will, an inheritance. Only under these conditions it is possible to analyze the structures of this discourse and to discern its history without submitting to the pressure of breaking with the logic of the end, of ending or radicalizing the end.

Until now there has been no way to think the end of art, to develop its forms or write its history, that is not already anticipated in Hegel. The end of art becomes a discourse through the exclusivity that includes all approaches to it, and thereby neutralizes them. Beyond the end of art, there is, for Hegel and after Hegel, no site for art. What concerns art is understood and described from the position of the end of art—not in the "thesis" of an end of art that would put into question the existence rights of modern art, but by discursivizing the motif, simultaneously opening and limiting its possible interpretations. This is the actual inheritance of the Hegelian *Aesthetics*, whose claims every reflection on art, from Nietzsche and Heidegger to Adorno and Derrida, has had to confront. Hegel's achievement (and the problem of reading the text rumored to be his[51]) consists in having initiated the end of art as a discourse, without ultimately reconciling the heterogeneous interpretive attempts into an all-inclusive super–end of art (which is what all attempts to outbid Hegel, whether by Schelling before him, or after him by the avant-garde, have tried to do). There is neither one end of art in Hegel, nor is each particular end of art identifiable as a sublation (*Aufhebung*) in the Hegelian sense. Alongside the end of art as sublation appear relatively unspectacular forms of ending. The sublime, for instance, that Hegel sets within symbolic art, simply falls away; other art forms dissipate in everyday consciousness. And it is by no means decided that the end of art that organizes the sequence of symbolic, classical, and romantic artistic periods, and which also determines the relation of philosophy and art, qualifies as a properly dialectical instance of Hegelian "sublation."

Hegel's quasi-democratic pluralization of a single end into many different ends initiates the end of art as discourse. The end of art since Hegel could become, with Hegel, a discourse, because in Hegel, talk of the end of art itself is unending: Hegel without end. Hegel's privileged position as the founder of a discourse does not result from the fact that he sublated the broad horizon of possible meanings of the end in the speculative concept of sublation, thereby making the end of art final. The reverse is the case; it is his philosophy of beauty that first makes available the diverse positions within the discourse on the end of art, albeit at a high price, for henceforth every position, every evaluation, and every interpretation of an end to art always and forever occur in the name of Hegel, his art, and its ends.[52]

The end of art as discourse in the sense outlined above poses questions different from those that arise in the acute conditions of the application of this topos. Here, what is at issue is no longer a refutation of the end, outbidding the latest version with something even more up-to-date, nor are we concerned with radicalizing or ending the end of art. The questions are different: Who can claim the competence to decree or to deny an end to art, and how is this competence acquired? What political questions are at stake with the end of art? What forms and practices of representation become possible or necessary, what speech acts and strategies of argument are pursued in texts that discuss the end of art? Is something like a history of the end of art even conceivable, and what would that history be, when its object intrinsically resists historicization and cannot be presupposed as a fait accompli, since we still speak under its conditions? What proportional relation between continuity and discontinuity is appropriate to such a tangled object as the long history of an always new and at the same time always outdated end of art? Are there texts or objects whose movements of thought not only actualize and instrumentalize the end of art, but also indicate possibilities for reflecting on the end of art as a discourse under its discursive conditions? Can they modify the discourse while continuing it? Can one describe the history of the end of art as a history of the always new discovery and modification of the end of art as discourse, in the course of which one does not find the end of the end of art, but an emancipation from ending under the conditions of an end, a setting free of the end in its endless possibilities? If one listens to those who tell their histories of the end of art, and so find themselves linked in a chain of similar tales, can one learn something about the mechanisms of transmission and the construction of tradition? Put methodologically: can one derive a genealogy of modernity from those who have contributed to the discourse on the end of art since Hegel, and who have, perhaps even without realizing it themselves, altered it?

The end of art—this is the book's claim—has not just been played out variously and repetitively, but the playing out occasionally provides glimpses of the rules of the game, the discursive conditions under which it is played. At the end of the end of art one does not find an end, but a beginning: the discovery of the end of art as a discourse of modernity. This double dimension of the end of art as inner-aesthetic theorem on the one hand and the exterior arena of its discovery as discourse on the other determines the dual perspective from which each interpretive reconstruction of the end of art from Hegel to Heidegger proceeds. The immanent reconstruction of the end of art and its forms in selected texts is accompanied and supplemented by the concurrent attempt to gesture beyond the immanence of aesthetics toward the *history* of aesthetics in modernity. A strange duplicity of the end of art thereby comes to light. Certainly the end is, so to speak, ambivalent in itself, to the extent that its meaning always oscillates between the poles of telos as completion on the one hand and finitude on the other. But the paradox of the end of art as a figure of thought in the aesthetic discourse of modernity is something else. Precisely this figure, in whose name the autonomy of art in one way or another is established, becomes the occasion for a reflection on the unity of autonomy and heteronomy. If the end of art is a discourse in Michel Foucault's sense, it is a form of knowledge. But because the end of art is a rumor, and thus cannot be an object of knowledge, the knowledge that emerges in the discussion of the end of art must concern something other than the end of art. This other object of knowledge is knowledge of the connection between autonomy and heteronomy, which is the exterior or flip side of aesthetic discourse since the "Querelle." The reconstruction of such knowledge, as the horizon within which concrete objects of knowledge are first constituted so that the question whether in any given case this or that sort of end of art is at issue, is what Foucault calls archeology. In what follows, however, we will not be trying to pursue the possibility Foucault himself hesitantly suggests of applying the concept of archeology to other domains such as philosophy or art.[53] The texts analyzed here are not objects of an archeological reconstruction. Rather, their authors are themselves shown to be archeologists of modernity. However different their texts and their attitudes, however various the philosophical and historical assumptions with which they worked, these authors always reveal themselves as archeologists, museologists—in short, as theoreticians of the constitution and transformation of tradition in modernity. With the end of art, Hegel, Nietzsche, Heidegger, Benjamin, and Adorno found themselves in a tradition. What they then made of it, the different ways in which they covered up and discovered its continuities, and what falls to us from this, this is all the object of their interpretation. The knowledge that their analyses attempt to develop, and the point of the end of art from Hegel to Adorno: Through the end of art, these authors become theoreticians of modernity *as* a tradition. We will have to show how their insight into the traditional character of modernity differs from what is usually understood, in either a positive or negative sense, by tradition. In a preliminary way, we can say that the use of concepts such as tradition and inheritance (*Überlieferung*) serves a polemical function, suggesting that the accelerations, radicalizations, and transformations that the end of art experienced in the nineteenth and twentieth centuries do not amount to any increase in reflexivity, supposedly the hallmark of post-Hegelian modernity according to standard accounts of modernism in literary and art history. The term *tradition*, because it signifies what is presumably opposed to the obsolete, the forgotten, or the suppressed in modernity, indicates as well that with the end of art we are concerned with, commitments cannot necessarily be understood simply as reflective advances, and perhaps not even as developments, whether of a continuous or discontinuous sort.[54]

3

The end of art is not only the hinge between aesthetics and anti-aesthetics, but it also falls between the disciplines that have competence to address it. Art history and literary studies are each here as competent and incompetent as intellectual history and philosophy. The relation between aesthetic theory and practice is particularly problematic, a relation whose inclusion within the purview of the end of art finds its historical emblem in the proximity of Hegel's and Goethe's deaths. The virulent competition, at least since Plato, between philosophy and art is sharpened under the conditions of the end of art as discourse to an antagonistic principle that binds the competitors firmly to one another. The topos has a philosophical origin, but Hegel himself already had to admit that a turn to aesthetics presupposes the existence of genuine poetical works. As a philosophical decree, the end of art always arrives too late or too soon. And yet art cannot end itself, for it would then no longer be art. It requires therefore a prior philosophy, or art itself becomes philosophy where it strives to reach its end.[55]

With the exception of the epilogue, which gives, late but emphatically, the final word to a poem by Hölderlin, the authors treated in the following pages belong to the canonical tradition of aesthetic philosophy. They are authors, that is, who fall outside the domain of competence of literary criticism. But where the end, and in particular the end of art, is not simply a philosopheme, but is always also a discourse with narrative structure and so functions in literary terms, representatives of these disciplines have not only the right, but perhaps even the duty, to read philosophical texts. Furthermore, if it is the case that the distinction between aesthetic practice and aesthetic theory is both established and hindered by the end of art, then no single discipline can claim sole competence over the end of art. The question whether the end of art is an edict of the philosophers or an immanent dynamic of art can only arise within the order of that discourse, for only within the order of discourse does this appear as a problem.[56] This means that in reading these texts, the focus will be on their respective ends of art; other systematic and quasi-official philosophical concerns will be discussed only where they pertain directly to the problem of the end of art. Shifting attention from philosophical issues to the texture of the end of art will, I hope, help disclose new aspects in familiar material.

The authors—Hegel, Nietzsche, Benjamin, Adorno, Heidegger, and Hölderlin—are canonical, but their connection here is not immediately obvious. The limitation to exclusively German-speaking authors refers to the fact that the end of art, as a descendant of German idealism, is a discourse with national overtones. It is well known that the rise of aesthetics and so-called autonomous art in Germany, the "overdue nation," represents a sort of provisional compensation for national-state identity, that aesthetics is also a supplement to the nation. (Since Heidegger's problematic interpretation, the controversial, if unquestioned, chief witness to this nexus is Hölderlin. Our reading of his poem "Voice of the People" is therefore postponed until the final chapter.[57]) The artistic philosophical tradition since Romanticism has shown itself particularly susceptible to what, since Walter Benjamin's famous artwork essay of 1936, has been called the "aestheticization of politics." Often enough, the end of art signals a fatal aesthetic self-transcendence and overestimation of art, which makes itself absolute in announcing the end of art.[58] The end of art provides something like a yardstick for measuring the hypostatizing evaluation of art over against other domains. From Schelling to Wagner's *Gesamtkunstwerk* to the avant-garde and on to what Benjamin diagnosed as the aestheticization of politics, the disastrous political and social consequences of such attempts have been manifest. (It is not least these politically fatal potentials of the discourse on the end of art that lie behind the anti-aesthetic consensus of recent theoreticians.[59]) The reference to the national dimension of the discourse on the end of art is not intended to suggest that the end of art is a uniquely German matter. Kierkegaard, Blanchot, or Bataille, to mention only a few, also participate in the discourse of the end of art. But limiting ourselves to the German tradition helps foreground the political aspects. With Heidegger or Nietzsche, the connection between aesthetics and national politics may be obvious. That Walter Benjamin, hardly a nationalist, also speculates in his *Trauerspiel* book on a rebirth of German art is less well known. And it is just as surprising to find that Hegel's *Aesthetic* of all theories has critical contributions to make to an understanding of the process in which nationally specific artistic production arose from extra-European origins.

There is, admittedly, one (French) author whose absence in connection with these authors cannot be ignored. Jacques Derrida has not only rediscovered, as it were, the European and in particular the German philosophical tradition, because his reading conceived what was at stake in this tradition in a new way, but he is the decisive contemporary reference point for the difficult relation of philosophy and art, which no analysis of the end of art can hope to avoid. That an encounter with Derrida is nonetheless lacking here does not testify to a conviction that he has either departed from or demolished the aesthetic tradition.[60] His reflection on the problem or repetition, inscription, and authorship in the debate with Searle, his consideration of the apocalyptic tone in Kant or the problem of style in Nietzsche, the interpretation of the Van Gogh paintings in Heidegger's artwork essay, and much more doubtless represent genuine contributions to the problem of the western philosophical tradition. But they answer to something other than questions of the *aesthetic*.[61] And therefore Derrida would deserve a separate discussion that cannot be undertaken here, since we are concerned with the end of art as the central motif of the aesthetic tradition.

Admittedly, the selection remains incomplete in other respects as well. Lukács is missing, as is Marcuse, both of whom certainly reflected on the end of art (as opposed to Adorno, who represents a curious exception, because his texts belong only to the periphery of this discourse, despite being almost obsessed with the end of art). These and others have not been included because the selection was made in terms of the extent to which each author contributed to the discovery of the end of art as discourse. The authors selected have all long been seen as founders of traditions; they organize the field in which the tradition of aesthetics can so far be perceived. But their canonical status as great representatives of German philosophy of art is, for the present study, merely an arbitrary sign for the fact that these theoreticians of the end of art achieved insights into the history of aesthetics in modernity. It is this, and not their status as classics, that sanctions their conjunction under the rubric of the end of art.

CHAPTER 2

Hegel Without End

I

"For the beauty of art is beauty *born of the spirit and born again.*"[1]
The statement appears at the start of Hegel's *Aesthetics: Lectures on Fine
Art.* Although emphasized, the enigmatic formulation does not belong to
the usual Hegel citations associated with the end of art. For although a
double ancestry of art would seem to presuppose an end, because what is
born again must also have died, Hegel elides this ending here. But how is
one to understand the relation of birth and rebirth without reference to a
death?

In the introduction, where Hegel is not yet arguing systematically,
but for methodological reasons staying close to the received philosophical-historical and art-historical notions, he distinguishes natural beauty,
which had played a central role in idealistic philosophy of art since Kant's
third Critique, from the beauty of art that excludes the former from consideration. Nature may be beautiful, but Hegel leaves no doubt "that the
beauty of art is *higher* than nature" (1:2). This distinction of "beautiful"
and "higher" proves to be of fundamental significance for the entire *Aesthetics.* It informs, for instance, the qualitative difference between beautiful classical and a no-longer-so-beautiful but, with regard to truth, higher
romantic art. On the basis of this distinction, which originates in the difference between natural and artistic beauty, the latter is designated as the
proper domain of spirit. Thus Hegel continues, "and the higher the spirit

and its productions stand above nature and its phenomena, the higher too is the beauty of art above that of nature" (1:2). And because the absolute essence of spirit cannot be relativized or proportioned, Hegel can conclude that "everything beautiful is truly beautiful only as sharing in this higher sphere and as *generated by it*" (1:2, emphasis added). Once natural beauty has been revealed as a deficient modality, "which in its substance is contained in the spirit itself" (1:2), it is eliminated from the proper sphere of aesthetics; the beauty of art alone bears the seal of spiritual productivity. Art is the child of spirit.

This argument in support of the artistic creativity of spirit explains why artistic beauty should be said to be spirit-born, but not why it should be said to be born *and then reborn*. In order to clarify this formulation, one must consider the relation Hegel takes to hold between art and reality. Spirit-born art performs a rebirth of bad, transitory reality, which it thereby fashions into "a higher reality, born of the spirit" (1:9). On account of its spiritual ancestry, art is capable of giving reality a new birth as and in the work of art, by revealing its sensuous aspect as insubstantial illusion, as *Schein*. But this explanation too requires the death or dying off that Hegel's turn of phrase eclipses. For Hegel, death always has "a double meaning: (a) it is precisely the immediate passing away of the natural, (b) it is the death of the purely natural and therefore the birth of something higher, namely the spiritual realm to which the merely natural dies in the sense that the spirit has this element of death in itself as belonging to its essence" (1:349). Thus birth, as well, must have a double meaning, and must also signify that silenced death that Hegel replaces with "rebirth."

Yet another reading is conceivable. For Hegel, art's success and failure consists in "displaying even the highest [reality] sensuously, bringing it thereby nearer to the senses, to feeling, and to nature's mode of appearance" (1:7–8). This is the source of art's mediating function. It is a response to the opposition between spiritual and sensuous that tends toward their overcoming. That such an opposition exists at all is already the result of an operation of spirit. "The breach, to which the spirit proceeds, it is also able to heal" (1:8). "It generates out of itself works of fine art as the first reconciling middle term between what is merely external, [. . .] and the infinite freedom of conceptual thinking" (1:8). The apparently tautological addition of "and reborn" proves to mean not only what heals and eliminates the contradiction between externality and thought, but also what reproduces and repeats it. And indeed, art not only responds to a breach, but also originates with one: the distinction between form and meaning. "It is with this attempt alone that there arises the proper need for art" (1:333). (Later we will show that, although Hegel occasionally claims that classical art achieves the beautiful identification of form and meaning toward which symbolic art was only groping and that romantic art has lost, it, too, is afflicted by this rupture.) But the problem with this interpretation is that, however meaningfully one can speak of a rebirth of reality and a rebirth of the contradiction, in the sentence in question—"For the beauty of art is beauty born of the spirit and born again"—artistic beauty is not just the subject, but equally the object of a rebirth.

Thus only one explanation remains. The birth and rebirth of the beauty of art indicates its dual relation to spirit, which creates art not only as an intermediary, but also rediscovers itself in art. The "power of the thinking spirit," Hegel writes in the introduction, "lies in being able not only to grasp itself in its proper form as thinking, but to *know itself again* just as much when it has surrendered its proper form to feeling and sense" (1:12–13, emphasis added). At the moment of this anagnorisis, in which artistic beauty is recognized, rediscovered, and reborn, it is no longer what as art it once was or might have been, but is reborn as philosophical knowledge of the beautiful. The addition of "reborn" marks the transition of art into its philosophical comprehension, which seals first and last the spiritual ancestry of art. Knowledge of the beautiful is distinguished from beautiful knowledge as a higher rebirth from profane birth.

But the consequences of this (orthodox Hegelian) interpretation for the relation of art to philosophy are quite un-Hegelian. If "born and reborn" expresses the double-sidedness of artistic beauty as the work of art on the one hand and its philosophical concept on the other, then the qualitative breach between art and philosophy, between the "beautiful" and that "higher" dimension, disappears. This differentiation loses its organizing power when the path from spirit-born art to its rebirth in philosophy passes through its death. The copula "and" in the phrase "born and reborn" dispenses with sublation, or at least silences it and consequently obscures the difference between philosophy and art—with the effect that philosophical reflection threatens to participate in an unsettling way in artistic beauty. In fact, beauty is the least lively effect of art's philosophical recognition, but Hegel's elliptical exclusion of the end—one formulation among many, true; but emphasized and set in a very prominent place—suggests that beauty has perhaps migrated into philosophical aesthetics, and in the place of a knowledge of beauty only beautiful knowledge is to be had. In a certain sense, this is indeed the case in the *Aesthetics*. Hegel's most successful interpretations, of the Egyptian sphinx or Shakespeare for instance, are beautiful, classical interpretations of not-yet-beautiful (symbolic) or no-longer-beautiful (romantic) art.

In every reflection on artistic beauty, in every philosophy of art, art is already passé. If art is taken to be beautiful—and for Hegel this is the case only where beauty has been philosophically recognized—this beauty is part of the past. Art can only be beautiful to the extent that it is known, is reborn as knowledge, and therefore has passed into the past. In Hegel's first definition of artistic beauty, art is already in the past, but has passed in such a way that there is literally no place between birth and rebirth for an end, no site, no location. Instead, art stands at the outset of an endless critique, but always already past. Whatever beautiful art is, it perishes and dissolves between birth and rebirth. The end of art is the process of art, and it passes not from art to philosophy (or vice versa), but passes away between art and philosophy. This is no emancipation of art that would allow the end of art to achieve its own autonomous logic. Under the rubric of the end, art is as heteronomous as philosophy.

In another passage of the introduction, Hegel offers a somewhat less enigmatic version of the same point. The task of the lectures is to show "what the beautiful is and how it showed itself." The beautiful in the way that it once showed itself is to be awakened to the presence of higher life in philosophical knowledge. Art is thus always only no-longer-beautiful art, and being past becomes a determination of beauty. The beautiful showed itself; it has always merely *been* beautiful, and if beauty is anywhere present, it is as beauty reborn in philosophy or religion. This means on the one hand that philosophy, the self-appointed judge of art, whose first and definitive act was the banishment of artistic beauty into the distant past, is at the same time infected by beauty and as a consequence provides the site for a rebirth of art. Art is past and always passing, but it finds no end in that expiration and perseveres in philosophy. On the other hand, art as art has the option of being or becoming or even having been something other than beautiful or true. The desire to unleash the potential of this latter suggestion has inspired all recent readings of Hegel in the wake of Derrida's Bataille exegesis.[2]

In the sense of the two-edged phrase "Hegel without end," a reading of Hegel's end of art has to consider how the past-tense character of art as such, its endless passing away, which figures so prominently in all radicalizing Hegel interpretations,[3] relates to the historically and geographically concrete end of art in its classical phase. For Hegel believes that the classical art of ancient Greece is the very end point at which the possibilities of art are completed, and by the same token, exhausted. Almost everything in this relation depends upon the concept "recollection,"[4] which echoes rediscovery, recognition, and rebirth.

2

Like "sense," "this wonderful word" (1:128) or "sublation" (*Aufhebung*), "recollection" belongs to those speculative concepts whose polysemia is concentrated into a single word.[5] Alienating transformation, internalizing adaptation, and productive transposition are brought together in Hegelian recollection in a manner he occasionally illustrates by analogy to the process of digestion. In Hegel's aesthetics, recollection embodies the transition from the art-religion of the classical phase to (Christian) religion, where "the Absolute has removed from the objectivity of art into the inwardness of the subject" (1:103). Religion is art internalized and recollected in the rites of a worshipping community, "in which objectivity is, as it were, consumed and digested, while the objective content, now stripped of its objectivity, has become a possession of mind and feeling" (1:104).[6] Internalizing recollection owes its emphasis to spirit, in whose essence it lies to return to the interior.

But the simpler effects of recollection are no less significant, and above all for art under the auspices of its transition into religion and philosophy. Art profits from recollection. Memory grants it an almost automatic generality, for which it has always had to struggle, because art "always simultaneously touches on the accidental" (1:12). Temporal distance effaces particularities and thus sets the stage for generalizations. The preferred subjects of classical artists testify to recollection's prerogative. That "the ideal artistic figures are transferred to the age of myths, or, in general, to bygone days of the past, as the best ground of their actualization" is due to recollection, for it "automatically succeeds in clothing characters, events, and actions in the garment of universality, whereby the particular external and accidental details are obscured" (1:189). The task of art, to rid appearance as far as possible of its sensuous particularity without its ceasing to be appearance, accords with recollection, because it "brings about automatically, owing to our memory, that generalization of material with which art cannot dispense" (1:264).

However, the privilege recollection enjoys as tending toward generality conflicts with the equally fundamental role the *Aesthetics* reserves for fantasy or imagination. Hegel's obstinate insistence on creative fantasy as the material of poetry has been counted by the majority of critics among the most regrettable aspects of his philosophy of art.[7] In order to preserve the spiritual heritage of poetic art, Hegel considers not language, but creative fantasy alone as the material of poetry. Stubbornly he clings to this position, even when it leads to patent absurdities, as, for instance, the assurance that a poetic work suffers not the slightest in translation, or the claim that in reading, the voice of the author is always heard.[8]

Hegel's aesthetics demands from the artistic ideal that creative fantasy on the one hand and recollection on the other coincide. Invention and discovery, autonomous formation and the material encountered, have to become identical. Now one might think that recollection in its complex plurality of meanings provides the medium for such identifications. In the act of recollection, discovery and invention are fused together into a higher "reencounter." But this is exactly what Hegel's text resists, as if recollection were unable to accomplish the unification and internalization of inventive creation on the one hand and found materials on the other. Hegel's examples demonstrate that the latent competition between discovery and invention persists. The "genuine mode of production" of

artistic *fantasy* [. . .] can be compared with the characteristic mentality of a man experienced in life, or even of a man of quick wit and ingenuity, who, although he knows perfectly well what matters in life, what in substance holds men together, what moves them, what power dominates them, nevertheless has neither himself grasped this knowledge in general rules nor expounded it to others in general reflections; rather, what fills his mind he just makes clear to himself and others in particular cases always, real or invented, in adequate examples, and so forth. (1:40, emphasis added)

But where the aging philosopher seeks argumentative support in an example, his comparison is off,[9] and Hegel quickly corrects himself: "Yet such a kind of fantasy rests rather on the recollection of situations lived through, of experiences enjoyed, instead of being creative itself. Recollection preserves and renews the individuality and the external fashion of the occurrence of such experiences, with all their accompanying circumstances, but does *not* allow the universal to emerge on its own account. But the productive fantasy of an artist is the fantasy of a great spirit" (1:40, emphasis added). Here the passive character of recollection, its lingering at the particular that elsewhere leads to generalization, is exposed critically as a limitation. In another passage, Hegel reverses himself again, noting that "in general great individuals are almost always signalized by a great memory" (1:281). In recollection, the conflict of discovery and invention does not come to rest, which is why Hegel speaks in the one case of recollection (*Erinnerung*) and in the other of memory (*Gedächtnis*).

This latent rupture in the concept of recollection has been worked out with great precision by Paul de Man in his essay "Sign and Symbol in Hegel's *Aesthetics*."[10] He discovers in the interior of recollection an unavoidable forgetting, one that enables the mechanisms of sublation without itself being accessible to sublation. Recollection does not unify, but splits into recollection on the one hand and memory on the other: "The surprise, in Hegel, is that the progression to thought depends crucially on the mental faculty of memorization [. . .]. Memorization [*Gedächtnis*] has to be sharply distinguished from recollection and from imagination. It is entirely devoid of images [*bildlos*] [. . .] But it is not devoid of materiality altogether."[11] In this split de Man locates the material trace as writing that retracts the primacy of fantasy behind Hegel's back: "Memory, for Hegel, is the learning by rote of *names*, and it can therefore not be separated from the notation, the inscription, or the writing down of these names. In order to remember, one is forced to write down what one is likely to forget. The Idea in other words, makes its sensory appearance, in Hegel, as the material inscription of names."[12] In this sense, recollection is "a truth of which the aesthetic is the defensive, ideological and censored translation.

Memory effaces remembrance."[13] De Man can therefore say of the end of art: "Art is 'of the past' in a radical sense, in that, like memorization, it leaves the interiorization of experience forever behind. It is of the past to the extent that it materially inscribes, and thus forever forgets, its ideal content."[14]

This dimension of the concept of recollection (or remembrance) was expounded most radically by Hegel himself in a famous passage of the *Phenomenology of Spirit*. At the start of the chapter on "The Revealed Religion," one finds that passage on the vanished religion of art, which for us, now that "God is dead,"[15] is no longer sensuous expression, but merely a fragmentary remnant of that moral life in which it arose:

The statues are now only corpses from which the living soul has flown, just as the hymns are words from which belief has fled. The tables of the gods provide no spiritual food and drink, and in his games and festivals man no longer recovers the joyful consciousness of his unity with the divine. The works of the Muse now lack the power of the Spirit, for the Spirit has gained its self-certainty from the crushing of gods and men. They have become what they are for us now—beautiful fruit already picked from the tree, which a friendly Fate has offered us, as a girl might set the fruit before us. It cannot give us the actual life in which they existed, not the tree that bore them, not the earth and the elements which constituted their substance, not the climate which gave them their peculiar character, not the cycle of the changing seasons that governed the process of their growth. So Fate does not restore their world to us along with the works of antique Art, it gives not the spring and summer of the ethical life in which they blossomed and ripened, but only the veiled recollection of that actual world (*PS* 455).

The orphaned world of art is its recollection. We orient ourselves among objects in a museal way, and our relation to artistic objects remains entirely external: "it is an external activity, that wipes from these fruits a few drops of rain or specks of dust, as it were, and sets in place of the inner elements of the surrounding, generating, inspiring reality of the ethical the extensive scaffolding of the dead elements of their external existence" (*PS* 455–56). Only a few sentences later, Hegel invests in the dialectical capital of this merely dead recollection, for the spirit of fate "that presents us with those works of art" is "more than the ethical life and reality of that people, for it is the *inwardizing recollection* [*Er-Innerung*] of the spirit that was *externalized* in them" (*PS* 456). This hasty assurance contradicts the image of the artwork as the plucked fruits of a former moral life, which remain untouched by the emphasis on internalization in the concept of recollection. The girl who presents the fruit figures as an allegory of "friendly fate" and as muse of this fate: "But, just as the girl who offers us the plucked fruits is more [. . .], so, too, the Spirit of Fate is more than the ethical life" (*PS* 456). The internal fissure of recollection, which de Man noted in the opposition of recollection and memory, occurs here between the museally petrified fruits on the one hand and the girl who presents them on the other. The girl has to signify both that the objects no longer have meaning as well as what meaning it is they no longer can have.

In light of this passage from *Phenomenology of Spirit*, Jean-Luc Nancy has suggested in his own book *The Muses* a reading of the end of art in Hegel that is not satisfied with uncovering an obstinate materiality of recollection but attempts to overcome Hegel's aesthetics from within. Nancy's reflections, in which aesthetics simultaneously implodes and releases the possibilities of a nonaesthetic aesthetics that will nonetheless not be a counter- or antiaesthetics, are the most recent and quite likely most radical actualization of Hegel's end of art.[16]

"Why are there several arts and not just one?" is Nancy's initial question.[17] He believes that the plurality and inner particularity of the arts are sufficient to interrupt the dialectical movement,[18] the process of sublating the external in inwardizing recollection. In an essay concerned with the relation of art to religion and philosophy in Hegel, Nancy shows that the sublation of art in religion not only remains incomplete, but is also tantamount to a liberation of art for itself in its partial and plural particularity. Nancy chooses poetry, which Hegel takes to be the medium of the self-dissolution (*Selbstauflösung*) of art, because its sensory determination and therefore its artistic character is threatened by the immanent tendency of poetry toward interiority, to demonstrate that the plurality of the arts manifests itself just at the moment of its threatening dissolution, because poetry finds itself compelled to borrow from music and painting. This same dynamic is at work, Nancy claims, in the relation between poetry and the prose of thought, for the latter must make use of poetry, which lends it a body. To the extent that art is reborn in the prose of thought, this is also a rebirth of the essential plurality of art. "The point of art's dissolution is therefore *identically* and *essentially* the point of the reaffirmation

of its plastic independence and of the correlative and no less essential affirmation of the *intrinsic plurality of the moment of this sensuous, perceptible
plasticity*" (43).

This thesis of the impossibility of sublating art at its boundaries and
in its plural particularity is modified in the second part of Nancy's essay
in the course of a reading of the passage from the *Phenomenology* cited
above, on the girl with her fruits. Nancy argues that the process of "re-col-
lection" in the emphatic sense in fact does not sublate the merely external,
as would be necessary and even notorious in Hegel, for the works are still
always presented *gesturally*. Nancy does not insist on a difference between
the girl and her fruits, but reads the passage in such a way that this difference, without being sublated, disappears into gesture. On account of this
gesture, the girl is irreducibly both art and the friendly indulgence of fate,
that is, both what is recollected, what becomes self-consciousness of spirit
as spirit, as well as the consciousness of art as art outside of the religion of
art and outside of religion, which sublates art. "A form turns out to represent nothing; it puts nothing into form except the graceful consistency of
the form itself. [. . .] In the infinite movement of the gesture of presentation, dialectical logic is interrupted: spirit is not going to reengender itself
in greater conformity with its pure spirituality by hollowing out its negativity. The gesture suspends this movement. By suspending it, the gesture
interrupts the sense of the dialectic, but it presents the form: the *Präsentie-
ren* that is the sole office of the girl" (53–54). And because there is nothing
to see in the gesture but gesture itself, Nancy concludes: "The girl exposes
art that consents to its own disappearance: not in order to be resuscitated
but because it does not enter into that process. The 'beautiful fruits' are
detached from the tree, and their presentation is the consenting to this be-
ing-detached, mortally immortal. What if art were never anything but the
necessarily plural, singular art of consenting to death, of consenting to existence?" (54–55).

Nancy's interpretation of the nonrepresentative gesture itself cites a
philosophical gesture that is indigenous to quite another aesthetic tradition, and is related to the Kantian concept of favor (*Gunst*).[19] At one point
Nancy in fact names Kant as the author of the end of art, which Hegel
radicalized and articulated. "This is not exactly a certification of exhaustion, but it is the first form of a certification of 'end,' through the ambigu-

ous motif of a finishing of art that is always begun again" (86). Under the rubric of the end of art not only do aesthetics and anti-aesthetics mutually limit each other, but also the apparently antipodal strands of the aesthetic tradition, Kant's aesthetic experience on the one hand and Hegel's aesthetics of presentation on the other.

One can of course wonder whether Nancy's attempt to transfer Hegel's end of art into his own heteronomous logic of particular arts—the inversion, as it were, of the *Gesamtkunstwerk*—is ultimately immune to the regression into a utopian, hypostatizing end of art. In the last essay of *The Muses*, Nancy unfolds Hegel's end of art as the end of every relation between image and art. *Aisthesis*, which gives aesthetics its name, becomes the withdrawal of perception: "that if art remains defined as a relation of the image to the Idea, or of the image to the unimaginable [. . .] then it is art as a whole that withdraws along with the image. This is indeed what Hegel saw coming. If his formula has known such success, if it has been amplified and hijacked, it is quite simply because the formula was true and art was beginning to be done with its function as image. Which is to say, with its ontotheological function" (93–94). It seems that only a radicalization of the Hegelian end may hope to escape the logic of the end as sublation.

Thus, if we do no more than take the step onto the limit of ontotheology, the step that succeeds Hegel, following Hegel but finally outside of him, the step into *the extremity of the end of art*, which ends that end in another event, then we are no longer dealing with the couple of the presenting sensible and the presented ideal. We are dealing with this: the form-idea withdraws and the vestigial form of this withdrawal is what our platonizing lexicon makes us call "sensible." *Aesthetics* as the domain and as thinking of the sensible does not mean anything other than that. (97)

Werner Hamacher's judgments about Hegel's end of art are just as radical but markedly more skeptical toward Hegel. His analysis of the end of art is based on Hegel's exposition of classical comedy in the *Phenomenology of Spirit*. Hamacher discovers art as the agent of the deconstruction of self-consciousness as such. But he discloses the horizon of possibilities implicit in Hegel's thoughts on comedy only to insist that although the potential of a radical development can be found in Hegel, it is bounded and limited there, because the "end for Hegel is the conceptualized end, and therefore [remains] the privileged mode of self-empowerment and self-ap-propriation."[20] By restricting exclusively to Attic comedy the radicalized disappearance in the play with masks, Hegel protects it, or, as Hamacher implies, prevents it from infecting other genres, epochs, and philosophy itself. The end of art in Attic tragedy is in one and the same movement the discovery and the denial of possibilities: "The thesis of the end of art in comedy—however radically art is conceived there as the agent of the political, religious, philosophical and aesthetic disintegration of self-con-sciousness—this thesis also has the sense of terminating the end of art and of limiting the radicality of the experiences of finitude and happiness it opens."[21] And here emerges the stumbling block of all radicalizing readings of the *Aesthetics*. They founder on classical art. As art's highest fulfillment, classical art arrests all endless ending. All the rupturing and duplication of the beautiful comes to rest uniquely and forever in a zone from which all processes of unification and internalization are excluded, because this art is "corporeal, not inwardized, present" (1:607). The perfected art of the clas-sical period is not only an art of ending, an endlessly perishable art, but it is also the end of all attempts to temporalize the end.

To gauge the status of classical art and its end, one should be careful not to attribute to Hegel a narrow-minded classicism. Classical art is the organic and organizing center of the *Aesthetics* not on account of an ideal-istic prejudice, but is the result, as Hamacher correctly argues, of Hegel's need to transpose the endless perishability of art into a geographically and historically secure end (and in the *Phenomenology* a limited poetic genre—namely, tragedy). The primacy of classical art results from Hegel's attempt to situate and limit the end and the ends of art into *one* single ending. This attempt may be said to be successful as well as unsuccessful. It fails in that it is possible to demonstrate that the artistic ideal has already dissolved be-fore its end, in the transition from symbolic to classical art, and that this contamination of art with its prehistory debunks *avant la lettre* the singu-lar closure of the ideal. At the same time, however, Hegel indeed succeeds in restricting the protective attempt to classical art. Rather than denounc-ing this limitation as Hegel's narrow-mindedness, one should, with Hegel, describe it as a virtual, displaceable drawing of boundaries, one that first permits the different possibilities of the end, including the unrestricted actualization that Nancy or Hamacher undertake. It may be that classical art, whose systematic priority in Hegel's *Aesthetics* has disquieted all modern reflections on art, is the site where modernity was invented and discovered, and where it can be rediscovered in a different manner. The usual criticism of Hegel's privileging of classical art is itself a classical prejudice, beholden to a concept of classicism that is foreign to Hegel. Hegel's classical art was always already more modern than many ultramoderns today are willing to admit.

3

In the artistic presentation of the human figure, classical art renders congruent form and content. Received material and inventive fantasy merge. As corporeal, unrecollected present, this art is classical, timeless; and just as utterly as it is art, it is at an end. This art can claim the status of Ideal because in it the identity of beauty and ethical substance is manifested as art.

But the potential conflict within recollection between discovery and invention does not spare the aesthetic ideal, which is supposed to uniquely accomplish the "correspondence of the concrete Ideal with its external reality" (1:252). Thus the fact that free invention is foreign to classical art still requires legitimation. "Of course we are accustomed to rate a free production of the imagination higher than the manipulation of material already available, but the imagination cannot go so far as to provide the required harmony so firmly and definitely as it already lies before us in actual reality where national traits themselves proceed from this harmony" (1:256). If one provisionally excludes the site of this "actual reality," the heroic age, in which the beautiful is at home in the preindividual ethical substance,[22] then here it is the past per se that is declared appropriate for art. The identity of real existence and poetic times, ethical substance and the religion of art, is in a certain way only the deferred legitimation of the aesthetic primacy of the past. But this prerogative of the past subsequently reveals itself as subject to another law. The idea of "being at home and domesticated," which returns like a leitmotif in connection with classical art, occupies in Hegel's discussion of classical art the site of the conflict-ridden concept of recollection. All the tensions between discovery and invention are neutralized in the postulate of being at home: "The general law which in this connection we can assert consists in this, that man in his worldly environment must be domesticated and at home" (1:252). This law governs not only the presentation of figures within the artwork and the relation of art and historical reality, but also determines—and this is decisive—above and beyond historical distances, the relation of each present to art, "which may demand ability to understand and be at home in the work of art" (1:264–65).[23] Not only should the figures in an artwork appear to be at home in their world, but the readers and audience must be able to recognize themselves in this world and become at home in it. "Our interest in what is over and done with does not arise from the pure and simple reason that it did once exist as present. History is only ours when it belongs to the nation to which we belong" (1:272). It turns out then that the "mortal side" (1:277) of the artwork also participates in this familiarity, these national particularities, because "it always carries details in itself which separate it from the characteristics proper to other peoples and other centuries" (1:265).

The past takes precedence not because it can be generalized, but because only in the past, with its distant, foreign, no longer familiar aspects, can the changes be undertaken that correspond to a demand for familiarity. *Anachronisms*—symptoms of not being at home in the work of art—are therefore a constitutive feature of the artwork: "Even the most excellent piece *requires* remodeling from this point of view" (1:277). Hegel does attempt to establish a hierarchy of modes of familiarity. In classical times, art presented what was absolutely at home in this phase; postromantic art, on the other hand, has available to it "everything in which man as such is capable of being at home" (1:607). But the genealogical derivation of classical art from the symbolic (proto-)art relativizes the absolute being at home, for classical art shows itself to be at home only to the extent that it reworks older, extant material, which remains present as anachronisms.

In his discussions of anachronism in classical art, Hegel differentiates between different forms. What falls under the rubric of props, concerning "merely external things," is contrasted with "the more important kind of anachronism": in which "in a work of art the characters, in their manner of speech, the expression of their feelings and ideas, the reflections they advance, their accomplishments, could not possibly be in conformity with the period, level of civilization, religion, and view of the world which they are representing" (1:277). Hegel defends the right of these anachronisms against the claims of a normative realism: "Such a transgression of so-called naturalness is, for art, a *necessary* anachronism" (278). For Hegel, art is always under pressure to eliminate particularities, but to the extent that this occurs in the form of necessary anachronisms, difficulties arise for an apparently placid and perfected classical art.[24]

The section in the *Aesthetics* following these comments is therefore entirely governed by Hegel's need to limit his concession to a "necessary anachronism" in art, and to distinguish it from what he calls "an anachronism of a higher kind" (278). This occurs "if insights and ideas of a later development of the religious and moral consciousness are carried over into a period or nation whose whole earlier outlook contradicts such newer ideas" (1:278). There is, however, no basis for differentiating the artistically appropriate and therefore sanctioned violation of naturalism from the illegitimate contradiction "of a higher kind." Because no artwork is free of anachronisms, and because the relation of the phases of art is also anachronistic (romanticism anachronistically cites the symbolic phase), it seems questionable whether anachronism as the principle of sublating the naturalism in art can really be restricted in the way Hegel prescribes. Rather, anachronism flourishes in the interior of art (and in its philosophical interpretation).

The chapter on the genesis of classical art from the symbolic leaves no doubt that the achievement of classical art consists in nothing but a "higher" anachronism. Only the reckless transformation and overcoming of symbolic art, which finds anachronistic entrance into classical art, is what makes art classical. The ideal character of the classical phase, where everything is "domestic" (1:261) and art reaches its highest determination, is not alone an expression of the indigenous ethical substance. It has this character only because classical art is concerned with nothing but the transformation and colonizing of foreign, past, non-Greek protoart from the symbolic period. Only in this process is protoart alienated from itself and thereby fashions classicism's identity: "For the position we gave to classical art in general was that only through reaction against the presuppositions belonging of necessity to its sphere was it elevated to what it is as genuinely Ideal" (1:491). This genealogical derivation of classical art not only founds but also distorts its classicality, for the remnants of the symbolic often appear "varied and outrageous" (1:493) and contingent. "The remains of symbolic meanings peep through" (1:492). Even the classical artwork, in which the identification of form and meaning was to have been achieved, has echoes of earlier phases and is buffeted by obscure recollections of symbolic ambiguity. "Even in the field of classical art a similar uncertainty enters here and there, although the classical element in art consists in its not being symbolical by nature but in its being, in itself and throughout, distinct and clear" (1:309). In addition to the sudden emergence of the classical in the free artistic creation of awakening individuality, "where the lightning flash of genius strikes tradition" (2:722), there is also the genealogical derivation of this art from protoart: "In the instance before us, classical art of course *comes into being*, but that from which it develops must have an independent existence of its own outside of it, because classical art, as classical, must leave behind it all inadequacy, all becoming, and must be perfect in itself" (2:780).[25]

Hegel has good reason to risk this delimitation of anachronism. He needs to concede that classical art remains effected by the transcended symbolic protoart, for only when what has been overcome remains legible as a trace is its appropriation as the autonomous achievement of classical art recognizable, which "comes essentially into being only through such a transformation of what went before" (1:477). For the sake of the unrepeatable uniqueness of classical art, protoart cannot be annihilated without remainder, but must be recognizable as colonized, as appropriated, even if this sublation leads to a collision in the artistic ideal that threatens to unleash anachronism and call into question the perfection and therefore the end of art with respect to its highest determination.

The necessity of recognizing the symbolic *as* overcome in classical art forces Hegel to introduce a distinction between central and peripheral features that by rights should not occur in classical art. Classical art is "a milieu which yet, like life in general, is at the same time only a transitional point, even if at this point it attains the summit of beauty and in the form of its plastic individuality is so rich and spiritually concrete that *all notes harmonize with it*, and moreover, what *for its outlook is the past* still occurs as an accessory and a background, even if no longer as something absolute and unconditioned" (1:437, emphasis added). The work of art, in its perfection requiring no hermeneutic, which "in knowing itself, [. . .] points to itself" (1:427) because it "means [*Bedeutende*] itself and therefore intimates [*Deutende*] itself" (1:427), is disfigured by distortions.

Of course, one can object here, as always, that the symbolic remnants in classical art are symptomatic of the dilemma faced by all art. Even perfect art suffers, according to Hegel, from being sensuous appearance and not yet either religion or philosophy. But through the fissure between main and peripheral features, externality and essentialness, a hermeneutic insecurity enters, one that otherwise has no place in Hegel, because the normative ideal of classical art is also the sublation of interpretation. Hegel unfolds the hermeneutic problematic at a time and in a place where questions of interpretation and its possibility are historically and systematically at home. This is the realm of symbolic protoart, which not only provides classical art with the necessary material for its labor of transformative sublation, but also supplies the conditions through which the identification of form and meaning advances to a transhermeneutic ideal. This protoart must accomplish the literal distinction between form and meaning. It falls to symbolic art to shape and articulate the task whose fulfillment is reserved for classical art.

In the discussions of symbolic art anachronism also finds its proper site. There Hegel attributes to it, as a mode of becoming classical, "independent existence" (2:780). Because classical art already operates anachronistically, it cannot be the home of anachronism, but only that time and art in which we can no longer be at home and in which its contemporaries are likewise not yet at home. As the home of all incommensurability between presentation and content, including all forms of anachronism, symbolic protoart gains a secret privilege that diminishes the stature of classical art. Emphasis must be shifted from the classical phase as the realized artistic ideal (and therefore the perfected end of art) to the end of symbolic art, because it harbors the "becoming" of classical art.

In the chapter on the symbolic, Hegel finds himself confronted with massive problems of representation and exposition. What is an appropriate and not already anachronistic way to speak about an art in which we, as descendants of classical antiquity, are not and should not be at home? Hegel is concerned not to impose any later interpretive notions on these protoartistic works. Thus he is greatly troubled by the question of whether or not the Egyptians knew what they were doing with their pyramids. The contemporary debate on Creutzer's interpretation of myth can only partially explain this considerable hesitation. Indeed, the chapter on symbolic art is the only place in the *Aesthetics* where Hegel seems to entertain something like a doubt about his own practice, which commits a higher anachronism, inasmuch as the beginnings of art are interpreted from beyond art.

The symbolic is a legitimate place for doubts because here doubt and dubiousness reign supremely. Everything depends upon bringing together subjective and objective doubtfulness which seems to be achieved with the leitmotif of the "task." "Egypt is the country of symbols, the country which sets itself the spiritual task of the self-deciphering of the spirit, without actually attaining to the decipherment" (1:354). This dictates Hegel's own task, namely, "interpreting the riddles of Egyptian art and its symbolic works as a problem remaining undeciphered by the Egyptians themselves" (1:354). At the end of this chapter on symbolic art, so concerned with the dubious, there is one doubt more: "The demand [. . .] is simply this, that the external appearance and its meaning, the thing itself and its spiritual interpretation, must not [. . .] remain as their unification a linkage which is symbolical or sublime and comparative. The genuine representation is to be sought, therefore, only where the thing itself through and in its external appearance affords the interpretation of its spiritual content" (1:426).

The necessary anachronism threatens to demolish the artistic ideal and to disperse its unique finality. Hegel dismisses it therefore into the protoart of the symbolic phase, whose eliminating supervention classical art accomplishes. The end of symbolic protoart is not, however, an ultimate sublation, but remains rather a dubious, ambiguous end, and this suddenly opens unexpected possibilities of rereading Hegel's interpretation of classical art.

4

"The symbol, *in the meaning of the word used here*, constitutes the beginning of art" (1:303, emphasis added). The symbol is a sign brought into the service of a determinate meaning, which must always somehow be "used" (1:305) in order to be a symbol. Symbolizing is an operation, as practiced by Hegel in the chapter's very first sentence, which makes a specific use and assigns a task to a sign, in this case the linguistic sign "symbol." The symbol is capable of becoming protoart, because it serves signifying purposes that are not intrinsic to it. At the same time, however, it can be instrumentalized only if a quasi-natural meaning is presupposed. The ambiguity of the symbol consists therefore only secondarily in the question of how it is to be understood. This doubt can only arise because the symbol already presupposes an essential affinity between form and meaning. This is why "the symbol by its very nature remains essentially *ambiguous*" (1:306). Thus the symbol marks the unrestricted dominance of the ambivalence between discovering and inventing, which first must be distinguished and clearly separated before classical art can proceed to unify them again. That the confrontation between these aspects has not yet occurred lends the symbol its characteristic ambiguity. The task is to eliminate this equivalence—or, as Hegel puts it, this "indifference" of the two sides of the symbol—in such a way that the ambivalence between internal significance and external signifying function evaporates. At the close of the symbolic phase, these two sides diverge until only the arbitrariness of positing meaning remains. The similarities one thought to have discovered are revealed to be meanings that one has invented and produced. The end of the symbolic phase of art consists in the recognition of this situation. Only then does the struggle for an appropriate relation between form and meaning enter into artistic consciousness. Classical art can now (re)unite what fell apart at the end of the symbolic period.

This collapse belongs to the stage of so-called conscious symbolizing, which dissolves and overcomes the earlier stages of originary symbolism and the sublime. But the transition is not marked as sublation in the emphatic Hegelian sense. Instead, symbolic art suffers a rather profane end; to be more precise, this art ends in the profanity of the quotidian: "still this unification is not a higher form of art at all but rather a clear but superficial mode of treatment which, limited in its content and more or less prosaic in its form, deserts the mysteriously fermenting depth of the symbol proper, and strays down from the height of sublimity into common consciousness" (1:380). Thus, before the beginning of art in the genuine sense of its highest determination, it comes anachronistically to an end of art that is no sublation, but a mere disappearance.

In the introductory section on the symbol, Hegel had noted how the end of symbolism was to be understood and how its essential ambiguity could be eliminated. On the one hand, he predicts what does indeed happen to the comparative art forms. Doubting comes to an end when the two sides of the symbol are strictly distinguished from one another and their relation is explicitly formulated. But Hegel also mentions, if only in passing, another way of limiting the symbolic. Its dubiousness is dissolved practically, so to speak, by means of the convention that has already decided about the connection and its significance, without making this explicit: "No doubt its ambiguity is removed from the symbol, strictly so-called, if, on account of this very uncertainty, the linkage of the sensuous picture with the meaning is made *customary*, and becomes more or less *conventional*" (1:307–8, emphasis added). Hegel is right to be leery of granting this practical resolution of the dubious character of the symbol much weight, for if classical art is in fact not the self-conscious distinction of the sides of the symbol, but simply and without much sublation the effect of a taming into a convention, then things do not look promising for the heroic perfection of this art.

From this end, in everyday praxis, no direct way leads to the lonely heights of classical art. With the dissipation of art into quotidian consciousness, a wretched, because undialectical and dubious, end confronts the sublating transformation of tangled symbolism by classical art. This makes the end of symbolic art itself ambiguous. The end of symbolic art is itself still a symbol. As symbolic, this ambiguous end points to an essential affinity between profane death and heroic sublation. It consists in nothing other than the convention, for conventions determine the prose of the everyday while being also present in classical art "as" a secondary feature. Classical art transforms the symbols of protoart into conventions. By only allowing animal representations, for instance, as subsidiary features and conventional accessories, classical art turns what preceded it into tradition. It invents the quotidian tendency toward the profane as tradition and convention. What is invented in classical art, what is founded there and established, is an inexhaustible reservoir of possibilities to discover, collect, and rearrange. Its manifestation as creative individuality is only one of these possibilities. Conventions can be denounced, suppressed, transformed, and degraded; one can accuse or praise them. But there is only one place where conventions are produced. The imaginary home of anachronicity, in which tradition and convention are invented in order to be rejected, transformed, or sublated, is the museum.

Classical art is devoted, Hegel writes, to the "preservation" of the old gods of protoart from the symbolic era. The classical site of preservation of these old gods and their accessories is the museum. Hegel could have watched from his window the construction of the first official museum in Berlin while composing the lectures on aesthetics. Classical art, as it is conceptualized in his lectures, presents us with a museum. Only there the tension between invention and discovery finally disappears, for in the museum the logic of collection establishes the difference between invention and discovery. That the heart of Hegel's aesthetic, classical art, is a museum (housing the prehistory of art) does not mean that here art is laid to rest. Quite the contrary; Hegel is the first theoretician of a modernity that is unthinkable without the museum, whether the moderns take up residence in it comfortably, whether they merely refurbish it or revolt against it. Modernity has done all of this in the name of the end of art. Understood as museal archive and "museum without walls" (André Malraux), Hegel's classical art is not the philosophical interment of idealist prejudices, but the exhibition of modernity, the—anachronistically—transplanted discovery in antiquity of the modern possibility of establishing traditions. But Hegel's *Aesthetics* also shows that only where such conventionalizing mechanisms have been preserved—that is, only as long as there are museums, not merely real museums but also textual archives such as Hegel's aesthetics and within them the imaginary site of classical art—does the possibility persist of collecting otherwise, ordering the materials differently and selecting them differently, and even breaking down the museum's walls. As a museum, classical art is not the death of living art, but the (re)birth of modernity.

Boris Groys has traced the logic of modern innovative art back to its museal conditions of possibility. "The modern art museum is therefore not a graveyard, but, if you like, a church for things. There they experience their conversion, their second birth, their parusia. [. . .] Only such newborn things can modernity call artworks."[26] What Groys writes about the paradox of modern artistic subjectivity is, despite his aversion to Hegel, indebted to Hegel's aesthetics. Hegel knew that the "lightning-flash of individuality" is not the opposite but rather a mode of conventionalizing, a specific effect of museumizing: "free subjectivity can only show itself free because the museum relieves it of the labor of artistic production, by itself assuming this labor."[27]

Groys's essays on the *Logic of the Collection* were written under the impact of a contemporary crisis of the museum. It consists not only in the increasing competition between modern art and the media that threaten to make the museum superfluous. The rapid proliferation of ever more museums also indicates a crisis, threatening an end of art in a different way, for the danger arises "of totalizing the museal gaze and of understanding the entire world as a museum."[28] With that, Groys claims, the museum becomes ideology. His essays are therefore dedicated to the relation "between the logic of museal collection and different modern ideologies of the collected world."[29]

Groys is not the first to accuse Hegel's "totalizing" philosophy of wanting to archive and resolve each and every thing from the vantage point of the end of history, but his aesthetics proves immune to the ideology of a world as total museum. For the application of the museal logic in that museum represented by classical art is confined exclusively to the art of that period. The borders, however, that reign in this classical museum are not fixed but should be considered virtual, for only where boundaries can be drawn and museums erected do substitutions and changes remain possible. (That to name a boundary is to transgress it is something Hegel already knew how to criticize in Kant. That a boundary can only be transgressed where new boundaries are drawn, by sorting or collecting differently, is something his *Aesthetics* continues to demonstrate to this day.)

All of this changed with Nietzsche. As the antipode of a Hegel constantly scolded as totalitarian, Nietzsche threatens not only the limits of art, but runs the risk of a totalization that Hegel's end of art had not excluded, but controlled. This is usually considered Nietzsche's aestheticism. But this is an insufficient designation for the problem that Nietzsche uncovered. The following chapter seeks to demonstrate how Nietzsche, as opposed to Hegel, actually released the end of art from its Hegelian restrictions—and therefore deserves to be considered the ancestor of all attempts at radicalization. At the same time, however, he resisted the temptation to hypostasize and totalize the end of art and thereby art itself.

CHAPTER 3

Nietzsche's Retrograde Motion

The living is merely a type of what is dead, and a very rare type.

—NIETZSCHE

I

From the birth of tragedy to the eternal return, Nietzsche[1] systematically avoids proclamations of an end, and thereby heeds the law of his philosophy. Under the dictate of becoming and the optic of life, there is no longer any need for an end, least of all for an end to art, whose emancipation from its metaphysical presuppositions is only accomplished when art has overcome all need of a "beyond," including all longing for its own termination. Nietzsche deeply mistrusts any "philosophy [. . .] that knows some finale, some final state of some sort, every predominantly aesthetic or religious craving for some Apart, Beyond, Outside, Above" (*GS* 34; *KSA* 3:348).

But precisely this rejection and avoidance of any references to an end to art by this first theoretician of decadence, who once defined decadence as "the will to the end" (*CW* 155; *KSA* 6:12), predestines his work as an exceptional case of the end of art. Because his thought critically excludes the end, Nietzsche himself can mark the end of *that* art that since Hegel has stood under the sway of the end of art and suffered the suspicion of not being art. In this respect, Nietzsche appears as Hegel's mirror image. Whereas many critics prefer to ignore the destructive pluralizing of the end in Hegel, Nietzsche tempts one to fill the empty spot of the end of art with nothing other than an end of art. In both cases, the discourse of the end of art ignores its own conditions: *because* his philosophy knows no end of art, Nietzsche *must* be the finale. This paradox does not just effect an end of art. The very Nietzsche who would have nothing of an end figures prominently in a whole series of phantasmagoric endings and scenarios of overcoming. He signs for the end of God, metaphysics, and the subject. "Nietzsche" signals a radical break in modern self-understanding. Jürgen Habermas, who criticizes Nietzsche from a certain position within this self-understanding, called Nietzsche the "turning point."[2]

Like Hegel, whom he is thought to have overcome, revoked, and terminated,[3] Nietzsche also predicts the paradigms of his own interpretability. "I am, to express it in the form of a riddle, already dead as my father, while as my mother I am still living and becoming old. This dual descent, as it were, both from the highest and the lowest rung on the ladder of life, at the same time a *decadent* and a *beginning*" (*EH* 222; *KSA* 6:264), is what identifies him. Therefore, he continues in *Ecce Homo*, "I have a subtler sense of smell for the signs of ascent and decline than any other human being before me; I am the teacher par excellence for this—I know both, I am both." This self-authorization as first and last allows him to proclaim himself the critical genealogist of all beginnings and all endings;[4] at the same time, however, it compels posterity to celebrate or criticize him as renewer, destroyer, or victor.[5] All subsequent readers must confront the question of how to deal with the *founder* of genealogy, which knows no foundings and no terminations but only transitions. There is no more penetrating critic of all need for endings or beginnings than the Nietzsche who sees himself as beginning and end. Such is the "Janus face" characterizing all great insights according to Nietzsche (*EH* 289; *KSA* 6:328); and such is the problem reading Nietzsche.

In the early *Untimely Observations* Nietzsche is already pursuing a double strategy of critically questioning the end as a function of all techniques of periodizing *and* simultaneously underscoring the impossibility of circumventing it. His discussion of the categories "monumental," "antiquarian," and "critical" history makes this clear. In contrast to modern historicism, within which life withers, these categories represent for Nietzsche a life-promoting encounter with history, because they all actually operate ahistorically for the sake of life. The three modes are neither properties of history nor forms of historiography, but describe their relation under changing constellations of past and present life. Monumental and antiquarian history are committed to continuity, and their praxis also ensures their own survival. The monumentalizing historian, who seeks protection in history from resignation, becomes a part of the "continuity of what is great in all ages" (*UO* 98; *KSA* 1:260) and has a claim to "a place of honor in the temple of history, where he can, in turn, serve later generations as a teacher, comforter, and admonisher" (*UO* 97; *KSA* 1:259). The antiquarian historian by contrast prepares new fields of activity for his colleagues. "By attending with caring hands to what has subsisted since ancient times, he seeks to preserve for those who will emerge after him the conditions under which he himself has come into being" (*UO* 103; *KSA* 1:265). Antiquarian and monumental history both establish continuities, but they differ in the way in which past and present are related to one another. The antiquarian historian draws conclusions from the present about past and future. "'It was possible to live here,' he tells himself, 'because it is possible to live here and will in the future be possible to live here'" (*UO* 103; *KSA* 1:265). The monumental historian believes the reverse, and he expects to find in the past justification for his present plans. This type of historian reasons "that the greatness that once existed was at least *possible* at one time, and that it therefore will probably be possible once again" (*UO* 98; *KSA* 1:260). Both tend to obscure discontinuities and to ignore that something might have come to an end. Monumental historians manage this by homogenizing the scattered past for their own purposes: "with what violence the individuality of the past must be forced into a general form, its sharp edges and its lines broken in favor of this conformity!" (*UO* 99; *KSA* 1:261). The antiquarian historian overlooks the contingent transitional cases, by placing the substrate of an identical "we" beneath them. "With this 'we' he looks beyond his own transient, curious, individual life and senses himself to be the spirit of his house, his lineage, and his city" (*UO* 103; *KSA* 1:265).

While monumental and antiquarian history posit a continuum beyond the unruly heterogeneity of transitions, critical history aims exclusively at discontinuity. What is past is dissolved and condemned in order to free the present from the spell of the past. This puts critical history and the life it serves in danger of denying continuities per se, and so of sawing the branch on which it sits. "For since we are, after all, the products of earlier generations, we are also the products of their aberrations, passions, and errors—indeed, of their crimes; it is impossible to free ourselves completely from this chain" (*UO* 107; *KSA* 1:270).

But not only critical history must insist upon an end; even the strategies that establish continuities and so deny that something can come to an end must speculate with endings. By isolating particular facts and attempting in their various ways to eternalize them, they too depend upon an end. Whether history is viewed as worthy of termination and ripe for interruption, as in critical history, or whether facts are observed in closed-off independence, innovation remains impossible; no new or different history takes place any longer. Admittedly, no history at all takes place, and thus no new history, when nothing is ended. Nietzsche's own strategy rests on this double insight into the necessity and the problematic of any ending. The "origin of historical cultivation—as well as its intrinsic and wholly radical contradiction with the spirit of a 'new age' and a 'modern consciousness'— this origin *must* itself, in turn, be understood historically, history itself *must* solve the problem of history, knowledge must turn the goad upon itself— this threefold *must* is the imperative of the spirit of the 'new age,' provided that there is really something new, powerful, life-promoting, and original in it" (*UO* 141; *KSA* 1:306). Because Nietzsche's own reflections are subject to this imperative, one cannot expect from him an end of the end, because even a history of history cannot entirely avoid the end as a periodization factor. Nietzsche does not provide an end of the history of the end, but only the endless and endlessly variable histories of history.

Under the title "From First and Last Things," Nietzsche prescribed the task ahead of the thinker at the end of metaphysics and thus at the end of myth:

Then, however, he needs to take a *retrograde* step: he has to grasp the historical justification that resides in such ideas, likewise the psychological; he has to recognize that they have been most responsible for the advancement of mankind and that without such a retrograde step he will deprive himself of the best that mankind has hitherto produced.—In regard to philosophical metaphysics, I see more and more who are making for the negative goal (that all positive metaphysics is an error), but still few who are taking a few steps back; for one may well want to look out over the topmost rung of the ladder, but one ought not to want to stand on it. The most enlightened get only as far as liberating themselves from metaphysics and looking back on it from above: whereas here too, as in the hippodrome, at the end of the track it is necessary to turn the corner. (*HA* 23; *KSA* 2:41–42)

Not only do the *Untimely Observations* manage the trick of both pos-

iting and revoking an end, but they also force (at least the early) Nietzsche
to ascribe an end to art. What Nietzsche at first calls "critical history" and
later genealogy is in fact nothing other than the art that stands in service
to life: "Only when history allows itself to be transformed into a work of
art, into a pure aesthetic structure, can it perhaps retain or even arouse
instincts" (*UO* 132; *KSA* 1:296). Only where historical (trans)formation
knows itself to be an aesthetic act can knowledge become historical and
still serve life. Only there is it able to accomplish this double movement, to
know and to be. It is the prerogative of art to achieve this. The vacancy of
the site of an end to art in Nietzsche results, then, from the omnipresence
of art. Together with the closely related concept "life," the term "art" already in the early *Untimely Observations* marks an ultimate instance. Scholarship continues to concern itself with the question whether the "vitalism"
of the early and middle Nietzsche is finally an "artistic metaphysics," or
whether his aestheticism is in the last analysis a vitalism.[6] An aphorism
from *Human, All Too Human*, in which the end of art plays a significant
role, proves that this alternative is pointless.

Art is above and before all supposed to *beautify* life [. . .]. Then, art is supposed
to *conceal* or *reinterpret* everything ugly, those painful, dreadful, disgusting things
[. . .]: it is supposed [. . .] in the case of what is ineluctably or invincibly ugly to
let the *meaning* of the thing shine through. After this great, indeed immense task
of art, what is usually termed art, *that of the work of art*, is merely an *appendage*.
A man who feels within himself an excess of such beautifying, concealing and re-
interpreting powers will in the end seek to discharge this excess in works of art as
well; so, under the right circumstances, will an entire people.—Now, however, we
usually start with art where we should end with it, cling hold of it by its tail and
believe that the art of the work of art is true art out of which life is to be improved
and transformed—fools that we are! (*HA* 255; *KSA* 2:453)

Although the aphorism starts by claiming that art serves life, beautifies it,
makes it bearable, and accords the meaning to it that man needs in order to survive and to endure life, it then reveals the idea of wanting to influence life by means of art as mere illusion. Art is not in service to life,
knowledge, or morals, but all these are already in service to art—a newly
conceived and unlimited art, however, in terms of which the prior object
domain "art" represents a derivation, a mere "appendage." "At the end" of
art and "ultimately," the artworks in a traditional sense appear, from which

in an invalid deduction art, its concept, beginning, and purpose for life are retrospectively concluded.

This inversion of the relations and their correcting restitution are performed by the rhetorical figure of hysteron-proteron, which Nietzsche's aphorism not only denounces, but also simultaneously marshals for its own purposes. Only at the end of the reading can one determine that the beginning is not that canon of vulgar-Hegelian aesthetic motifs, different from their originals only to the extent that the concept of life has replaced Hegelian spirit. With its final turn, Nietzsche's text not only ensures that the illusory conclusion about the true connection between art, artwork, and life is artificial, rhetoric, and reinterpretation, but clearly that the second inversion, which (re)turns the things to their proper positions, is also artificial. Because it is here also a matter of mere transposition and reinterpretation, it can make no claim to be a restitution of the true state of affairs.

Because Nietzsche expands the boundaries of art not only conceptually but also by understanding it as a process of reinterpretation, art in neither its old, narrow sense nor its new, unlimited sense can claim priority.[7] As a consequence, art no longer means anything other than the possibility of endless reinterpretations. Art in Nietzsche is no longer a separate object domain, neither a determinate way of considering things nor a specific form of production. Rather, art is interpretation, reinterpretation of life by life, self-interpretation of life as the self-constitution of life. Art does not stand in service to life, but neither does life stand in service to art. These alternatives collapse in favor of endless possibilities of interpretation. Only with this transformation of art and life into interpretation does the world become infinite in its possible exegesis; art no longer has a site, because everything is art and all art is always the art of interpretation.[8]

If neither art nor life can be installed as metainstance, this does not yet solve the problem of their oscillating affinity. Martin Heidegger's critical Nietzsche interpretation throws a spotlight on this. His argument that Nietzsche's interpretation of the will to power is modeled on art in a traditional sense and therefore remains metaphysical can be transferred to the matters here at issue. One can ascribe an end of art to Nietzsche insofar as what was once limited to art does not find its end as art, but is dissolved by extending its boundaries. Art expands into previously unknown territories.

Whether one criticizes this expansion of art as a problematic aestheticization or welcomes it as a long-overdue modification of an outdated concept
of art is a secondary problem.

Although the claim that Nietzsche marks a new, as yet unknown and
above all anti-Hegelian end of art deserves skepticism[9]—"since we are, after all, the products of earlier generations"—it is hard to ignore the fact
that Nietzsche indeed releases the end of art from the sphere of aesthetics
once and for all, making it available as a model of interpretation for other
projects, in particular for the cultural philosophy emerging around 1900.
Nietzsche—and this is a difference from Hegel, in whose aesthetics art
endlessly terminates, without becoming or being anything else—exposes
art and its end to other contexts. The discourse of crisis that began around
1900 and then was radicalized against the background of World War I—
and in which Valéry, Husserl, and Simmel participate as much as Jünger,
Spengler, or Pannwitz—starts here. Art does not come to an end, but explodes, expands, and is emancipated as the possibilities of its application
multiply. These were available since Hegel, but Hegel himself, with his end
of art in the classical age, had simultaneously blocked many of the possibilities he had generated. Nietzsche activates this arsenal, suspending the
limitation that the end of art in Hegel placed on the heterogeneous interpretive potentials of the end of art.

It is difficult to fully determine Nietzsche's diffuse influence on these
developments. But at least one of his central aesthetic concepts lends a
certain unity to the multifarious discourses of crisis. Again and again, the
"plurality of styles"—a radical variant of Hegel's anachronism—appears
as the seal of a loss of unity and a symptom of crisis. A characteristic expression of this can be found in Paul Valéry's essay on the "crisis of spirit."
"An unparalleled horror has shivered Europe to its marrow. [. . .] But in
this moment, as if in desperate self-defense of its inner being and possession the entirety of its memories have once again arisen darkly. Its great
men and its great books tumble confusedly before it. . . . And in this spiritual confusion, under the pressure of this terror educated Europe lived fe-
verishly through its innumerable thoughts once more."[10] The crisis is the
museal confusion of different styles. There is perhaps no discourse of crisis
in the early twentieth century that does not invoke the specter of plurality of styles.[11]

Indeed, Nietzsche (re)discovered for modernity an emphatic notion of style opposed to the negative phantasmagoria of a plurality of styles. As style, art and life grow together into culture, for "culture is a unity of artistic style that manifests itself throughout all the vital self-expressions of a people," as the *Untimely Observations* has it (*UO* 9; *KSA* 1:163). The opposition is between "absence of style" and "the chaotic hodgepodge of all styles" (*UO* 9; *KSA* 1:163). As the epitome of a unity of art and life, style is not reducible to either art or life. This suggests that an interpretation of the end of art in Nietzsche would have to proceed by beginning with a detailed analysis of Nietzsche's theory of style. With reference, but also in opposition to Heidegger's interpretation of the "great style," the French Nietzsche reception has long shown how fractured and irreducibly heterogeneous Nietzsche's seemingly homogeneous concept of style actually is.[12] It also became obvious that no serious engagement with the concept of style in Nietzsche can avoid its link with the other central concept of distance.[13] In *Ecce Homo* Nietzsche writes: "Distance; the art of separating without setting against one another; to mix nothing, to 'reconcile' nothing; a tremendous variety that is nevertheless the opposite of chaos—this was the precondition, the long, secret work and artistry of my instinct" (*EH* 254; *KSA* 6:294). The problematic relation between distance and style is first unfolded, albeit in different terminology, in the *Birth of Tragedy*, whose tragic staging of an end to art in the form of the death of tragedy served as a model for many of the modern discourses of crisis. A sequence of four aphorisms on the end of art in the narrow sense of the end of literature provides a convenient prologue to reading the "drama" that Nietzsche stages in his *Birth of Tragedy*.

2

Aphorism 221 of the fourth section of *Human, All Too Human* ("From the Souls of Artists and Writers"), whose devastating verdict against the entire aesthetics of autonomy, including the iconic Goethe, already seemed scandalous to contemporary literary historians, still upsets the guild.[14] In the section entitled "The Revolution in Poetry," Nietzsche attributes to German literature since Lessing and French literature since Voltaire, in gestures as crude as they are seductive, a mere insubstantial "experimentation" (*HA* 103; *KSA* 2:181). Their first and last innovation consisted in a unique and irrevocable "breach with tradition" (*HA* 103; *KSA* 2:182), in the wake of which "art moves toward its dissolution" (*HA* 104; *KSA* 2:183). The history of modern literature knows no end, because it is nothing more than a long decrepitude—that is, an expiring history, a ceaseless "going down to destruction" (*HA* 104; *KSA* 2:183). In addition to exotic curiosities that Hegel had already associated with romantic art—"all that has grown up in hidden places, the primitive, wild-blooming, strangely beautiful and gigantically irregular" (*HA* 103; *KSA* 2:182)—art gains something else that it never had before: the history of its development. For an art seized by its dissolution "ranges—which is extremely instructive, to be sure—through all the phases of its beginnings, its childhood, its imperfection, its former hazardous enterprises and extravagances: in going down to destruction it interprets its birth and becoming" (*HA* 104; *KSA* 2:183). What had to be painstakingly extracted from Hegel, the archiving of the genesis of art from symbolic protoart in the classical phase, becomes in Nietzsche explicit and programmatic. With the self-interpretation of its past, art establishes its development and produces for the first time the fact of its having become what it is. Only by dissolving does art become historical, does it discover that it has a history. Since the middle of the eighteenth century art has been the recollection, the memory, the historical commemoration of the fact that there was once art. Along with Byron, Goethe—although only the Goethe of "the second half of his life" (*HA* 104; *KSA* 2:183), the Goethe of the poem "Re-encounter" in *West-östlicher Divan* and the epic *Hermann and Dorothea*—embodies the insight in both the interruption of tradition as well as this becoming-history of dying art: "Thus he lived in art as in recollection of true art: his writing had become an aid to recollection, to an understanding of ancient, long since vanished artistic epochs" (*HA* 104; *KSA* 2:184). In a word, Goethe "understood" the art that the Greeks and the French still "practiced" (*HA* 104; *KSA* 2:184). Arthur Danto, who likes to cite Hegel as an authority for his own thesis of the end of art, should find Nietzsche a more appropriate witness with more generous calculations. According to him, the end of art can be dated from around 1750 and the beginning of its history. Afterward art is at best, as in late Goethe, (art) history, and recollection of what has long since passed, and at worst it remains, as in early Goethe, bound to the path of revolution, victim to its deluded idea of innovation, while it aimlessly experiments here and there. After the "breach of tradition," art lives historically and parasitically from the end of (great, long since past) art.

The paradox of this theory of degeneration is, however, that art only has a history and can be an object of a development once it is degenerating. Only from this point on can something like an end (of a development or of a history) come into view. What has no history or development can also have no ending. Two things follow from this. First: Whatever may have happened to art at its breaking point, when revolutionary attitudes and innovative experiments began to prevail, can under no circumstances be its end, because before this there was neither history nor development for art, and so no end. Second: An end of art first becomes possible with an art that is no longer (great) art. And because it is no longer art, this art can just as little have an end as can the great, passed art. The non- or quasi-art of self-demolition and dissolution that follows the breach with tradition is not a terminal art, an art of the end, a symptom of degeneration, but just the opposite—a renewed resumption of the ruptured tradition qua recollection, a rebirth of art out of the spirit of history and *as* its history. We may have Nietzsche to thank or blame for the expansion of the confines of art, but he is also the first participant in the discourse of the end of art who radically uncouples art from ending, because neither on this side nor the other of the breach in tradition is there an end of art. The breach itself remains undetermined, unmotivated, and enigmatic, an empty place—entirely comparable to the elliptical hiatus between the birth and rebirth of art at the outset of Hegel's *Aesthetics*. This empty field organizes the historical trajectories, makes changes localizable, without itself participating in them or being integrated into them.

In order to argue conclusively that art neither *before* nor *after* the breach in tradition has or is an end, it is necessary to demonstrate that that great art that is supplanted after the breach in tradition by that "revolution in poetry" actually was and knew no development. Further exegesis is required to prove that point, for it seems initially as if Nietzsche wanted to attribute a stringent development precisely, and only, to the art of classical antiquity and the Middle Ages, while modern art strays in leaps and bounds along the "path of revolution" without any developmental law of its own.

Here as elsewhere (and like Hegel), Nietzsche argues that art first becomes genuine art and leaves behind the preartistic "naturalization" (*HA* 102; *KSA* 2:181) when it has learned "to limit itself to what is most severe (perhaps also most capricious)" (*HA* 102; *KSA* 2:181). Long practice in walking while fettered results in art's highest achievement; according to Nietzsche, the development of modern music has attained this summit: "Here we see how the fetters grow looser step by step, until in the end it can appear as though they have been wholly thrown off" (*HA* 102; *KSA* 2:181). This appearance of freedom, the grace of an art in "self-imposed fetters" (*HA* 102; *KSA* 2:181), Nietzsche calls the "supreme outcome of a necessary development in art" (*HA* 102, translation modified; *KSA* 2:181). The adjective "necessary" is odd, given the fact that in poetry there has not been "such fortunate, gradual development" (*HA* 102, translation modified; *KSA* 2:181). When a development can be more or less fortunate, it must be contingent and leaves no room for a "necessary development." Moreover, this necessary "development" or emergence is actually no such thing at all, whether gradual or "constant," but it merely gives the impression of development; it appears as if the fetters had been tossed aside. This art therefore does not develop at all, but rather in its fetters it evokes, if things go well, the appearance of an unfettering, an emergence, or a development. The art of art consists, then, in not developing, in remaining fettered, in order to evoke the appearance of freedom and development. This art can have no end, because it knows no development.

The appearance of a gradual evolution from self-imposed fetters is opposed by the appearance of modern art that neither develops nor appears to, but "moves towards its dissolution," because it is no longer anchored in anything. When Nietzsche writes that "even the most gifted can achieve only a continual experimentation once the thread of evolution has been broken" (*HA* 103; *KSA* 2:181), he must be taken literally. The thread, the fetters, the fastenings are torn. Because it is unfastened, modern art can look forward to no evolution. Without ground and connectedness it collapses; instead of appearing to solve its restrictions, it dissolves. But only then can art establish what it never before had: a beginning, a becoming, albeit one that lies behind it and has no future to look forward to.

Aphorism 221 belongs together with two other aphorisms in which the fate of art is not considered immanently and historically, but is sketched in terms of its metaphysical presuppositions. From this broader perspective as well, art has no end, but even more clearly than in "The Revolution in Poetry," it knows only transitions. Under the title "The Beyond in Art," Nietzsche writes in aphorism 220 that the arts have always been "the glorifiers of the religious and philosophical errors of mankind, and they could not have been so without believing in the absolute truth of these errors. If belief in such truth declines in general, if the rainbow-colours at the extreme limits of human knowledge and supposition grow pale, that species of art can never flourish again, which, like the *Divina Commedia*, the pictures of Raphael, the frescoes of Michelangelo, the Gothic cathedrals, presupposes not only a cosmic but also a metaphysical significance in the objects of art" (*HA* 102; *KSA* 2:180). The concluding sentence demonstrates that this is not an end, but the transfiguring transformation of art into its history—indeed, its invention *as history*: "A moving tale will one day be told how there once existed such an art, such an artist's faith" (*HA* 102; *KSA* 2:180). Art does not end; it does not go under, but goes over into the world of tales, of the chimerical, that provokes the subjunctive of indirect report. Art and artists' faith will one day have existed in the way tales claim dragons and monsters existed.

Aphorism 222, which follows "The Revolution in Poetry," also precludes an end to art, circumvents it by proceeding directly to "What is Left of Art" (*HA* 105; *KSA* 2:185). Not transfigured into legend, but transformed into a drive for knowledge, once again the doctrine taught by art appears: "to take pleasure in existence" (*HA* 105; *KSA* 2:185). "One could give up art, but would not thereby relinquish the capacity one has learned from it. [. . .] the intensity and multifariousness of the joy in life it has implanted would still continue to demand satisfaction" (*HA* 105; *KSA* 2:185–86). And Nietzsche concludes that the scientific man "is the further development of the artistic" (*HA* 105; *KSA* 2:186).

The retrospectively transfiguring transformation of art into its legendary history in aphorism 220 and the prospect of the scientific man as the continuation of the artistic man in aphorism 222 are linked despite their differing accents. Their common denominator is not art, but an *aesthetic attitude*, to which belongs the legend of displaced, great art just as much as the notion of an artist mutating into a scientist. The last aphorism, number 223, confirms the nexus between those two models; it provides a sort of prophetic retrospection that brings together the motifs that had been bound in image and saga in the three preceding aphorisms. "Just as in old age one remembers one's youth and celebrates festivals of remembrance, so will mankind soon stand in relation to art: it will be a moving recollection of the joys of youth" (*HA* 105; *KSA* 2:186). This extension of the present into a future that will have come to pass, leaps over or evades precisely the end, inasmuch as it presents itself as a reconstruction of a prehistory. This last aphorism in the sequence picks up the motif of recollection that already resonated in the legend of the "moving artists' belief" and that Goethe was taken to exemplify in the aphorism on "The Revolution in Poetry." Nietzsche confirms once more that a genuine understanding and feeling for art can commence only with this art of recollection. The opposition between "practice" and "understanding" is superseded by a "grasping" that is neither pure praxis nor conceptual completion: "Perhaps art has never before been grasped so profoundly or with so much feeling as it is now, where the magic of death seems to play around it" (*HA* 105, translation modified; *KSA* 2:186).[15] And as if he were recounting a legend, Nietzsche appends the history of the Greek city in southern Italy, whose population "on one day of the year continued to celebrate their Greek festival and did so with tears and sadness at the fact that foreign barbarism was triumphing more and more over the customs they had brought with them; it is to be doubted whether the Hellenic has ever been so greatly savoured, or its golden nectar imbibed with so much relish, as it was among these declining Hellenes" (*HA* 105; *KSA* 2:186). Art is again in bondage, but instead of lying in "self-made fetters," it suffers the chains of foreign domination; transplanted and indentured to other commitments, art now is what survives as mere relic. But in analogy to an art that becomes historical, gaining its development as art only with its dissolution, here, too, art becomes fully art only now: never was "its golden nectar imbibed with so much relish, as it was among these declining Hellenes." The extreme of pleasure and emotional intensity means as well an extreme of autonomy under conditions of heteronomy. Exiled, an exotic relic of itself, art becomes autonomous. Moreover, because the faith of artists has become extinct, the relic becomes an object of ritual adoration, a reliquary: "The artist will soon be regarded as a glorious relic, and we shall bestow upon him, as a marvelous stranger upon whose strength and beauty the happiness of former ages depended, honors such as we do not easily grant to others of our own kind" (*HA* 105–6, translation modified; *KSA* 2:186). Aesthetic attitude is ignited not by art but by art's relics. Recollection, ritual adoration, in Benjamin's terms the "cult value" of art is based on—not art, or its end, but on its history. Aesthetic attitude, the adoring, disinterested devotion, the "festivals of remembrance" are only possible once (great) art no longer exists. Aesthetic perception and aesthetic experience arise when their presumed object is no longer perceivable: "The sun has already set, but the sky of our life still glows with its light, even though we no longer see it" (*HA* 106; *KSA* 2:186). Art is always only art's colorful reflection. The aesthetic attitude is a type of postartistic behavior; it arises from the ruins and relics of something that can only be called art when it no longer exists. No path leads back to what art once was: "The best in us has perhaps been inherited from the sensibilities of earlier ages to which we hardly any longer have access by direct paths" (*HA* 106; *KSA* 2:186). Aesthetic attitude, aesthetic perception, is a detour that follows no end and faces no end—none, at least, that would somehow still be accessible beyond the detour, which always leads away from art and leads art on.[16] Whether as science or as the legend of a faith of artists, the aesthetic attitude is belated without end. There is no way to conclude from an aesthetic attitude that there is something like an object domain of art, or that it could end. Aesthetic behavior, strictly speaking, has no object, and although the concept of recollection and the legend of artistic faith might seem to suggest it, not even the end of art could be its object. Nietzsche's genealogy of the aesthetic attitude and the artistic gaze, which rules as much in history as in science, makes it impossible to map art onto either the traditionally limited or the newly expanded notion of art. To the extent that the artistic drive is an ex post facto effect and arises through detours, it cannot be determined as a final instance in either the name of life or the name of art. Art is not the apotheosis of life, and life is not the apotheosis of art.

Although art is omnipresent, it is not omnipresent as a constant drive but as a permanent detour and eternal afterthought, and so it enjoys no privilege. Even the end of art, central in all four aphorisms, is a detour and the effect of a reinterpretation. All that remains of the end is, in the middle of the aphoristic sequence, that enigmatic "breach of tradition" that marks a change that might look like an end but in a puzzling way remains entirely indeterminate and open.

Although the *Birth of Tragedy* deals in much larger historical expanses, it is also organized around such an enigmatic turning point. Already in antiquity, whose artists according to these aphorisms, still "practiced" what the moderns at best "understand," poetry itself dies along with tragedy: "Tragedy is dead! Poetry itself has perished with her!" (*BT* 76; *KSA* 1:75).

3

"Greek tragedy met an end different from that of her older sister-arts: she died by suicide, in consequence of an irreconcilable conflict; she died tragically" (*BT* 76; *KSA* 1:75). Where the end of art itself adopts tragic features—where tragedy is no longer, as with Hegel, the apex and end point of what art can achieve, but on the contrary, the end of art is conceived *as* tragedy, presented, or more correctly staged—it has become possible to evade and simultaneously neutralize the characteristic tension between the end of art as perfection and as finitude. Tragedy is, after all, that genre in which death is meaningful and meaningless at the same time. The constitutive ambivalence between the end of art as salvation and decay is made semantically available in the tragic staging of the end. The death of the hero amounts to salvation; this is how Nietzsche interprets the tragic figure of Oedipus, classically in the sense of Schelling's theory of tragedy: "though every law, every natural order, even the moral world may perish through his actions, his actions also produce a higher magical circle of effects which found a new world on the ruins of the old one that has been overthrown" (*BT* 68; *KSA* 1:65).

In the *Birth of Tragedy*, Nietzsche discovers or invents this only apparently original affinity between the end of art and tragedy, because on the ruins of the tragically dying tragedy a new order of "tragic knowledge" will be founded. The tragic staging of the end of art as the death of tragedy is the step by which the end of art is dissociated from art in order to live on in the discourses of cultural criticism. Nietzsche's "tragification" of the end in his *Birth of Tragedy* has turned out to be most productive for cultural criticism. As tragedy, the end of art once again reveals its founding power. But contrary to Nietzsche, who, as the reading of his book on tragedy will demonstrate, marks his staging of the end in the form of tragedy *as* staging, strategy, and representation, in many cultural-critical discourses the new nexus of the end of art and tragedy survives unimpeded by such refractions.

Perhaps there is no theory of tragedy upon which the shadow of Hegel does not fall. Nietzsche is quite explicit about the Hegelian ancestry of his book: "it smells offensively Hegelian, and the cadaverous perfume of Schopenhauer sticks only to a few formulas" (*EH* 270; *KSA* 6:310).[17] The Hegelian echoes are not limited to the dialectic of the opposition between Apollonian and Dionysian, or the position of tragedy as the pinnacle of art, in which "the antithesis is sublated into a unity" (*EH* 271; *KSA* 6:310). Nietzsche also shares with Hegel a number of aesthetic convictions. Like Hegel who famously excluded nature from the domain of artistic beauty, Nietzsche is deeply skeptical of art's pretensions to naturalism (*BT* 140; *KSA* 1:151). And even where their differences seem greatest, for instance between Hegel's emphasis on the role of developed individuality for art and Nietzsche's abandonment of just this individuality in the Dionysian, there is nonetheless a common narrative structure, as the following reading seeks to demonstrate.[18]

Above all, Hegel and Nietzsche share a surprising consensus, despite opposing valuations, on the topic of the end of art. In Nietzsche, as well, one learns that prose begins among slaves (*BT* 78; *KSA* 1:78), and if, in one version of Hegel's end, it falls to philosophy to transcend art, in Nietzsche, art dies similarly under the destructive influence of the intellectual forces of Socratism: "Here *philosophic thought* overgrows art and compels it to cling close to the trunk of dialectic" (*BT* 91; *KSA* 1:94). In addition to this explicit reference to Hegel and the tradition, Nietzsche also deploys interpretive hints that justify this dependence while simultaneously relativizing its significance by depicting it as a presentational procedure, indebted to a narrative technique.

His book "stammered [. . .] as if in a foreign tongue," Nietzsche writes in the later foreword, the "Attempt at a Self-Criticism" (*BT* 20, translation modified; *KSA* 1:15). That more is at stake than a self-critical assessment of infelicitous formulations is evident from the persistence of the topic of translation in the volume overall. Nietzsche wanted his book appreciated as a translating achievement. Thus Wagner does not really mean Wagner, but instead is a figure and a name necessary for something else that Nietzsche had "to transpose and transfigure [. . .] into the new spirit" (*EH* 274; *KSA* 6:313–14). Not unlike the exiled Greeks of southern Italy, celebrating their own festivals on foreign soil, transposition and translation are dominating motifs throughout the book. The problem of science "installed on the terrain of art, for the problem of science cannot be recognized on the terrain of science" (*BT* 18, translation modified; *KSA* 1:13). Under this premise, nothing in the book can be seen any longer in its own terms, but must be considered the effect of a transposition or translation.[19]

When Nietzsche writes in *Ecce Homo*, looking back on his first publication, "I had *discovered* the only parable and parallel in history for my own inmost experience" (*EH* 271; *KSA* 1:311), he is making the same claim about the status of his genealogy of tragedy as the book itself does: namely, that the entire theatrics of tragedy is not there for its own sake, but merely to provide "Hellenic analogies" for quite other themes that must be translated into the language of tragedy and the history of tragedy. That much the text says directly: "For to us who stand on the boundary line between two different forms of existence, the Hellenic prototype retains this immeasurable value, that all these transitions and struggles are imprinted upon it in a classically instructive form; except that we, as it were, pass through the chief epochs of the Hellenic genius, analogically in *reverse* order" (*BT* 121; *KSA* 1:128). The *Birth of Tragedy* is thus an exercise in "critical history," a rewriting of the past for the purposes of the present, the result of a "retrograde movement." What lends the Greeks their character as unique models is not some lost essence of tragedy but the prototypical character of tragedy's historical development. Greek exemplarity lies in tragedy's mortality. At issue is not the birth of tragedy or its hoped-for "rebirth" (*BT* 121; *KSA* 1:129), but at issue is the tragedy of tragedy, its development and entanglements, its dramatic dénouement and above all the tragic demise of tragedy.

As an instructive example and a parallel, as analogy and medium of translation, tragedy is legitimated not only by its development, but also internally, for in tragedy the principle of reinterpretation and translation is presented and staged. Nietzsche selects Rafael's painting "Transfiguration" to illustrate the "demotion of appearance to the level of mere appearance" (BT 45; *KSA* 1:39) that characterizes tragedy. In tragedy appearance becomes visible as appearance, and just as the privileged status of tragedy is the result of a translation, so translation is also its innermost principle: "Dionysus speaks the language of Apollo; and Apollo, finally the language of Dionysus: and so the highest goal of tragedy and of all art is attained" (*BT* 130; *KSA* 1:140).

In order to make appearance appear as appearance, a rhetoric is needed capable of producing this effect. Analogy and transfiguration, and above all translation, provide the means through which appearance shows itself as appearance, without this representation having to exclude itself from the general domain of appearance. The *Birth of Tragedy* is all smoke and mirrors, where one thing always makes something else appear and one thing appears as another. Even the categories of Dionysian and Apollonian are introduced quite explicitly as mere analogies, in order to illustrate further visions and analogies. The Dionysian as the experience of fusing with primal unity does not manifest itself, but is revealed only with the help of Apollonian visions. Even the imageless and nonrepresentational art of music is only "a copy of this primal unity, assuming that music has been correctly termed a repetition and a recast of the world" (*BT* 49; *KSA* 1:44). Even music, presumably the most direct art, is already an echo, a reflection, a repetition and rebirth, not yet fully transfigured, but still no longer only itself.[20]

This appearance-world of the *Birth of Tragedy*, its cosmos of reflections and reflexes, presents itself in Nietzsche's text *as translation and transfiguration*. The nexus between the presented principles within tragic art and the principle of their presentation in the *Birth of Tragedy* thus appears in the costume of translation and analogy. This imbrication of the development of tragedy and its presentation offers a solution to the epistemological dilemma that Nietzsche confronts: How is knowledge of appearance possible under the premise of appearance? In the language of tragedy, this becomes: How is a knowledge of tragedy that is simultaneously tragic and knowledge possible? How is "tragic knowledge" possible?

The fifth chapter, in which Nietzsche's theory of art departs from the paths of traditional aesthetic theory up through Schopenhauer, also marks the point where the problematic limits of his own theory emerge. Nietzsche's attempt to escape the tradition conjures forth the specter of aestheticism. The chapter in question is ostensibly concerned with the lyric; Dionysus and Apollo enter in the guise of Homer and Archilochus, the representatives of epic and lyric poetry, respectively. Firmly rejecting the conventional subject-object dichotomy that had still governed Schopenhauer's interpretation of lyric quoted earlier in extenso, Nietzsche unfolds his radically antisubjective understanding of lyric that culminates in the famous assertion of an artist metaphysics: "For to our humiliation *and* exaltation, one thing above all must be clear to us. The entire comedy of art is neither performed for our betterment or education nor are we the true authors of this art world. On the contrary, we may assume that we are merely images and artistic projections for the true author, and that we have our highest dignity in our significance as works of art—for it is only as an *aesthetic phenomenon* that existence and the world are eternally *justified*" (*BT* 52; *KSA* 1:47). The claim of this aesthetic theodicy is so radical, however, that from now on, all aesthetic efforts, including Nietzsche's own contributions to the aesthetic discussion, are surrendered up hopelessly to an indifferent world of appearances. If we are "merely images and artistic projections" of the primal unity, then our consciousness and knowledge of this dignity as artwork is worthless, because "our consciousness of our own significance hardly differs from that which the soldiers painted on canvas have of the battle represented on it" (*BT* 52; *KSA* 1:47). That is, it is no consciousness at all. With that, "all our knowledge of art is quite illusory, because as knowing beings we are not one and identical with that being which, as the sole author and spectator of the comedy of art, prepares a perpetual entertainment for itself" (BT 52; *KSA* 1:47). Whoever knows about this essence cannot merge with it, and whoever merges cannot at the same time know it. Only the "genius," Nietzsche claims, in accordance with the aesthetic tradition since Kant, *knows* something about the essence of art, to the extent that he "in the act of creation coalesces with this primordial artist of the world" (*BT* 52; *KSA* 1:47–48). But the subsequent image, together with the fact that such knowledge can only be expressed in an image, confirms just how problematic and paradoxical this condition is: "for in this state he is, in a marvelous manner, like the weird image of the fairy tale which can revolve its eyes and behold itself" (*BT* 52, translation modified; *KSA* 1:48).[21] This paradox of the self-observing image is not only particular to artistic creation, but may be considered an allegory of the epistemological paradox of the book as a whole, which demands simultaneously knowing distance from and immediate participation in its object.[22] Thus Nietzsche claims in the preface that his ideal readers would be "artists who also have an analytic and retrospective penchant" (*BT* 18; *KSA* 1:13). Nietzsche desires those whose artistic creativity is matched by their ability to maintain distance.

Strictly speaking, it is not just a matter of that impossible site where distance and participation can coexist, but also of a third aspect: the knowledge of their coexistence. Keeping with the image, it is a matter of that site from which the image beholding itself can in turn be observed. If tragedy can be seen as a realization of the fairy-tale figure, in that participants and audience both perceive themselves "transformed before one's own eyes" (*BT* 64; *KSA* 1:61), the *Birth of Tragedy* aims to validate a view of the self-observing image. Like Euripides entering and exiting as a scornful hero and founder of a new order, so Nietzsche enters with and in his book. Greek tragedy is not only evidence of the need "to see while at the same time longing to transcend all seeing" (*BT* 140, translation modified; *KSA* 1:150), but it also fulfills this need, because "it is the magic of these struggles that those who behold them must also take part and fight" (*BT* 98; *KSA* 1:102). This last sentence no longer refers to tragedy, but to its tragic development in the course of history. Thus one needs more than just tragedy to accommodate the epistemological demand of knowing and participating; one needs a tragedy of tragedy, the dramatic staging of its history.[23] Tragedy is not (yet) the unity of distance and participation, but this unity is first and only given in the knowledge of this truth. Only this knowledge is tragic knowledge; it is modern, entirely un- even anti-Greek: "The Greeks, as the Egyptian priests say, are eternal children, and in tragic art too they are only children who do now know what a sublime plaything originated in their hands and—was quickly demolished" (*BT* 105–6; *KSA* 1:110). Tragedy and its essence remain mere play, a prologue to tragic knowledge, whose actuality is indexed as a reconstructed prehistory. Taken in itself, tragedy as a work of art contains no tragic knowledge; the artwork is neither model nor prototype for aesthetic knowledge; it is not something to be interpreted, but is itself already an interpretation. Hence only the historical development of tragedy can claim to be a model. The past character of tragedy and the fact that its inventors did not know what they were doing—like the artists in Hegel's symbolic phase—are signs that art is always constructed from a position that must lie beyond art. Tragedy alone is not enough. There must be a tragedy of tragedy; tragedy must be simultaneously the subject and object of the *Birth of Tragedy*.

In this scenario, the event of tragedy's historical demise is crucial. The tragic death of tragedy is absolutely necessary if this book about tragedy is to be a product of tragic knowledge. Only the death of tragedy can seal the tragedy of tragedy; only this tragic death can legitimate the "Hellenic analogies." The death of tragedy constitutes the point of contact between the essence of tragedy and its tragic presentation. But just this point is the most puzzling in the entire text. Where one expects tragedy and the tragedy of tragedy to coalesce, their differences emerge instead.

Precisely when Nietzsche's account of the death of tragedy finally establishes the nexus between the end of art and the tragic, it turns out that the new orders of tragic knowledge are *not* guaranteed by sacrificial death, by the tragic death of tragedy, but that this honor falls to its reckless executioners. Euripides, the mocker in the sense of Nietzsche's interpretation of Prometheus, and Socrates, the founder of the new art of Platonic dialogue, are the true heroes of the tragedy of tragedy. In the beginning of the fifteenth chapter, Nietzsche writes of Socrates: "It must now be said how the influence of Socrates, down to the present moment and even into all future time, has spread over posterity like a shadow that keeps growing in the evening sun, and how it again and again prompts a regeneration of art—of art in the metaphysical, broadest and profoundest sense—and how its own infinity also guarantees the infinity of art" (*BT* 93; *KSA* 1:97). Socrates corresponds to Oedipus as the ideal type of the tragic man, "who eventually, through his tremendous suffering, spreads a magical power of blessing that remains effective even beyond his decease" (*BT* 67; *KSA* 1:65). The other tragic hero is "sacrilegious Euripides" (*BT* 74; *KSA* 1:74), under whose violent hands tragedy died, but who, like Prometheus, is a tragic figure, through the "dignity" he "confers on tragedy" (*BT* 71; *KSA* 1:69). To the extent that Socrates and the posttragic poet Euripides are the actual heroes of the piece, Nietzsche's genial synchronization of tragedy and the tragedy of tragedy exposes a hiatus, because only *after* its death, with Euripides and Socrates, does the tragedy of tragedy begin.

Strictly speaking, already the prelude to tragedy appears tragic. The tragic hero of this prelude is again not tragedy itself, but the "tragic myth."

Before tragedy can begin, the tragic myth must, like the mythological race of titans, be defeated. The hero of the tragedy of tragedy before the tragic death of this genre is myth: "This dying myth was now seized by the new-born genius of Dionysian music; and in these hands it flourished once more [. . .]; it rises once more like a wounded hero, and its whole excess of strength, together with the philosophic calm of the dying burns in its eyes with a last powerful gleam" (*BT* 75; *KSA* 1:74). There is tragic dying even before there is tragedy, and there is tragic dying and knowledge of it once tragedy has passed away.

What sort of death is the tragic death of tragedy, what status does it have, when tragedy and the tragedy of tragedy do not coincide in it, but diverge? Instead of a single tragic death, the *Birth of Tragedy* offers simultaneously three death scenes, as if tragedy would not stay dead, because it must always die again in a new and different way. Tragedy, Nietzsche had written in the first sentence of chapter 11, "died by suicide, in consequence of an irreconcilable conflict, that is, tragically" (*BT* 76; *KSA* 1:75). Tragedy did not die simply, but in a complicated way and repeatedly. When Nietzsche claims that an irreconcilable conflict drove tragedy to suicide, he not only refers to the tension between Apollonian and Dionysian, which is responsible for the "previously described impression of the discordant and incommensurable elements in the nature of Aeschylean tragedy" (*BT* 81; *KSA* 1:80). More importantly, tragedy died from itself, from its own incommensurability. It died from its failure to resolve the conflict between participation and distance, this presentational conflict that Nietzsche attempts to resolve by presenting the development of tragedy tragically. Or, conversely, by presenting it tragically, tragedy died from it. The death of tragedy is meant to be the solution, the dramatic denouement of the entire production, but his death does not take place—because it happens too frequently. Thus tragedy dies on the one hand by suicide, on the other hand it dies, likewise tragically, at Euripides' hand: "And just as myth died on you, the genius of music died on you, too. Though with greedy hands you plundered all the gardens of music, you still managed only copied, masked music. And because you had abandoned Dionysus, Apollo abandoned you" (*BT* 75; *KSA* 1:75). But third, tragedy continues to die unendingly, for petrified into "a monument of its exceedingly painful and violent death" (*BT* 76; *KSA* 1:76), it survives in the New Attic comedy: "When a new artistic genre blossomed forth after all, and revered tragedy as its predecessor and mistress, it was noted with horror that she did indeed bear the features of her mother—but those she had exhibited in her long death-struggle" (*BT* 76; *KSA* 1:76). The lethal inner conflict that killed tragedy is finally the fact that it dies and must die, but nonetheless cannot be done away with once and for all. Its end is as overdetermined and polysemic as was the end of symbolic art in Hegel.

Within the tragedy of tragedy that Nietzsche stages for the sake of tragic knowledge, the death of tragedy, just like the "breach in tradition" from *Human, All Too Human*, constitutes a dramatic vacancy that belongs no longer or not yet into the dramatic process that it founds. But whereas in the aphorisms on the twilight of art Nietzsche conceives as a "breach in tradition" an end to art that is no end, because it remains entirely undetermined and underdetermined, in the book on tragedy, the end of art is an overdetermined end, because tragedy falls victim to murder, commits suicide, and perpetuates its agony in the new genre. So extreme is this overdetermination that one can maintain not only that the death of tragedy is the vacant and therefore no longer tragic moment in the tragedy of tragedy, but also the opposite: this puzzling, overdetermined, and multiplicitous death of tragedy is perhaps the *only* tragic moment in this drama. If the death of tragedy is indeed the only tragic moment in this tragedy, then the *Birth of Tragedy* would become at this point the tragedy of tragedy of tragedy.

Because the tragic death of art in Nietzsche remains a vacancy, both in the underdetermined breach in tradition of the aphorisms as well as the overdetermined death of tragedy in the *Birth of Tragedy*, it could be filled, interpreted, even occupied with the death of art itself. "With the death of tragedy a great vacancy arose" also means that the death of tragedy is this great vacancy. This end of art remains an empty site, a blind spot, that precludes the end. Only as a free space that cannot be occupied because it is overoccupied does the death of tragedy gesture ostensibly at the fictional character of the production of which it is a necessary part, but in which it no longer participates. This dimension of the *Birth of Tragedy*, its ironic play with itself, no longer belongs to tragedy, whether as the tragedy of tragedy or the tragedy of the tragedy of tragedy. As Nietzsche assumes an ironic distance from all tragedy and from tragic knowledge as well, his book becomes comedy. Under the title "The Muse as Penthesilea," Nietzsche writes: "'Rather perish than be a woman who does not *charm*.' Once the muse is thinking like that, the end of her art is again in sight. But this end can be comic as well as tragic" (*HA* 236, translation modified; *KSA* 2:420). This end with an open outcome is also an inheritance from Nietzsche and remains part of the Hegelian heritage.

It is taken up, among others, by Walter Benjamin, who plays a strange game with Nietzsche's *Birth of Tragedy* in his *Origin of the German Mourning Play*. If Benjamin did not exactly ignore Nietzsche's double play, then he certainly rendered it one-sided.

CHAPTER 4

Counterplay: Benjamin

I

Benjamin's famous essay on "The Work of Art in the Age of Mechanical Reproduction" (1935) bids farewell to the (anti-)idealistic hopes of euphoric modernism for an unlimited art at a point in time when, with fascism, the politically disastrous implications of these hopes stood clearly before him.[1] As Benjamin put it in the programmatic closing formulation of the essay: "Thus the aestheticization of politics that fascism carries out. Communism responds to this with the politicizing of art."[2]

As with Hegel, it has become customary to refer to Benjamin's "theses"—he himself understands his reflections in these terms (*GS* 1:473; *I* 218)—and so the debate over the validity and justification of the end of auratic art continues. But the significant influence of this text—in which Benjamin's supposed turn from metaphysics to historical materialism is thought to be at stake—rests on the singular status the artwork essay assumes in his oeuvre. The reconstruction of this version of the end of art in modern technology must take a detour through other texts by Benjamin, not in order to deny its uniqueness, but in order to determine its specific features. Above all, *The Origin of the German Mourning Play* (1927) cannot be avoided. In light of this text's striking proximity to Nietzsche, it becomes evident that Benjamin's artwork essay intends neither an end of art nor an end to its ending; or rather, such intentions can only be attributed so long as one ignores the horizon that his treatise on the baroque had opened. For by way of an end of art, Benjamin stumbles across the theory of an allegorically understood modernity. His point is not the departure, overcoming, or obsolescence of auratic art, but the rediscovery of Hegel's classical museum as the allegorical structure of modernism.

One may speculate whether the "the best" in Benjamin's Trauerspiel book derives from Nietzsche's *Birth of Tragedy*, but the conception of his work on Trauerspiel certainly is indebted to a subterranean Nietzsche reception,[3] of which, admittedly, only critical peaks occasionally emerge. Benjamin was neither the first nor the last to remark on the "abyss of aestheticism . . . [into which] this brilliant intuition was finally to see all its concepts disappear."[4] His brief polemical comments on Nietzsche in the Trauerspiel book leave one with the impression that their actual purpose is to divert attention from the possibility that his idiosyncratic archeology of German Trauerspiel is a competing parallel and countertheory to Nietzsche. They invite the suspicion that despite all the obvious differences—in particular of course the programmatic shift in focus from tragedy to Trauerspiel—Benjamin pursues similar goals, follows similar rules of representation, and therefore also provokes similar questions.

Already Benjamin's formulaic and stereotypical aestheticism reproach, which would be much more appropriately leveled against the dominant tendency of contemporary Nietzsche reception, for instance in Volkelt, than against Nietzsche himself, evokes as many parallels as it denounces. "For what does it matter whether it is the will to life or the will to destroy life which is supposed to inspire every work of art, since the latter, as a product of the absolute will, devalues itself along with the world?" (*GS* 1:282; *O* 103).[5] If Nietzsche's night of aestheticism renders all artworks gray, Benjamin's antiaesthetic figure par excellence, allegory, does not fare much better, for the Midas hand of the allegorist also produces "a world in which the detail is of no great importance" (*GS* 1:350; *O* 175). The antiaesthetic counterlogic of allegory leads ultimately to an abyss in whose depths knowledge loses itself: "But this is also the bottomless pit of contemplation" (*GS* 1:404; *O* 231). And what does it matter, one might ask, whether one finds oneself in the abyss of aestheticism or the bottomless pit of contemplation?

More profoundly than the tendentious one-sidedness that characterizes Benjamin's encounter with Nietzsche's theory of tragedy,[6] their common enemy proves the two books' competitive affinity. Each author faults historicism for the failure of understanding a literary genre—baroque Trauerspiel in Benjamin, Attic tragedy in Nietzsche. Benjamin resolutely pursues the critique of historicism that Nietzsche had founded. Their interest in historical objects is determined by reference to the present. The "Hellenic analogies" that Nietzsche seeks in Wagner's opera correspond to Benjamin's actualization of baroque Trauerspiel in the light of contemporary modernism, in particular expressionism. If, according to Benjamin, it was the baroque achievement "to see the power of the present" in the medium of antiquity (*GS* 1:278; *O* 100), he himself is attempting to recognize in the medium of the baroque his own present moment.

It is as insufficient to imagine that Benjamin's reference to his present moment is exhausted by contemporary artistic productions as it would be to see in Nietzsche's work simply an attempt to lend historical legitimacy to Wagner's musical drama. The actualization lies more in the experiment of revolutionizing an entire tradition of aesthetic thought by means of the genealogical reconstruction of a single artistic genre. Thus Benjamin turns to Trauerspiel above all because it contradicts the normative standards of idealist aesthetics. Its invectives against aesthetics are said to be even more authoritative and permanent than the correctives launched by the early romantics (*GS* 1:352; *O* 176). Benjamin does not merely attempt to rehabilitate an obscure genre, but credits the German baroque with a "deep-rooted intuition of the problematic of art." He exhibits baroque Trauerspiel as "a corrective [. . .] to art" as such (*GS* 1:352; *O* 176). Nietzsche uses tragedy in order to circumvent the schematism of aesthetics in favor of a genealogy of tragic knowledge. Nietzsche's demand for tragic knowledge corresponds to Benjamin's notion of the Idea, for only by being conceived as an Idea does Trauerspiel become what it is.

The latent affinities between Benjamin and Nietzsche turn into acute rivalries with regard to the political, and above all the national political implications of their reference to the present. That Nietzsche insists on the national impetus of his reflections, in which Germany becomes the site of a reawakening of tragedy (that at least is the hope, quickly revised and on occasion denied in the course of the text), would seem at first to distinguish him from Benjamin, who emphatically resisted virulent German self-assertions in the wake of Nietzsche. This resistance is one reason for his interest in the thematically and formally "un-German" Trauerspiel.[7] None-theless, Benjamin's book is concerned with the specifically *German* Trau-erspiel. Neither Spanish nor Shakespearean drama, but only the German Trauerspiel has a claim to being interpreted as Idea. This concentration on the German variant of baroque drama ought not to be belittled as a con-cession to the academic discipline of German studies, in which Benjamin hoped to be professionally certified. He systematically elaborates Trauer-spiel as a specifically German phenomenon whose historical significance rests precisely on its aesthetic failure. German Trauerspiel could not find the path to transcendence that the drama of Calderón, Shakespeare, and to a certain extent the romantics were able to reach by detours and back roads, and so, Benjamin seems to suggest, in the last analysis, illegitimate-ly. Benjamin's explanation of the historical conditions of this failure in the Protestant Germany of the seventeenth century does not absolve Trauer-spiel from its failure. Quite the contrary: its aesthetic negativity alone con-stitutes its unique quality. Trauerspiel refuses to be judged according to traditional aesthetic criteria, and because it remains aesthetically incongru-ent, German baroque drama amounts to an objection to art as such. This procedure of revaluing aesthetic values is itself borrowed from the baroque and introduced in exemplary fashion at the outset of Benjamin's text. Just as the emancipation from Greek domination lay in the baroque misunder-standing of Aristotelian authority, so Benjamin liberates a part of German literature from the misleading conditions within which it lay bound. And it is not insignificant that the specifically German overcoming of antiquity was accomplished by the un-German Trauerspiel, which carried antique tragedy as "the fettered slave on the triumphal carriage of the baroque Trauerspiel" (*GS* 1:278; *O* 100). The rank and greatness of baroque Trauer-spiel lies in such "failure." To put it differently: the Trauerspiel successfully avoids the seductions of aesthetic self-reflection.

With regard to Nietzsche's *Birth of Tragedy*, the question arises wheth-er this "German" failure and its dialectic in Benjamin's book meets the standards of the theory of tragedy, or whether this triumphant failure is in the last analysis an endless Trauerspiel. Is the failure of German Trauerspiel to be understood as the failure of the defiantly silent hero of tragedy, who thereby founds a new community or society, or do we face an endless and pointless failure? Or should one say that Benjamin's book calls into ques-tion these alternatives?[8]

The question is relevant because Benjamin's Trauerspiel book converges with Nietzsche's tragedy book in its theory and practice of presentation. Despite its forbidding learnedness, the epistemo-critical prologue to the Trauerspiel book, devoted to the philosophical elaboration of the Idea, leaves little doubt that the emphatically formulated concept of presentation (*Darstellung*)—"presentation as digression" (*GS* 1:208; *O* 28)—was learned from Nietzsche. Presentation determines the interplay of three elements: idea, concept, and phenomenon. The connection between idea and concept is provided by the notion of an "objective interpretation" of the phenomenon.[9] Obviously, this is quite compatible with Nietzsche's presentational practice in the *Birth of Tragedy*. In the second of the *Untimely Observations* Nietzsche had written, "It would be possible to conceive of a historiography that does not contain a single drop of common empirical truth and that yet could lay claim in a high degree to the predicate of objectivity."[10] In Benjamin's Trauerspiel book we find: "And so the real world could well constitute a task, in the sense that it would be a question of penetrating so deeply into everything real as to reveal thereby an objective interpretation of the world" (*GS* 1:228; *O* 48).[11]

The imbrication of tragedy and tragic presentation as undertaken by Nietzsche has in Benjamin's case long been recognized as the strategy of dramatizing his book on Trauerspiel as a Trauerspiel and with this mode of presentation in the concept of the tractatus validate philosophical presentation. But in contrast to Nietzsche, Benjamin insists much more decisively and explicitly on the distinction between the object and its presentation, which he trusts (and assumes) can resist the temptations of the abyss: "Only by approaching the subject from some distance and, initially, foregoing any view of the whole, can the mind be led, through a more or less ascetic apprenticeship, to the position of strength from which it is possible to take in the whole panorama and yet remain in control of oneself" (*GS* 1:237; *O* 56). One must thus remain steadfast precisely there, where Nietzsche apparently failed, as he admitted that it is the magic of such struggles that whoever observes them must also fight them. (That Nietzsche, however, did not fight the same struggles he observed, but only developed their possibilities, the preceding chapter sought to demonstrate.) If Benjamin's Trauerspiel book is also a reflection on the end of art, then the question arises whether his text, which acknowledges the difference between its object and its presentation, does not in the end surrender the "anchor" it invokes, and falls into the abyss over which he appears to leap in the *Ponderación misteriosa* of the concluding chapters.

In contrast to Nietzsche, who is at least occasionally committed to a rebirth of tragedy, Benjamin's theory depends unambiguously on the Hellenic uniqueness and unrepeatability of tragedy. "It must still be possible to write tragedies"; overturning this "axiom of cultural arrogance" (*GS* 1:280; *O* 100) is what Benjamin's theory hopes to accomplish. Up until now, Benjamin claims, all investigations of tragedy, and above all those in the wake of Nietzsche, have failed to ask themselves whether tragedy is even still a possible form, and not rather a form bound to past historical conditions. And although one might justifiably ask whether tragedy for Benjamin (and moreover for Nietzsche as well) qualifies as art after all, Benjamin leaves no doubt that it is irretrievably finished. But with the end of tragedy, the dialectical conception of the tragic end has also disappeared: "Tragic death has a dual significance: it invalidates the ancient rights of the Olympians, and it offers up the hero to the unknown god as the first fruits of a new harvest of humanity. [. . .] Death thereby becomes salvation: the crisis of death" (*GS* 1:285–86; *O* 107). Neither for Nietzsche nor for Benjamin is the historical demise of tragedy a tragic event.

Trauerspiel is diametrically opposed to the irrevocable end of tragedy. Internally determined as an endless repetition without progress, a "play with no proper end" (*GS* 1:314; *O* 135), German Trauerspiel is a form that resists its perfection: "Nowhere but in Calderón could the perfect form of the baroque Trauerspiel be studied" (*GS* 1:260; *O* 81). Here it finds a "conclusion" that is superior to the German Trauerspiel (*GS* 1:260; *O* 81). Thus Trauerspiel, in contrast to historically bound tragedy, is a form that "still has a future" (*GS* 1:292; *O* 113). The end of the dialectical end, exemplified in the conclusion of tragedies, this end with surplus value, is opposed to an open-ended form that lacks any formal ending, for Trauerspiel "has 'no proper end, the stream continues on its course'" (*GS* 1:314; *O* 135). Of all possible plays, Benjamin selects Hölderlin's translation of the Sophoclean tragedy *Antigone* to support his claims regarding the continuing resonance of the Trauerspiel form. That the German translation of a Greek tragedy—and since Hegel *the* Greek tragedy—should demonstrate the open future of Trauerspiel suggests that the antitragic Trauerspiel, for all its distance from tragedy, is not entirely separated from it, and is better regarded as its counterplay. In fact, the rigid antagonism between tragedy and Trauerspiel, between a singular tragic end and an endless play, between a form bound to its historical moment and one with a future, is mitigated in a few crucial passages.[12] One of these passages concerns Benjamin's interpretation of Platonic dialogue, although he neglects to mention the decisive role the Platonic dialogues had already played in Nietzsche's book on tragedy.

Benjamin turns to Platonic dialogue after he has confronted Schopenhauer's "ahistorical" interpretation of Trauerspiel and tragedy with a long quotation from Franz Rosenzweig, in order then to gesture toward the "still open future" of Trauerspiel: "Here it is a question of its [the form of Trauerspiel] past. This leads us far back to a turning-point in the history of the Greek spirit itself: the death of Socrates. The martyr-drama was born from the death of Socrates as a parody of tragedy. And here, as so often, the parody of a form proclaims its end" (*GS* 1:292; *O* 113). This interpretation derives, down to the details of its formulation, from Nietzsche. If the shipwrecked Greek poetry saves itself in Nietzsche on the barge of Platonic dialogue,[13] in Benjamin, the end of tragedy is equally the origin of Trauerspiel. What Benjamin calls the "turning-point" is in Nietzsche a "vortex of world history" (*BT* 96; *KSA* 1 100). With the death of Socrates as one version of the end, the foundation of a future community in tragedy, is separated from another version, the pointless martyrdom in an endless Trauerspiel.

But at this turning point, the lucid distinction between the two forms is suddenly obscured, for the productive, singular dialectical end in tragedy appears now problematic and opaque: "The solution is always, it is true, a redemption; but only a temporary, problematic, and limited one" (*GS* 1:296; *O* 116–17). In place of the dialectically satisfying, transparent end, we find the "awe which surrounds the inscrutable conclusion" (*GS* 1:296; *O* 117). And reversed, pivoted at the turning point, the new version of the end in Trauerspiel suddenly reveals a quasi-tragic dimension in the form of Platonic dialogue.

The war which the rationalism of Socrates declared on tragic art is decided against tragedy with a superiority which ultimately affected the challenger more than the object challenged. For this does not happen in the rational spirit of Socrates, so much as in the spirit of the dialogue itself. [. . .] The dialogue contains pure dramatic language, unfragmented by its dialectic of tragic and comic. The purely dramatic quality restores the mystery which had gradually become secularized in the forms of Greek drama: its language, the language of the new drama, is, in particular, the language of the Trauerspiel. (*GS* 1:297; *O* 118)

With this surprising interpretive swerve at the turning point of Platonic dialogue, which Benjamin had already called "the irrevocable epilogue of tragedy" (*GS* 1:296; *O* 117), the antagonism between the two forms dissolves. Trauerspiel restitutes and restores what had broken apart in the process of secularization: the authentic mystery of the purely dramatic.

This approximation of tragedy and Trauerspiel can only be convincingly explained with reference to Benjamin's enigmatic discussion of origin as vortex and turning point. "Origin is an eddy in the stream of becoming, and in its current it swallows the material involved in the process of genesis. That which is original is never revealed in the naked and manifest existence of the factual; its rhythm is apparent only to a dual insight. On the one hand it needs to be recognized as a process of restoration and reestablishment, but, on the other hand, and precisely because of this, as something imperfect and incomplete" (*GS* 1:226; *O* 45).[14] By and since Hegel, the end of art has been seen from this perspective, which understands reestablishment not as a recuperative conclusion, but as a function of opening and openness and so as a "retrograde movement." Hence, the end of art should number among the few original phenomena in Benjamin's sense.

In any case, this surprising turn in Benjamin means that with the destruction of the symmetrical opposition of Trauerspiel and tragedy, the opposition between the end of tragic ending and endless play also collapses. These two modalities of ending can now no longer be as rigidly distinguished from one another as it at first appeared. But this suspended end, the ambivalence of the end of the end, is not Benjamin's last word. He saves his final turn for the ultimate finale.

The self-divided and dual-sided end is eventually superseded by a third end that resolves any confusion. This end falls within the purview of neither Trauerspiel nor tragedy; this end no longer even falls within art: "The powerful design of this form [that of Trauerspiel] should be thought through to its conclusion; only under this condition is it possible to discuss the idea of the German Trauerspiel" (*GS* 1:409; *O* 235). At the end of his book, Benjamin proceeds to bring an end to this open-ended form. Trauerspiel can end neither aesthetically nor tragically, but only theologically. And because Benjamin's book on Trauerspiel is conceived as a Trauerspiel, that is, allegorically, the end of the book, where the deus ex machina, the *Ponderación misteriosa*, appears is also the point at which, with the divergence of theology and art, the object and its presentation explicitly diverge. Here the panorama of the abyss unfolds: "In the form of knowledge instinct leads down into the empty abyss of evil in order to make sure of infinity. But this is also the bottomless pit of contemplation. Its data are not capable of being incorporated in philosophical constellations" (*GS* 1:404; *O* 231). Trauerspiel and the book about Trauerspiel could only be concluded theologically. Their respective forms of ending have not yet left the gravitational field of art; no form can determine its own end. The final interpretation in the last sentence of Benjamin's book, that German Trauerspiel "preserves the image of beauty" until the Last Judgment (*GS* 1:409; *O* 235), is no longer an insight of Trauerspiel, for "it is conceived from the outset as [. . .] a fragment" (*GS* 1:409; *O* 235). Only its theological and philosophical interpretation completes the Trauerspiel as Idea. This shelters Trauerspiel from the reproach of having transgressed the confines of its generic boundaries and aesthetic limitations in the attempt to bring itself to an end. (Such transgression had been the core of Benjamin's criticism of romanticism in his dissertation.[15])

The question remains whether Benjamin's finale also resolves the tension between the tragic and the endless end, whether their lingering competition and affinity also subsides. He does write: "All this vanishes with this *one* about-turn, in which the immersion of allegory has to clear away the final phantasmagoria of the objective and, left entirely to its own devices, re-discovers itself, not playfully in the earthly world of things, but seriously under the eyes of heaven" (*GS* 1:406; *O* 232). But only *as* allegory. Ultimately, only a God could determine the difference between end and endlessness, tragedy and Trauerspiel. Benjamin does not provide a final answer to the question of their relation, and thus the relation of different modes of ending remains unclear. Any answer is henceforth only allegorical. For whether in the triumphant close of the book Benjamin becomes a Hamlet who brings allegory to self-determination, or whether that, too, is only allegory, must remain undecidable.[16] Just as unresolvable is the question of whether or not the redemptive end is really an ending, or whether it is in the last analysis itself an endless Trauerspiel. In the words of Samuel Weber: "Benjamin's 'end' is itself 'ostentation' and held fast by an allegory that comes to no end but only endings, significant but without sense."[17]

With this amalgamation of ending and endlessness, Benjamin renders manifest a latent dimension of the end of art since Hegel. Under the conditions of allegory, the difference between a (dialectical) end and an endless ending is no longer available. The consequences of this situation find expression in Benjamin's studies of Baudelaire. After the acrobatics of the Trauerspiel book, there Benjamin finds himself again under the earnest skies of modernism. The Baudelaire studies are informed by the concept of allegory Benjamin had developed in his studies of the baroque. The relationship between antiquity and modernity that Benjamin had worked out on the eccentric terrain of the seventeenth century—the problem of the ancients and the moderns set on the terrain of the baroque—proves to be essentially allegorical. Hegel discovered and invented modernity with antiquity; Nietzsche searched for the future of modernity in the prehistory of antiquity. Benjamin follows suit and explicitly grasps the relation of antiquity and modernity as allegorical: "The interplay between antiquity and modernity must be transferred from the pragmatic context in which Baudelaire finds it into the allegorical" (*GS* 1:661). The pragmatic context is Baudelaire's claim that "all modernity be truly worthy of being at some time antique" (*GS* 1:584). The allegorical context in which Benjamin wants to situate Baudelaire[18] is characterized by antiquity's and modernism's shared transitoriness and their unavoidable exposure to increasing devaluation: "That within which in the final analysis modernity and antiquity are most alike is this vulnerability" (*GS* 1:586). Everything that comes into being as something new is vulnerable in this way because only what is new can grow old: "True, Paris still stands; and the great tendencies of social development are still the same. But the more permanent she remains, the more vulnerable becomes the experience of her that had stood under the sign of the 'authentically new.' Modernity has remained the least like itself; and the antiquity that was supposed to be hidden with it actually presents the image of the out-of-date" (*GS* 1:593). Modernity has not remained like itself because its hope for innovation and for an end—that is, for revolution—has not been fulfilled. With this perspective, Benjamin opts for a theory of modernity that knows no original tragedy, but only endless Trauerspiel. The poet may still be the "stand-in for the antique hero" (*GS* 1:584), but the drama of modernity is, as in Hegel, feigned tragedy, tragedy *as* (mourning)-play. "For the modern hero is not a protagonist—he plays the hero. Heroic modernism reveals itself to be a Trauerspiel, in which a heroic role is available" (*GS* 1:600). In other words, Trauerspiel is the allegory of tragedy. For the theory of modernity, this means that "Modernism in the end becomes a role that perhaps only Baudelaire himself could fill. A tragic role, in which the dilettante who, in the absence of other forces had to take it on, would often make a comical figure [. . .]. But he [Baudelaire] had something of the actor in him, who played the role of 'poet' on a stage before a public that no longer needed the real thing, and so gave him leeway only as an actor" (*GS* 1:662). Through the detour of baroque Trauerspiel, Benjamin transposes the end of art into a theory of modernity that can only play what it presents as reality. The paradox is not only that with this insight the assurance that there had once been an "authentic poet" whose time has passed becomes senseless. The true paradox is above all that the discoveries that become possible with the end of art as a discourse only remain possible as long as an end of art is posited, thought, and acted out.

What Benjamin achieves with the concept of acting for the theory of modernity—and this also means the affinity to Hegel that he achieves—seems to be missing from the artwork essay. Benjamin's later text, by insisting emphatically on an end of art, seems once more to stake out the claims for a heroic modernity that the studies on Baudelaire had already revealed as allegory. By contrast, the artwork essay seems to promise a future beyond the end of art. Perhaps this lure is chiefly responsible for the enduring popularity of this text.[19]

2

In fifteen sections, Benjamin's essay diagnoses the decay of the aura as a symptom of modernity. The mode of reception corresponding to the auratic artwork is contemplation. Both aura and contemplation are anchored in the concept of *cult value*, which is opposed to the *exhibition value* of a work of art that is not only reproducible, but has from the start been conceived with reproduction in mind. On the receptive side, film demands and promotes distracted attention, whose structural characteristics Benjamin derives from the tactile reception of buildings. The other central theme of the essay is the modern masses, whose rise Benjamin brings into temporal and causal connection with the new technologies of reproduction. Fascism and political reaction have an interest in suppressing the revolutionary character of the new media, in which the masses confront themselves for the first time. The star cult testifies to the politically motivated but anachronistic attempt to reanimate the lost aura. These are Benjamin's theses. They were controversial then and remain so today.

If, in contrast to the diffuse Baudelaire studies or the eccentric Trauerspiel book, "The Work of Art in the Age of Mechanical Reproduction" appears to be an accessible, grounded, and at the same time more pointed text, that does not mean that it is unambiguous. Quite the contrary— precisely its decidedly ambivalent posture toward the end of auratic art predestined it to canonical status.[20] On the one hand, the text preserves a perspective toward an end of art in which all would be well if we were only to jettison our outmoded aesthetic criteria and surrender our idealistic prejudices that fascism perpetuates by aestheticizing politics. On the other hand, the text shows traces of tender melancholy. When Benjamin lovingly describes the last flashes of the disappearing aura in the faces of the dead in early portrait photographs, the pathos of a possible renewal mingles with the sorrow of departure. It is not least this simultaneous endorsement of contradictory evaluations of the end of (auratic) art, widely discussed as Benjamin's covert ambivalence (whether fortunate or unfortunate) toward the decay of the aura, that has ensured the survival of his essay's provocations.[21]

It has been said, quite rightly, that Benjamin's text is the "dramatization of a crisis."[22] What needs to be elaborated is the extent to which Benjamin was aware of this, so much so that one can argue that the text does not describe a crisis in art but stages one. This would prove that Benjamin's earlier insights into the role-playing of modernity inform the artwork essay as well. Benjamin works through an end of art, but the way in which he does marks it as a production. In continuing the discourse of the end of art, Benjamin also offers reflections on the conditions of rendering the topos relevant. Here, too, this dual insight depends on a particular technique of presentation.

In order to distinguish Benjamin's technique of presentation from his presentation of technology, it makes sense to view the artwork essay first through Adorno's eyes—that is, critically. The stylistic rupture between this text and Benjamin's earlier and later work did not escape Adorno: "A certain simplification of means is unmistakable."[23] Long before the "precipitous conclusion"—"Thus the aestheticization of politics that fascism carries out. Communism responds to this with the politicizing of art"—the essay lacks the familiar subtlety.[24] Somewhat crude oppositions and analogies that often seem arbitrary make up its structure. Historical events and processes are rather recklessly related to film as their telos. Dadaism, for instance, had already striven for the effect that new technologies can now achieve effortlessly. In general, art has always had the purpose of stimulating demands that could only be satisfied in later times (*GS* 1:500; *I* 237). These apodictic propositions can hardly be legitimized by the lapidary objection that historiography for Benjamin is always oriented on the "now-time" (*Jetztzeit*); as if we could ever be sure what "now" is. The urgency of the present moment, in Benjamin's emphatic use of this word, its "actuality" (*Aktualität*), must first be demonstrated. Only then can one understand his remark in a letter that the artwork essay attempts "to determine the exact point in the present toward which my historical constructions will be oriented as toward their vanishing-point" (*GS* 1:983). The site of the now-time is not itself given, but must first be located. This is the meaning of Benjamin's excerpt of a fragment from Turgot for the *Arcades Project*: "Before we are able to inform ourselves about the given state of things, Turgot says, they will have already changed repeatedly. Thus we always experience too late what has occurred. And therefore one can say of politics, it has the task of *predicting the present*" (*GS* 1:1237, emphasis added). Benjamin adds: "Precisely this concept of the present is what underlies the actuality of historical writing" (*GS* 1:1237).

With film, Benjamin discovered and invented an object that, as technology, satisfied a fundamental requirement of his own concept of presentation as it was first developed in the book on Trauerspiel. The objects he considers are not in themselves or already given, but constitute themselves in their presentation. But the affinities that hold between film and its theoretical-historical presentation in Benjamin's text are not simply analogies. The artwork essay is not put together in the same way as a film. No direct relations between text and film are at issue, but the similarities in the way object and method are proportioned in film and text, respectively. That this structural homology also has a temporal dimension follows from the addenda in which Benjamin writes "to indicate the particular structure of the work": "it does not apply the method of materialist dialectic to an historically given object, but rather unfolds it on that object that—in the realm of art—is *contemporaneous* with it" (*GS* 1:1049). Because the advent of film is by no means contemporaneous with the "discovery" of the materialistic method, that simultaneity must first be produced by the presentation. Because this kind of simultaneity can only be an effect of presentation, Benjamin's text takes on a performative dimension. His method demands that the objects—the materials, texts, data, and so on—first be elevated, qua presentation, to the state of simultaneity. This simultaneity that appears like a leitmotif throughout the text as the telos of all technical developments and accelerations shows up in the quoted note as precondition, but it is at the same time the result of a procedure that arises only in the presentation and can only be analyzed there.

Already the first sentence of the essay says as much: "When Marx undertook the analysis of the capitalist mode of production, this mode was in its infancy. Marx *arranged his investigations in such a way* that they had prognostic value. He *returned* to the fundamental relations of capitalist production, and *presented them in such a way* that they revealed what could be expected from capitalism in the future" (*GS* 1:473; *I* 217; emphasis added). The introductory indication of the methodological horizon of the work contains at the same time a presentational program, or more exactly, a method contained in the presentation alone, for Marx "arranged his investigations in such a way" and "presented them in such a way." Thus a specific mode of presentation enabled Marx to make his prognoses. But Benjamin's explanation of this procedure is contradictory. Because the capitalist mode of production "was in its infancy," it seems puzzling that Marx was able to "return" to something that was just beginning to establish its "fundamental relations."[25] The tiny hiatus in the first sentences draws attention to the temporal discrepancy that separates Benjamin from Marx. Accordingly, Benjamin writes in the subsequent section on the slower transformation of the superstructure in the course of the nineteenth century, "*Only today* can it be shown what form this has taken" (*GS* 1:473; *I* 218; emphasis added). Thus it is only when we understand that these characteristics of the Marxist method are visible *only today* that the apparent incoherence of these introductory sentences begins to make sense. What is true of the process that the sentences describe and perform is also true of what Benjamin says of film. It "presents a process that can no longer establish a viewpoint from which the apparatus involved in producing the film and that does not belong to the action is not in view of the spectator" (*GS* 1:495; *I* 232–33). The spatiotemporal discontinuity that the sentence describes shows that the past is always for Benjamin something constructed, presented, and thereby distorted. History only becomes history through representation. The specific form of the methodological demands that Benjamin accommodates with this sentence turns out to be an already completed practice of the procedure.

The procedure introduced in an exemplary way in the first sentences determines the entire structure of the essay. It does not describe "facts," but constructs them in its presentation. Although Benjamin, with one exception, systematically avoids the future tense and instead relies on the descriptive present tense with regard to film and the historical imperfect with regard to its precursors, his preface nonetheless invokes a future. The essay's "prognostic demands" are understood in terms of "theses on the developmental tendencies of art under contemporary conditions of production" (*GS* 1:473; *I* 218). Just as insistently, he emphasizes that the "concern of the present investigation" is not directed toward concrete "revolutionary criticism of social relations" by means of film (*GS* 1:492; *I* 231). That is to say, he is not presenting a program or a set of demands to be fulfilled. The peculiarity of the future dimension finds expression as well in a letter from the time when the essay was composed: "As far as I'm concerned, I'm attempting to direct my telescope through the fog of blood toward an aerial view of the nineteenth century, *which I am trying to paint in the strokes that it will have for a future state of the world, one freed from magic*" (*GS* 1:984; emphasis added). History must be written from the perspective of a future that does not yet exist.

That the text was written from the standpoint of a yet undecided future is evident from corresponding textual markers. In the afterword, for example, two contradictory interpretations of the relation between man and technology with regard to Italian futurism coexist in the same sentence. There the war provides evidence for the fact (present tense in the German original) "that society *was* not mature enough to make technology its organ, that technology *was* not developed enough to master the elementary social forces" (*GS* 1:507; *I* 242; emphasis added). The shift in tenses points to the temporal origin of the text. Only from the future can the present be depicted as past. Benjamin elides the conjunctive "either-or" that ought to link the two sides of the alternative. In the mute indecidability between the two possibilities a future speaks that withdraws from its own project, a future that can turn out one way or another, that is still to come.

Benjamin's own standpoint is thus not a fixed point, a critical position, but is the marking of a virtual point. In the movement of prospective and retrospective understanding, the fixed standpoint is obliterated. The justification, the necessity, even, of such "standpointless" thought increases with the emergence of film. Like Benjamin's text, film shows "a process in which no single viewpoint can be assigned to the spectator" (*GS* 1:495; *I* 232). Film can and must no longer be conceived in the categories and with the methods of traditional art criticism. The older discussion had its standpoint predetermined by the "stand-point of the original" (*GS* 1:476; *I* 230), from which the pursuit of a tradition must make its start. But with the invention of photography, this standpoint (*Standort*) has become a crime scene (*Tat-Ort*) (*GS* 1:485; *I* 226). This is how Benjamin characterizes Atget's photographs of empty streets. The criminological-juridical terminology suggests that from now on theoretical standpoints, too, are crime scenes, uncovered by their active prospective and retrospective understandings.[26]

Benjamin's anticipation of the future and his restriction to the reinterpreted return to the past is made possible and legitimated by the simultaneity of method and object. Strictly speaking, simultaneity is thus not a temporal category, but a function of presentation that constitutes temporality. What makes history as a conflation of future and past possible is itself not determined by either of these temporal dimensions. Certainly all of the developments Benjamin *presents* aspire to the telos of a simultaneity that supports the identity of presented object and presentation in film: graphic art "began to keep pace with printing" (*GS* 1:474; *I* 219). A bit later, "the process of pictorial reproduction was accelerated so enormously that it could keep pace with speech" (*GS* 1:475; *I* 219). And with the advent of film, the decisive temporal discrepancy in the development of superstructure and relations of production also disappears. But these phenomena owe their simultaneity solely to the simultaneity produced by the *presentation*.

That the simultaneity between method and object is temporal only in a secondary sense is evident above all in the details of the exposition. Benjamin repeatedly points to the gradual erosion and ultimate leveling of received differences that film brought about, among them the collapse of the criteria that had allowed reception to be distinguished from production. Traditionally, a small coterie of art producers confronted a wide mass of recipients. With the modern press that began to change, because it increasingly allowed readers to act as authors. This quantitative displacement is transformed with film into a qualitative difference. The same logic underlies the disappearance of the difference between theory and practice, between artistic production and critical reception. Benjamin hopes that the "greater analyzability" of film will promote the "tendency of a mutual penetration of art and science" (*GS* 1:499; *I* 236).[27] He justifies his hopes by way of an interpretive excursion into the past. In section 13, Benjamin refers to Freud in order to clarify with an analogy between film and psychoanalysis how the human being "presents his surroundings with its [the camera's] help" (*GS* 1:498; *I* 235). "*Film* has enriched our field of perception with *methods* that can be *illustrated* by those of Freudian *theory*" (*GS* 1:498; *I* 235; emphasis added). Benjamin attributes to the images of film the status of a method, while he reduces Freud's psychoanalytic method, inasmuch as it "illustrates" what first becomes authentic method in film, to the status of an image. Film is authentic method because the film image is presentation in which method and object have reached the point of simultaneity. Freud's methods have analyzed the field of perception, but only film has managed to glean a methodological structure from the field of perception itself. Put another way: film has ensured that "entirely new structural formations of the material come to view" (*GS* 1:500; *I* 236). With reproduction as a representational technique, matter has finally become what it always was in Benjamin's critical practice: presentation.

Benjamin's thought has often been called a "dialectic in stasis."[28] One immediately associates his fondness for enchantment, for holding fast, for immobilizing. The expression is valid, although primarily because of its ambiguity. As a dialectic of presentation, Benjamin's dialectic is not simply dialectics at a standstill, a dialectic in a static condition, but also a dialectic that reaches all the way into what would seem to be solid and immobile. More precisely, in its most extreme form, where everything external has become form and form has become object, the movement and the stasis of this dialectic are *simultaneous*; just as the two mutually exclusive ways of reading the preposition "*in* stasis" are *simultaneously possible*, and because they exclude one another, *impossible at the same time*.

If the reproductive technology of film dictates Benjamin's procedure—or, put another way, if Benjamin has raised film *as* a principle of presentation *to* the principle of presentation of his own text—then the question remains why this is nowhere directly stated in the text, but can only be deduced in an interpretative reading. Once again, only film can provide an adequate answer. In film there is no longer any object outside its own presentation: "what is really jeopardized [. . .] is the authority of the object" itself (*GS* 1:477; *I* 221). The object surrenders its authority to: its presentation. The dialectic of this process and of Benjamin's text consists in the fact that there is no longer *mediation*, neither between method and object, nor can presentation be charged with any mediating purpose, for it is itself the object (and the method), and therefore film is *pure immediacy*.[29] In footnote 19 (footnote 11 in Zohn's translation), Benjamin contrasts the role of props and actors in film with their roles on the stage and cites "Pudovkin's statement that 'the *playing of an actor* which is *connected with an object* and is *built around it* . . . is always one of the strongest *methods of cinematic construction*'" (*GS* 1:490; *I* 247; emphasis added). Film is indeed the lead *actor* in this text. Benjamin continues: "Film is the first art form capable of demonstrating how *matter plays along with man*" (*GS* 1:490; *I* 247; emphasis added). Matter is no longer dead material, but becomes as independent as classical artworks were for Hegel, above all those in which art comes to an end, as classical tragedy and comedy. This means nothing less than that film—not as a technological a priori, but as it is presented here by Benjamin—satisfies all the criteria of a classical work of art in Hegel. In and as film, presentation comes home.

As Hegel's emphatic end of (symbolic) art in classical art was secretly accompanied by the end of an art form in quotidian consciousness, Benjamin also knows about the role of usage in endings. In his presentation of film as presentation, matter becomes, as it were, *manifest* (*handgreiflich*). Terms drawn from the German root *Hand*—"grasp" (*Handgriff*), "manipulation" (*Handhabe*), "manifest" (*handgrieflich*)—constitute their own semantic field in his text. "The liquidation of the traditional value of the cultural inheritance is most clearly manifest (*handgreiflich*) in the great historical films" (*GS* 1:497; *I* 221). At another point: "Thus it becomes manifest (*handgreiflich*) that a different nature speaks to the camera from the one that speaks to the eye" (*GS* 1:500; *I* 236). The famous comparison between the magician and the surgeon is instructive for understanding the role of "manifest" (*GS* 1:495 ff.; *I* 233 ff.). The surgeon is manifest when he manipulates internal organs with his hand while not looking the person in the eye. His proximity to the organs is proportionate to his distance from the whole person. The precise and decisive but also strangely violent way in which Benjamin's text engages its material again derives from that material. Film accords with the need of the masses "to *get hold* of the object [. . .] in as great a proximity as possible" (*GS* 1:479; *I* 223; emphasis added). Likewise Benjamin calls photography and film "the most serviceable handles [*Handhaben*]" (*GS* 1:484; *I* 225) for grasping contemporary transformations. But such manipulations take place "covertly" (*unter der Hand*) (*GS* 1:505; *I* 240), in the same way as the tactile reception of buildings. The hand is not a means, but rather an immediate medium. This type of practical appropriation, the dissolution of the authoritative artistic tradition in its practical usage, the distracted, tactile reception, recalls Hegel's discussion of the transition of symbolic to classical art. Just as in Hegel the practical liquidation of art runs parallel to its emphatic sublation, so for Benjamin, as well, whose presentational technique stages the technology of film as unity of form and object, there is a practical disassembling.[30]

However uncomfortable this may be for all those who wave the banner of technological revolution and the ultimate destruction of aesthetic norms and dialectical presentation in Benjamin's name, what classical art was for Hegel is in Benjamin's presentation, film. Benjamin's promotion of the exhibition value over the cult value does not lie outside the walls of Hegel's classical museum.

3

The theory of the "aura," central to the artwork essay, is also subject to the principles of presentation outlined above. It differs from the examples already discussed, however, because aura, as opposed to the technological facticity of film, does not appear to be an historical fact. But just as with Benjamin's presentation of film, the thesis of the primacy of presentation also determines the exposition of aura. Benjamin's oft-noted ambivalence toward the decay of the aura, which emerges involuntarily in the morose description of the melancholy beauty of early portrait photographs, is also not merely a matter of subjective judgments, but is rooted in the object, the presentation, itself. The theory of the aura is characterized above all by its dual aspect. It is just as much a theory of history as it is an historical marker of the theoretical rupture from which Benjamin's considerations proceed.

In light of the rather pointless discussions over whether the collapse of the aura is to be celebrated to lamented, it is necessary to emphasize that the aura, ephemeral and altogether immaterial, is less a concept than a performative intervention. The theory of aura developed in sections 2 through 4 undoubtedly unfolds under the rubric of the last sentence of section 1. Nothing is more revealing for the analysis of modern technologies of reproduction, Benjamin writes, "than the way in which the two manifestations—reproduction of the artwork and cinematic art—*retroactively effect* art in its received form" (*GS* 1:475; *I* 220; emphasis added). More exactly: aura can only be described retrospectively, for the knowledge that the essence of art has up until now been constituted in the aura can only appear once it has lost this character. Thus aura as aura arises only in its loss.[31] The more detailed discussions of the concepts of authenticity and the original underscore this point: "A medieval image of the Madonna was not yet 'authentic' at the time it was fashioned; only in the subsequent centuries did it become so, and perhaps most emphatically only in the last" (*GS* 1:476; *I* 243). Authenticity is a receptive effect, and at the start we do not find an original, but the reproduction that first makes possible the concept of the authentic. Only subsequent to reproducibility does authenticity become "authentic." Authenticity is thus originally and constitutively compromised, for it did not have its origin within itself, was not rooted in the authentic, but rather in its opposite, reproducibility: "The invention of the woodcut may be said to have struck at the root of the quality of authenticity even before its last flowering" (*GS* 1:476; *I* 22). This, then, exposes the other elements of idealist aesthetics, such as creativity and genius, to the suspicion that they, too, are merely belated effects. If there has never been authenticity in itself, but only as an effect, then there was also never an aesthetics that could be overcome in Benjamin's text.

In the same way as authenticity, the aura is essentially determined by its disappearance. Its decay does not invade aura from without; rather, the decay produces it in the first place. That aura appears only in its disappearance determines the content and the scope of its definitions. The distance that Benjamin adopts toward any definitive explanation is immediately evident in the definition: "the unique appearance of a distance, however close it may be" (*GS* 1:479; *I* 222). One can grasp the definition of aura as little as the aura itself. The explication of the aura does not proceed from a preordained standpoint, but unfolds in a series of steps and from various perspectives. In section 2, the aura is conceived in connection with the category of authenticity and exemplified by artworks. In section 3, by contrast, Benjamin introduces the aura as a dimension of historically variable sensory perceptions, and illustrates its concept by means of natural objects. At one point the aura is defined as the sensitive nucleus of time (*GS* 1:477; *I* 221) characteristic of the work of art; elsewhere Benjamin writes that the perception of the aura "withers" like a degenerate organ (*GS* 1:477; *I* 221), and finally: "the peeling of an object from its husk, the smashing of its aura" (*GS* 1:479; *I* 223). Peeling—a process that recalls the liberation of shock effect from its moral packaging—is apparently not the same as smashing, which tends to evoke more a nucleus than a peel. But precisely the immediate proximity of both formulations, secretly tied together by the affinity between nucleus and peel, gestures toward the objective ambivalence of the process in question.[32] Destructive dismantling and the careful unveiling of what is essential belong together like far and near.

This ambivalence does not mitigate the critical-destructive potential of the aura. Although Benjamin is attempting to rewrite history "in its name," the aura is as much the result of a tradition in shock as it is the act of shocking that tradition. Thus the aura is not a concept in the conventional sense, but more in the Hegelian sense: act and result in one. For a concept such as the aura even to become thinkable is a sign that art no longer has an aura. But that Benjamin describes the history of art in terms of its aura, and, above all, how he does this, lends the concept performative qualities. The theory of the aura itself contributes actively to the "liquidation of the traditional value of the cultural heritage" (*GS* 1:478; *I* 221).

A footnote to Hegel supports the fact that this liquidation is not a resurrection or rebirth, but encompasses a certain kind of retraditionalizing. Hegel alone, Benjamin feels, had recognized the essential polarity between exhibition value and cult value. Admittedly, such a distinction could find no place in the idealistic system; but nonetheless, in Hegel it "announces itself as clearly as possible within the limits of Idealism" (*GS* 1:482; *I* 244–45). As evidence, Benjamin cites Hegel's remark that "fine art has arisen . . . in the church . . . , although it has already gone beyond the principle of the church" (*GS* 1:483; *I* 245). The analogue to this in Benjamin's essay: Authenticity appears at the point in its development at which there no longer is anything authentic.

The true problem that Hegel has bequeathed to all post-Hegelian reflections on art is not the end of artistic production but the end of the possibility of a reflection on art or aesthetics that does *not* involve the end of art. Benjamin's concept of the aura and his discussions of authenticity are part of this tradition. That the decay of the aura is, if not explicitly, then implicitly, "traditional," shows yet again that the liquidation of traditional value does not occur outside of the tradition, but is only possible by means of a return to the tradition.[33]

Benjamin does not repeat Hegel, does not radicalize him, does not outdo him; rather, he merely cites him, partially and reductively. But Benjamin left little doubt that citation is also destruction. Such a citational emancipation is what is ultimately at stake here. Where with Hegel the lightning of genius strikes the ossified art of the Egyptians, for Benjamin, "then came film and blasted this prison-world asunder with the dynamite of the tenth of a second, so that now, in the midst of its far-flung ruins and debris, we calmly and adventurously go traveling" (*GS* 1:499–500; *I* 236). The past is not arrested or recovered in its presentation, but liberated and exploded, that is, to invoke a central concept of the theses "On the Concept of History" and the *Arcades Project*, it is rendered *citable*. Tradition in the old sense wants to preserve its object, keep it the same, while citation both preserves and destroys, for no citation ever remains identical to itself. The citation preserves tradition *in that* it is constantly destroying it. For in the citation old and new are brought into simultaneity. In this sense Benjamin can demand of his *Arcades Project*: "This study must bring the art of citing without quotation-marks to its highest development" (*GS* 5:572). The elision of quotation marks indicates that the difference between material and commentary, interpretation and its object, and above all the difference between original and citing reproduction disappears. The production laws of film allegorize what citation without original might mean.

What this means for Benjamin's text, and further for its relation to the aesthetic tradition and to Hegel in particular, whom he cites literally and in his presentational techniques, can be seen in a passage of the text, probably its most difficult point. The passage, a distant relative of that enigmatic discussion of origin in the *Origin of the German Mourning- Play* concerns the relation of Benjamin's method to the methods of filmic production. "One might generalize by saying: the technique of reproduction detaches the reproduced object from the domain of tradition. By making many reproductions it substitutes a plurality of copies for a unique existence. And in permitting the reproduction to meet the recipient in his own particular situation, it renders the reproduced object actual and relevant [*aktualisiert*]" (*GS* 1:477; *I* 221). The grammatical subject of the sentence is the technique of reproduction. It must therefore be read as: The technique of reproduction reproduces reproduction. Only this second-order reproduction encompasses the process with which Benjamin is concerned. By "permitting the reproduction to meet the recipient in his own particular situation, it renders the reproduced object actual and relevant." Radicalized reproduction, which Benjamin calls here the reproduction of reproduction, makes possible the actualization of the object. In the relation of the different definitions of the aura to one another, but also in the relation of film and text, the process that Benjamin describes as the consequence of reproductive technologies plays itself out.

It is difficult to say exactly what Benjamin means by the reproduction of reproduction. But for the text and its procedure, the formula contains a decisive insight pertaining to the relation between presentation (in film) and presentation (in the text). What has so far been described as the simultaneity of method and object in presentation can now be grasped more precisely. Benjamin's text reproduces the process of reproduction in film as presentation. And only through the presentation of presentation raised to higher power in this text can film lay claim to the actuality Benjamin accords it. The reproduction of reproduction first makes it possible that cinematic presentation and its linguistic presentation can appear in simultaneity. Reproduction of reproduction does not merely determine the relation of the text to its object, but also marks the limits of their simultaneity. For film per se as technical a priori certainly is not capable of reproducing reproduction, but rather its presentation in Benjamin's text, film achieves it *as* performer (*Darsteller*) *in* Benjamin's presentation (*Darstellung*). With this, the difference between the technology of reproduction of film and its specific presentation in Benjamin's text is given its due, and the distinction that separates film as such from Benjamin's words on film emerges. It is also the site where Benjamin's difference from Hegel, whom he actualizes by reproducing, comes to light.

Attributing Hegelian echoes to Benjamin does not entail the assumption that his critical considerations of invectives and illuminating insights into modern technologies have lost their value and are now passé. Quite the contrary: only against this horizon can his theses be discussed, and Benjamin's text is likely to continue to provoke further actualizations in the future. Compared with this potential, it is perhaps the least and most ephemeral achievement of Benjamin's essay to have made the concept of tradition available to us once more. By liquidating the traditional value of our heritage Benjamin is able to rediscover a freedom in the concept that can be reinvested and transferred. "Reminiscence" (*Eingedenken*) is a reinterpretation of tradition Benjamin himself suggests, but it is hardly possible to distinguish tradition from renascence with final clarity, as Benjamin in his essay on the storyteller attempted to do by means of the distinction between "memory" and "reminiscence" (*GS* 2:453–54; *I* 97–98).

In a fragment titled "Problematic of the Tradition" that Benjamin wrote at the same time as his theses "On the Concept of History," one reads: "The tradition as the discontinuum of what has been [*das Gewesene*] in contrast to history as the continuum of events" (*GS* 1:1236). Tradition exists only *as* the discontinuum of what has been, of what is always differently uncovered, discovered, and invented. And therefore tradition needs continuity as its anticipated or observed end, as narrative strategy or allegorical structure. Because Benjamin calls this insight a "fundamental apo-ria" (*GS* 1:1236), it remains "impossible to play off tradition against history, discontinuity against the continuum, the essentially past against the event. It may be that the continuity of tradition is mere appearance. But then the very permanence of this appearance of permanence establishes the conti-nuity within it" (*GS* 1:1236). It is this mere appearance that Hegel, that Ni-etzsche, that Benjamin—each in his different manner—established.

CHAPTER 5

Afterthought: Adorno

The end is in the beginning, and still one goes on. . . .

—S. BECKETT

I

Adorno's aesthetic theory unfolds its stern aporetic between a good, utopian end and the false demise of art; between the ideal of a reconciled society that no longer has need of art and the distorted reality of a society that in eliminating art has banished the last trace of the individual.[1] Even the allegorical interpretation of the Homeric sirens in the *Dialectic of Enlightenment* (1944) as the origin of art in bourgeois society is governed by an end, despite all the ambiguity in its details. The very beginning of aesthetic pleasure coincides with an imagined end of the seductive song of the sirens; and because "all songs have sickened"[2] since Odysseus's fortunate-unfortunate encounter with the sirens, art continues to strive toward its end, whether this be its death or its convalescence. But even this speculative interpretation itself, however problematic it may appear today, is indebted to an end that precedes the allegorized origin of art. For on the first page of the Odysseus excursus in the *Dialectic of Enlightenment* one finds the laconic remark: "to celebrate the anger of Achilles and the wanderings of Odysseus is already a wistful stylization of what can no longer be celebrated" (*DE* 43; *GS* 3:61). Homer's epic is no more the beginning of art than is the episode of the sirens. The *Odyssey* is already a modern work of art, a dirge for itself, and the fact of its existence is just as paradoxical as are the possibilities of its interpretation. That the authors of *Dialectic of Enlightenment* do not conceal this, but on the contrary emphasize it, by referring in the first sentence of the Odysseus excursus to an end *be-fore* the dialectic of myth and enlightenment that will be developed via the epic as an end that lies before the bifurcated origin of art; that they subvert the pathos of their interpretation precisely by exaggerating it—this all points to an unexpectedly ironic and self-subversive dimension of the *Dialectic of Enlightenment*, whose hyperbolic excesses have irritated critics since Habermas.[3] Yet neither the notoriously exaggerated presentation nor the polemically exaggerated recourse to the end of art are sufficient to accord Adorno a place in the discourse on the end of art. It may be that he is the sharpest theoretician of the paradox of the end of art,[4] but a discourse-analytical approach can find little traction in his writings. The *conditio sine qua non* of Adorno's aesthetics draws its intensity from sources that only indirectly have anything to do with art's ending. Thus Adorno actually lies outside the tradition of authors discussed here, for he has little to contribute to a genealogy of modernity as developed by Hegel, Nietzsche, or Benjamin. At best, one may encounter such contributions along detours that lead away from the end of art to the margins of that discourse. But even if Adorno's end of art represents from a discourse-analytical perspective little more than an afterthought (*Nachspiel*), his restaging and sharpening of the elements of the discourse remain instructive, for here we see that not every deployment of such a discourse develops it, that not all talk about the end of art has the character of discourse. To retrace the detours to which Adorno's talk of an end of art leads is valuable not only for the sake of this negative demonstration, but also because it provides some surprising perspectives on Adorno's theory of art. Its main course not only has little to do with the end of art but perhaps just as little with aesthetic theory.

Therefore, the reading patterns practiced so far are no longer adequate to the object. The conditions that have allowed up until now a juxtaposition of rhetorical and discourse-analytical readings, of immanent reconstruction and the discovery of a discursive character, are not to be found in Adorno to the same extent. The following reflections proceed differently. They reconstruct the status of the end of art as a philosopheme in Adorno abstractly and systematically, in order then to confront this reconstruction in a second step with the rhetorical reading of selected texts. This reading is occasioned by the irritating effects of Adorno's version of the end of art, but quickly leads into areas and problems that lurk behind Adorno's obsession with this topos. Because Adorno's negative dialectics is, after all, an engagement with Hegel, it is also possible to gain from his texts some insights into the interplay of autonomy and heteronomy. However, even if it sounds absurd, it is questionable whether in the last analysis Adorno is concerned with art or even with aesthetic experience, or if these are actually functions of a latent theory of language.[5] What is linked to this theory of language is the fact that precisely Adorno's ubiquitous references to the end of art are more strongly inhabited than those of other authors by the tendency to hypostatize the end and thereby to fall into just the fatal overestimation of art that has characterized talk of the end of art since Schelling.

Adorno's dissertation on Kierkegaard offers a model for the "construction of the aesthetic" in his own philosophy of art and thus can be read as prelude to his epilogue. The aesthetic qualities and in particular the imagery of Kierkegaard's prose with which most interpretations begin play a role for Adorno only after his reconstruction of the aesthetic has rejected the customary idea that Kierkegaard's prose falls under the rubric of art. Adorno denies as chimerical the claim that Kierkegaard's philosophical prose continues the tradition of German romanticism: "Kierkegaard repeats the rhythm only externally."[6] For Adorno, evidence of a hostility to art even in the early Kierkegaard is documented by the involuntarily parodic features in his presentation of an aesthetic posture toward life. On a theoretical level, as well, Adorno denies any aesthetic claim Kierkegaard's concept of art might make, for what Kierkegaard calls "poetry" (*Dichtung*) is in Adorno's eyes not at all an aesthetic phenomenon, but rather a philosophical category of knowledge: "Without exception, the origin of the name poetry in Kierkegaard's work is transparently philosophical" (*K* 6; *GS* 2:12). (This may also hold—*cum grano salis*—of Adorno himself, who had few illusions about the aporetic nexus of art and philosophy.[7])

Adorno thus does not refute Kierkegaard's objections to art but rather strengthens them. The point of this strategy is admittedly the ultimately triumphant demonstration that the aesthetic is in fact never exhausted by art. On the contrary, Kierkegaard's criticism of art—in itself another end of art—is precisely the condition for Adorno's salvation of an aesthetic sphere that is no longer reducible to art, and is thus immune to Kierkegaard's critique of art. "The aesthetic as art finally falls, with whatever proviso, subject to the verdict" (*K* 15; *GS* 2:25)—but only *as art*. Adorno advances the aesthetic as a category of experience as an alternative to the aesthetic as art. "For just as Kierkegaard's verdict on the aesthetic sphere hardly matches with its contents, so its images are hardly restricted to the domain that his doctrine of existence has granted it" (*K* 132; *GS* 2:187). That an aesthetic sphere informed by image and imagination not only survives, but first appears with an end to art, is confirmed by Kierkegaard's image of the crucified Christ in a children's book, "insignificant from an artistic point of view." In Adorno's interpretation, Christ's passion becomes the passion of art, whose sacrificial death enables the resurrection of a purified aesthetic realm. Adorno writes of this portrayal of the Crucifixion: "His image goes beyond all art; it is 'insignificant from an artistic point of view' and yet itself an image; thus it rescues the aesthetic even as the aesthetic is lost" (*K* 133; *GS* 2:189). For the sake of aesthetic resurrection, art is crucified. Adorno's elegant demonstration that the "original experience of Christianity" remains for the iconoclastic Protestant Kierkegaard essentially linked to the image (*K* 133; *GS* 2:188–89), means at the same time that the "original experience" of the aesthetic for Adorno is implicated in religion to the same extent as Kierkegaard's religion is informed by aesthetics. With the sacrificial death of art for the sake of the aesthetic, Adorno's notion of the aesthetic reveals itself as latent theology. Perhaps Adorno, who clung throughout his life to the mystery of sacrifice as the threshold between the mythic and what is no longer mythic, suspected this connection when he wrote, "the later Kierkegaard's antagonism toward art cannot simply be reduced to the category of sacrifice," and sought to support his claim by pointing out that Kierkegaard "entirely excludes from the verdict on art the children's storybook image of the crucifixion" (*K* 136; *GS* 2:193).

The validity of the aesthetic as imagination—"the moments of fantasy are the festivals of history" (*K* 139; *GS* 2:197)—that Adorno finally attempts to install on the ruins of art, does not in the last analysis fall in the purview of the suffering Christ and also not under the rubric of nature, but rather is illustrated by the prepared stencil or blueprint. "We clipped out of a piece of paper a man and a woman who were man and woman in general in a more rigorous sense than Adam and Eve were" (*K* 138; *GS* 2:197). Adorno juxtaposes this image quite legitimately with Kierkegaard's analysis of farce, whose unexpected freedom is also owed to the stencil-like cutout, the stereotypical character of the genre. Adorno's own acting out of the various scenarios of an end to art, for all its pathos, has on occasion something of the farcical. And just this dimension counteracts the immanent tendency of his aesthetic theory to render the end of art and thereby art itself absolute.

2

The splitting of one end to art into several mutually contradictory ends, characteristic of the sirens interpretation in the *Dialectic of Enlightenment*, is a mode of pluralization typical of the theorem of an end of art well beyond Adorno. But in his work, the end's constitutive oscillation between finitude and perfection, catastrophe and redemption, yields particularly radical consequences. Symptomatic for the irritations that this ambivalence in the end of art can cause is Adorno's paradoxical posture toward art after Auschwitz. Although he made history with the famous verdict on the barbarity of lyrical poetry after Auschwitz (in the 1951 essay "Cultural Criticism and Society"), Adorno turned into a sharp critic of such verdicts when he had to confront them in 1968. "The moment art is prohibited and it is decreed that it must no longer be, art—in the midst of the administrative world—wins back the right to exist, the denial of which itself resembles an administrative act."[8] And with a view toward the rich tradition of the end of art in modernity he adds: "The verdict that it is no longer possible [. . .] is itself a shop-worn bourgeois gesture" (*AT* 252; *GS* 7:373). That the contradiction between Adorno's own verdict and his critique cannot simply be attributed to the contradiction between his theory and his practice is evident in the fact that each position taken in its own terms already contains and produces a contradiction. Thus when Adorno claimed that writing lyric poetry after Auschwitz was barbaric, he reflected in the same sentence on the impossibility of such a claim by adding, "And this corrodes even the knowledge of why it has become impossible to write poetry today."[9] Adorno's critique of the decreed end of art in the *Aesthetic Theory*, by contrast, is so radical that it begins to affect the core of his own construction of aesthetic modernity, for the critique of proclamations and postulates of an end of art imperceptibly passes over into self-criticism of his own theory of an aesthetic domination of the material in accordance with the standards of critical consciousness: "The utilization of available technical means in accord with the critical consciousness of art does *not* offer a solution to the dilemma of whether and how art is possible that [. . .] would be relevant in today's world; on the contrary, any solution demands the authenticity of a form of experience" (*AT* 218–9; *GS* 7:325; emphasis added).[10] This suggests that the end of art touches on aporias in Adorno's thought that his negative dialectics—that canon of aporias—can neither contain nor absorb.

Still, the preliminary delimitation of Adorno's apparently incompatible positions on the end of art—that everything is already impossible and that one must go on anyway—has some heuristic value. This juxtaposition marks the two poles between which the innumerable negativities of Adorno's aesthetics are suspended. These poles can be condensed into the formulae "afterthought" (*Nachspiel*) and "process" (*Vorgang*). In Adorno's reflections on the impossibility of art after Auschwitz the end of art is an index of postapocalyptic survival and afterlife. The contradictory meaning of the sentence on the barbarism of lyric after Auschwitz, continually misunderstood because continually instrumentalized, finds its most significant manifestation in the radicalization Adorno ventured in his *Negative Dialectics*. "Hence it may have been wrong to say that after Auschwitz no poem can be written. But it is not wrong to raise the less cultural question whether after Auschwitz it is still possible to go on living, whether someone who accidentally escaped and by rights should have been killed still can genuinely live. His mere survival calls for the emotional coldness, the fundamental principle of bourgeois subjectivity, without which there could have been no Auschwitz."[11] Referring also to his own life, Adorno develops a notion of survival after the end that finds its most poignant formulation in the famous opening sentence of *Negative Dialectics*: "Philosophy, which once seemed obsolete, lives on because the moment to realize it was missed" (*ND* 3; *GS* 6:15).[12] What is said here about the life of philosophy as survival and anachronistic afterthought holds also for art, whose development is closely tied to the collapse of metaphysical sense.[13] Art too is in a comprehensive sense merely and always an afterthought, just as the *Odyssey* is already—this temporal adverb, together with "no longer" a formulaically returning expression—a threnody for song. According to this logic, the end always already lies behind us and condemns what survives to an endless afterlife, whereby afterlife signifies both the temporal *post fi-*

nem as well as the fatal compulsion to repeat. The dictum against art after Auschwitz is thus no stricture, but an expression of the fact that after Auschwitz there is no longer any before Auschwitz, that whatever might, chronologically speaking, be prior history remains, historically speaking, posthistory.[14]

This logic of afterlife and survival contrasts with and accompanies a second logic, in which the end as acute process operates in the interior of artworks. This logic of process determines the relation of the artworks to one another, but also the relation of genre to particular work, and even of art to its interpretation. Both models are inherently temporal and dynamic. Art always comes into being as with something other as a relation, and indeed as an agon, because, as Adorno writes in "Art and the Arts," "Art requires something heterogeneous to it, in order to be art" (*GS* 10:439). This reference to something heterogeneous to art is not reducible to the relation of art to the social totality, although Adorno tends to privilege this and raise it to a paradigm. But also in another respect it holds that art is war. "Works of art," Adorno writes in *Minima Moralia*, are

each the mortal enemy of each. [. . .] For if the Idea of Beauty appears only in dispersed form among many works, each one nevertheless aims uncompromisingly to express the whole of beauty, claims it in its singularity and can never admit its dispersal without annulling itself. Beauty, as single, true and liberated from appearance and individuation manifests itself not in the synthesis of all works, in the unity of the arts and of art, but only as a physical reality: in the downfall of art itself. This downfall is the goal of every work of art, in that it seeks to bring death to all others. That all art aims to end art, is another way of saying the same thing.[15]

A statement about artworks in the *Aesthetic Theory* presents this idea in its most poignant abbreviation: "Ultimately their development is the same as their process of collapse" (*AT* 178; *GS* 7:266).

This double logic of the end as process and as epilogue of afterthought holds sway over Adorno's numerous negative formulas: ruin and disintegration, liquidation, destruction as well as deaestheticization.[16] None of these concepts signifies a fixed point of termination; all of them indicate processes. The specificity of the end of art in Adorno does not only consist in the fact that it appears in so many different and contradictory variations, but also that in every case, the end refers to a relation and process. For Adorno, the open ambivalence between catastrophe and convalescence, between a false decline and a conciliatory end under the conditions of modernity and after Auschwitz, is in principle undecidable. This undecidability reaches its most radical expression in the closing passages of Adorno's Beckett essay: "The last absurdity is that the peacefulness of the void and the peacefulness of reconciliation cannot be distinguished from one another."[17] In the dual logic of afterthought and process, this undecidability has become, so to speak, mobile and dynamic. In Adorno, therefore, art does not have an end, for it is perpetual crisis. And there is no instance to which one could appeal to judge whether the crisis results from the fact that art has paradoxically survived its end and preserves its existence as an afterthought of itself, or whether art announces its decline, anticipates it, and lives it out as an agon. "The end of art [. . .] did not occur," Adorno remarks in the *Aesthetic Theory*, with reference to Hegel's end of art, but "the gesture of self-imposed muteness and vanishing, art persists, as in a sort of differential" (*AT* 208; *GS* 7:309–10).

The aporia of an endless polysemic end of art informs Adorno's essay about the site that has, since Hegel, functioned as a stage for the dramatization of the end of art. In his essay "Valéry Proust Museum," Adorno dialectically relates Valéry's critique of the museum as the deathbed of art to Proust's celebration of the museum as the site of its rebirth. To the hypothetical question of whether the critic or defender of the museum is correct, Adorno responds, as might be expected: "In the litigation implicitly pending between them, neither Proust nor Valéry is right, nor could a middle-of-the-road reconciliation be arranged. [. . .] Each position passes over into the other" (*P* 183; *GS* 10:191).

Such passing over of one position into its opposite characterizes all variants of the end of art in Adorno. This is not to say that he is immune to the seductions of the end. Thus the abbreviated schema of process and afterthought must be subject to at least two objections. That is, it raises two problems. Although the logic of the afterthought and that of the process are linked and precisely their mutual limitation accounts for the undecidability of the end in Adorno and multiplies and divides every end, there are still traces of their latent incompatibility to be found in his writing. These traces mark a lack of consequence on Adorno's part. To each of the two logics there corresponds in Adorno's writing on art, and particularly on literature, a different canon of works. Whereas the irresolvable dialectic of the end as process is found for the most part in authors whom Adorno takes to be emphatically modern—Beckett, Joyce, and Kafka as well—the logic of the afterthought tends to dominate in the analysis of those authors whom he considers antiquated and hopelessly out of date. Only with great difficulty can authors such as Eichendorff, Borchardt, George, or Mörike be integrated into an aesthetic theory that has subscribed to the motto "il faut être absolument moderne," for these authors are not merely *no longer* modern (as are, for example, Wedekind or Ibsen), but rather they were *never* modern. The fact that it is precisely in the essays devoted to these authors that one comes across explicit reflections on a theory of language suggests that the latent tension between the two logics of the end responds to another tension in Adorno, the tension between a theory of language and its never quite achieved subsumption into a general aesthetic theory.

Adorno's inclination toward an (often religiously inspired) hypostatization of the end of art brings up a second problematic aspect. True, process and afterthought are movements, and their mutual imbrication refutes any attempt to distinguish between a good ending and a bad decline. But when Adorno asserts of art that "the quintessence of the determinate negation that art exercises is its own negation" (*AT* 36; *GS* 7:60), he is granting to the end of art a privilege that has proven to be a most problematic aspect of the history of the end of art—for the more emphatic the end of art, the greater the risk of aesthetic totalization. Where the end of art is promoted to the quintessence of the negativity of art, it occupies a metaposition that can neither be further legitimized nor reinscribed into the process of ending, just because as quintessence, it is already beyond the process. As the quintessence of the negativity of art, the end of art can only be communicated from an Archimedean point and as quasi-apocalyptic mystery.[18] This is the risk that Adorno's radicalization of the end as dynamic process runs; it is perhaps nowhere greater than in the *Dialectic of Enlightenment*, whose strongly apocalyptic tone is notorious. But it is precisely here, where Adorno appears to have succumbed to an apocalyptic tone, that other modalities of ending emerge that avoid the risks of his not always successful tightrope walk between temporalizing and hypostatizing. In this context a dimension of Adorno's thought comes to light that has until now often been neglected, a latent theory[19] of language that is worth considering at least as much as it is necessary to clarify the relationship it entertains to Adorno's end of art.

3

What the close of the Beckett essay formulates so pointedly—"The last absurdity is that the peacefulness of the void and the peacefulness of reconciliation cannot be distinguished from one another" (*NL* 1:274–5; *GS* 11:321)—can already be found in the excursus on the culture industry in the *Dialectic of Enlightenment*. There, the relationship between good art and bad culture industry is not merely antagonistic, but strictly reciprocal;[20] but the problematic presuppositions of the insights derived from apocalyptic thought also come to light.

Fifteen years ago, Martin Seel, among others, acknowledged that the authors of the *Dialectic of Enlightenment* contemplate the depredations they perceive in the U.S. culture industry with considerable fascination. But the discussion of this observation limited itself to cautious formulations and only considered in passing the possibility that the culture industry might function as both correlate and corrective to (bourgeois) art.[21] The true measure of the uncanny and fascinating affinity between works of high art and the rubbish of the culture industry appears, however, in famous or notorious, wildly exaggerated, and so to speak hysterical passages of the *Dialectic of Enlightenment*, such as the remarks on style and tragedy. Adorno and Horkheimer's interpretation of style in the culture industry reveals the fatality and corruption of genuine style in all art from the very beginning: "In the culture industry the notion of genuine style is seen to be the aesthetic equivalent of domination" (*DE* 130; *GS* 3:151). "Having ceased to be anything but style, it [the culture industry] reveals the latter's secret: obedience to the social hierarchy" (*DE* 130; *GS* 3:152). Of tragedy, they write: "The culture industry reveals the truth about catharsis as it did about style" (*DE* 144; *GS* 3:166)—namely, that it was always a lie. Cinema appears as the perverted realization of Schiller's theater project: "The tragic film becomes *in fact* an institution for moral improvement" (*DE* 152; *GS* 3:175; emphasis added). A passage in *Minima Moralia* shows quite unmistakably the catastrophic knowledge gained from a confrontation with the culture industry: "The archetypes of our time, synthetically concocted by film and hit-song for the bleak contemplation of the late industrial era, do not merely liquidate art but, by their blatant feeblemindedness, blast into daylight the delusion that was already immured in the oldest works of art and which still gives the maturest their power. Luridly the horror of the ending lights up the deception of the origin" (*MM* 226; *GS* 4:258). The culture industry is the great illuminator, it reveals, "discloses" (*DE* 155; *GS* 3:178) and illuminates; it is the discovery that can only occur at the end of days, on the last day of judgment. The epistemological pattern of this pervasive knowledge, which Adorno hardly ever granted to an artwork (with the possible exception of Beckett's *Endgame*), is the decline of art as apocalypse. The lexicon of illumination and revelation is unambiguous: "For centuries society has been preparing for Victor Mature and Mickey Rooney. By destroying they come to fulfill" (*DE* 156; *GS* 3:179). In the apocalypse, revelation and catastrophe coincide, for art is freed from its compulsion to lie once the culture industry has become the catastrophic revelation of universal blindness. This apocalypse is rhetorically staged in the form of a literalization of all metaphors. The objective social tendency of the age is consequently incarnated in the Antichrist of the subjective dark machinations of the general directors (*DE* 124; *GS* 3:145). With a characteristic formulation from the "Schema of Mass Culture" in the appendix to *Dialectic of Enlightenment*, "For mass culture, reification is no metaphor" (*GS* 3:334).

Rhetorical excesses of this sort inevitably result in the spread of indifference. Although the authors harness this indifference for the purpose of gaining knowledge about the fundamental problematic of art through the encounter with the culture industry, the apocalyptic rhetoric ultimately engulfs the epistemological intention, because it buries the difference between the object and critical knowledge of it. Thus the chapter on the culture industry not only forsakes all potential legitimation, but—as is well known—it jeopardizes any possibility of a critical intervention in the catastrophic process. Just because apocalyptic knowledge is a hermetic knowledge, whose signs can only be interpreted by the initiate, its legitimation has no other option than to surrender cognition and interpretation to signs of the end itself—signs that speak for themselves, needing no interpretation, signs that, as Hegel says, know and demonstrate themselves. This is precisely what happens in the chapter on the culture industry, whose signs come across as autonomous and self-significant. The objects and phenomena reveal themselves by letting themselves be recognized as the lies they in truth are. But just this effect of apocalyptic rhetoric allows for remarkable insights into the self-revelatory character of mass culture that have not been sufficiently reflected upon. (The question is, how does one deal with the fact that an American bank successfully advertises with a slogan of straightforward manipulation: "one day we will be your bank," or that the motto of the *Bildzeitung* [a German tabloid newspaper] is as ironic as it is hair-raising: "Shape [*Bild*] your own opinion!" Even the most advanced analyses of so-called popular culture can register these quasi-phenomenological self-interpretations paradoxically only in a vocabulary borrowed from the interpretation of high art, of self-reflection and irony.)

The self-revelatory and self-confessing character of the culture industry forces it to converge with art. In the *Dialectic of Enlightenment*, the authors summarize their nonplussed astonishment at this tendency of the lie to show itself barefacedly, which admittedly they exaggerate rhetorically, in the American phrase: "I am a failure, the American says—and that is that" (*DE* 211; *GS* 2:238). But "that" is not only "that," "that" is also art, high art, which like the culture industry goes on despite its own impossibility. In the confessional tendency of these phenomena, made recognizable by apocalyptic rhetoric, what was initially a reciprocal relationship between art and culture industry ultimately mutates into identity. The spectacle of the torments of Tantalus (*DE* 140; *GS* 3:162) provided by the culture industry can no longer be demarcated from the pains of art that Adorno compares, in the *Aesthetic Theory*, to the myth of "Sisyphean struggle" (*AT* 219; *GS* 7:326). Of course, these archaic forms of torment also mark Adorno's desperate attempt to rupture the continuum that his theory of the culture industry inevitably forms with his theory of art. Recoiling from the consequences to which his apocalyptic dramatization leads, its threat to annihilate the distinction between culture industry and art, and so in an effort to rescue the apocalyptically jeopardized difference between art and culture industry, Adorno invokes with Tantalus and Sisyphus a difference between passively suffered and actively self-inflicted suffering in the form of labor and effort. With no small effort itself, the second part of the excursus on the culture industry insists upon this difference: "Certainly every fixed work of art is nonetheless predetermined, but art strives to overcome the burdensome weight of the artifact through the force of its own construction, while mass culture identifies with the curse of predetermination" (*GS* 3:310).[22] The introduction of these criteria, however urgently they are required as a corrective to the leveling dynamic of the apocalyptic rhetoric, is based on the (incidentally gendered) opposition between strength and weakness, erection and impotence, work and laziness, that, although not uncharacteristic for Adorno's prose in general, falls below his own standards. For if the work of art according to one of its definitions is characterized by "stasis" (*AT* 176; *GS* 7:264), by a momentary balance between stillness and movement, construction and its dissolution, by the unity of strength and weakness, development and collapse, then the opposition ventured in the *Dialectic of Enlightenment* between effeminate culture industry and manly courageous artwork is itself weak.

Of course, the opposition between weak and strong rests in the last analysis on the opposition between mass production and individual production. Because the culture industry is concerned with capitalistic commodity production, the internal tensions of this product in comparison with individual creations have already been neutralized. But the attempt, as well, to stabilize the opposed terms with reference to individual and society is doomed, because it neglects the dialectic between individual and society that Adorno elsewhere mobilizes against static opposition. Thus all attempts to prevent the threatening collapse of art and culture industry by means of apocalypse become questionable—and that is probably a good thing; it speaks not against Adorno, but for him. Decades later, in Adorno's "Résumé of the Culture Industry" from 1966, where the apocalyptic energies are as throttled as the opposition between tension and relaxation fixed, the fatal consequences of what is now a successful opposition between art and culture industry are apparent. Nothing is left of the *dialectic* of Enlightenment that the chapter on the culture industry from twenty years earlier had revealed but sheer anti-Enlightenment. In this late essay, Adorno pays a high price for having rescued the important differences from the wreckage of apocalypse; his theses are indistinguishable from conservative resentment.

In other words: the exaggerated version of the apocalyptic scenario has significant advantages over the later mitigated variant, but it exposes a dilemma. On the one hand, the apocalyptic staging is an indispensable presupposition for any perception of the genuinely ominous tendency of the culture industry to annihilate all differences.[23] On the other hand, it is precisely this apocalyptic model that precludes all possibility of any further differentiation and critical intervention; the technique of uncovering can no longer be distinguished from what it has uncovered. The *Dialectic of Enlightenment* is thus as totalitarian as the system it conceptualizes.

But although the *Dialectic of Enlightenment* is the first victim of that terror of (bad) identity that it prosecutes, it also contains the following, initially enigmatic, sentence, which echoes Walter Benjamin's "reproduction of reproduction" from the artwork essay: "The perfect similarity is the absolute difference" (*DE* 145; *GS* 3:168). This is no longer a dialectical transition, but more a leap of faith: Only a God could save us.[24] This sentence cannot be justified in a philosophically discursive manner, but only at the level of presentation, what Herbert Schnädelbach referred to with a somewhat infelicitous formulation as the "narrative coherence" of Adorno's prose.[25] Only on this level is it apparent that the chapter on the culture industry is no apocalypse but rather its desperate parody. And perhaps Adorno's and Horkheimer's text had to accrue a certain anachronicity before this parodic dimension could emerge.

Now, Horkheimer and Adorno frequently use the term "parody" in the chapter on the culture industry. The omnipresent radio is apostrophed as the demonic parody of Max Weber's charismatic leader (*DE* 159; *GS* 3:183), and the culture industry as a whole is a parody of the fairy-tale never-never-land (*DE* 156; *GS* 3:179–80). The laugh tracks of American situation comedies are condemned in the following terms: "What is fiendish about this false laughter is that it is a compelling parody of the best, which is conciliatory" (*DE* 141; *GS* 3:163). But this ostentatious *use* of the concept of parody only serves the purpose of positing some difference between false and true conciliation, and thus of maintaining apodictically something that escapes the distinction. Because this use of the concept of parody depends on prior knowledge about the difference between the original and its parody, the good and the evil end, it presupposes a difference that no longer can be legitimated. Such a concept of parody and its use remain under the spell of apocalyptic rhetoric. But—and this is decisive—this parodic use of the parodied, while perverted, apocalypse is also the foil on which another parody, perhaps also the Other of parody, becomes legible. Adorno's and Horkheimer's text becomes genuine parody not where it uses the concept of parody in an instrumental fashion, but where it appears to surrender without reserve to apocalyptic tirade. At those moments when the authors take naïve recourse in the ancient vocabulary of apocalypse, their own text becomes readable as a parodic practice. As the consequence of an ever more perfect similarity between the original and its perverted parody, a difference is established that can only be registered *as* a difference against the background of a conscious use of parody as the quintessence of perversion. It is the difference between an instrumentalized concept of parody on the one hand and a parody that (like the function of farce in Kierkegaard's interpretation) cannot be calculated.[26] The parodic dimension of the text is thus not a proper feature, not an essential quality of the text in itself, but is an effect of a relation among its elements, apocalypse and its sometimes involuntary parody in contrast to the instrumentalized deployment of the concept of parody. Only in these excessive moments does the text catapult itself out of its own aporias. This alternative parody opens the interstitial space in which the nexus between a logic of process and a logic of afterthought becomes thinkable without reference to beginning or end points. The logic of afterthought is simultaneously the parody of the logic of process, and vice versa. Parody is a process in the sense that it can always only be an afterthought. If Adorno's texts today occasionally read like self-parodies *avant la lettre*, the time might have come to render this parodic dimension of his texts fruitful for their interpretation. It is not superfluous to emphasize that the concept of parody belongs to rhetoric and preempts recourse to the category of mimesis, which systematically distorts any access to Adorno's praxis and theory of language.[27]

4

Adorno developed this sense of parody through an encounter with a text in which the end has already taken place, which is in this sense afterthought and in which the desire to end and the inability to end make up the only process—a text, that is, in which the mutual limitation of afterthought and process is already achieved, and moreover, a text that in Adorno's interpretation becomes absolute parody, for Adorno parodies Beckett even as Beckett parodies Adorno. Adorno's reading of Beckett's *Endgame* owes its coherence and evidence to the stringent logic of parody: "The explosion of the metaphysical meaning, which was the only thing guaranteeing the unity of the aesthetic structure, causes the latter to crumble with a necessity and stringency in no way unequal to that of the traditional canon of dramatic form" (*NL* 1:242; *GS* 11:282). Reminiscence and parody are thus the central categories in Adorno's interpretation, which insists on the distinction between parody and negation, because parody negates what cannot any longer be negated: "In its emphatic sense, parody means the use of forms in the era of their impossibility" (*NL* 1:259; *GS* 11:302). There is nothing in Beckett's piece that cannot, Adorno insists, be read as parody. Poetry, education, the avant-garde, and humor are all parodied; the play parodies philosophy, existentialism in particular but Hegel's master-slave dialectic as well; even the trash heap of the culture industry is the object of parodic inversion. "The whole play is constructed by means of this technique of reversal" (*NL* 1:274; *GS* 11:320). As a universal technique of reversal, this parody, like the apocalypse in the *Dialectic of Enlightenment*, condemns all differences as indifference. The scornful parody of utopian hopes in the false never-never-land of the culture industry is no different from Beckett's indifference, which parodies what the chapter on the culture industry called a parody of the best and conciliation. "The distinction between absolute domination [. . .] and the messianic state [. . .] disappears," Adorno writes (*NL* 1:274; *GS* 11:321).

Adorno's interpretation culminates—and disintegrates—in his reading of the closing scene of the piece. At this point the distinction between difference and indifference dissolves once and for all. Parody parodies and negates the scheme of its interpretability. "Aside from the differences which may be decisive but may also be completely irrelevant, it [the scene] is identical with the beginning. No spectator, and no philosopher, would be capable of saying for sure whether or not the play is starting all over again" (*NL* 1:269; *GS* 11:314–15). Adorno closes the section with a sentence that parodies the movement of (negative) dialectics: "The pendulum of the dialectic has come to a standstill" (*NL* 1:269; *GS* 11:315). This ought to be the end of the essay, not because it is about the last scene of Beckett's play, but because with the claim that "the dialectic has come to a standstill" the parody continues to leave undecidable what Adorno goes on to force together into a significant, neither undecided nor undecidable, indifference. There, the pendulum of the dialectic is not exhausted, but rather "Benjamin's notion of a dialectics at a standstill comes into its own" (*NL* 1:274; *GS* 11:320). And just as if it should seal this arrival, the cited sentence from the closing passage appears: "The last absurdity is that the peacefulness of the void and the peacefulness of reconciliation cannot be distinguished from one another" (*NL* 1:274–5; *GS* 11:321). This indifference is an apodictic claim, revelation of a decision that, just as in the *Dialectic of Enlightenment*, can only be apocalyptically legitimated. In place of the apocalypse in the chapter on the culture industry, however, the Beckett essay substitutes an existentialism of death. "Hope skulks out of the world, which cannot conserve it any more than it can pap and bon-bons, and back to where it came from, death" (*NL* 1:275; *GS* 11:321). Not only Beckett's play draws from this its only consolation, but Adorno's "Attempt to Understand *Endgame*" as well. The problem for the essay, which is no counterexample but the exact pendant to the culture industry chapter, is not the end of art in apocalyptic form but the necessity of decreeing the end of modernity. When Beckett is read as Adorno reads him in his essay, nothing can succeed him. The end of art is suspended in order to triumph as the end of modernity, returning to death as the origin and end of all things. But just as in the chapter on the culture industry a difference emerged between parodic praxis and the *use* of the concept of parody, so in the Beckett essay the difference between the proposition that "the dialectical pendulum has come to a standstill" and the dialectic "comes home" covertly holds open the end and thereby a modernity that had seemed to find its end in this essay.

The effect of this self-contradictory (self-)parody in the wake of an interpretation commands sovereign mastery over the concept and technique of parody as Beckett's method does not exhaust itself in disturbances, but the metaphoric of the entire essay affects it. Beckett's mode of economic reductionism is parodically depicted by means of a generous metaphoric of corporeal ascesis. The occasional talk of insatiable "dégoût" (*NL* 1:243; *GS* 11:283), "detritus" (*NL* 1:247; *GS* 11:288), "homely fare" (*NL* 1:243; *GS* 11:284), the "existence minimum" as the remnants of existentialism (*NL* 1:243; *GS* 11:284), the reference to "the strict ration of reality and characters which the drama is allotted and with which it makes do" (*NL* 1:251; *GS* 11:292)—all of this is admittedly nourished by what Beckett himself already has to offer, but Adorno's paradoxical exaggeration of economic metaphors articulates at the same time the unpredictability of parodic practice. The last barb of Adorno's consequent parody of art as consumption appears only at the close, where with the indifference between nourishment and excrement Adorno also seeks to ensure that excrement might turn into its opposite: "Excretions become the substance of a life that is death. But the imageless image of death is an image of indifference [. . .]. In that image the distinction between absolute domination [. . .] and the messianic condition in which everything would be in its right place, disappears" (*NL* 1:274; *GS* 11:321).

But prior to this strictly calculated closing inversion—a parody of what was once catharsis and dramatic denouement, and thus negative dialectics—the parodic practice had long since conquered other domains. The organ that takes in nourishment but spits out sentences is the human mouth. This is where the secret of Beckett's parody and its parodic echo in Adorno's own text is located. "The objective decay of language, that bilge of self-alienation, at once stereotyped and defective, which human beings' words and sentences have swollen up into within their own mouths, penetrates the aesthetic Arcanum. The second language of those who have fallen silent, an agglomeration of insolent phrases, pseudo-logical connections, and words galvanized into trademarks, the desolate echo of the world of the advertisement, is revamped to become the language of a literary work that negates language" (*NL* 1:262; *GS* 11:306). This rebirth of chatter as aesthetic blessing is hardly inspiring. A bit more sharply formulated: Adorno's idea of literature that negates language is at best the hypostasing radicalization of the end of art as the end of language, and at worst itself mere chatter. But what comes off in Adorno's own prose as platitudinous invitations to parody gains some cohesion and credibility in light of his metaphorical economy. That this will have to suffice is evident from the context in which Adorno introduces his dictum on the law of Beckett's parody. At issue is the play's central scene—crucial for Adorno's own attempt to understand *Endgame* (and for any attempt to understand Adorno's exercise in incomprehensibility). As *parodia ultima*, this particular scene upstages any further attempts at parody by Adorno or Beckett: "The deadliest fear of the characters in the drama, if not of the parodied drama itself, is the fear, disguised as humor, that they might mean something. Hamm: We're not beginning to . . . to . . . mean something? Clov: Mean something! You and I, mean something! (Brief laugh) Ah that's a good one!" (*NL* 1:261; *GS* 11:305). After the citation, Adorno continues: "With this possibility, [. . .] the meaning of language disappears as well." That could mean at least two things, if language still means anything; on the one hand, language in its signifying function disappears; on the other hand, what is signified by language disappears (so that, for example, language ossifies into gesture). The ambiguous formulation of the disappearance of the meaning of language is only apparently another formulation for the idea of a literature that negates language. What is crucial is how the loss of language can be expressed in language and how the disappearance of meaning is interpreted. Adorno locates Beckett (as opposed to Joyce) in a literary tradition that knows that the semantics of language cannot be cast aside, for it is not in spite of, but because of its semantic dimension that language can no longer mean anything. The systematic distinction of the signifying from the mimetic elements bestows on the latter a conventionality that denies their mimetic origins. They become "a second-order convention" (*NL* 1:262; *GS* 11:306). This fundamental insight underlies Adorno's own parodic practice as well. Parody in this sense is not mimetic, not secondary and derivative; rather, it produces and invents the convention in the first place that can then be parodied. Adorno's remark that for Beckett literature negates language must be gauged against the sentence "with this possibility the meaning of language disappears." The gap and the difference between these sentences may be considered the figurative of Adorno's prose. In that gap persists the tension between negative dialectics as philosophical process and linguistic presentation as its parodic medium. A sentence such as "with this possibility the meaning of language disappears" parodies not only the dialogue of Beckett, but—*avant la lettre* and *post festum*—it parodies the later sentences about literature as the negation of language.

Not parody as concept but parody in practice operates in Adorno's prose as a kind of corrective, above and beyond the antithetical procedure that lets mutually contradictory positions annul each other. This excessive moment of parodic practice cannot be separated from the discursive content of his texts, because it always appears as relation and momentarily, in one way in the chapter on the culture industry, in another in the Beckett essay. If parodic practice indeed constitutes an important dimension in Adorno's thinking, this does not mean that his texts cannot be further interpreted, but it does require that their rhetoric (including its involuntary effects) be included in the reading, and can at times imply a rejection of thematic constraints. One should not rely solely on Adorno's terminology, even and precisely when parody as a concept is invoked.

That much Adorno himself already suggested in *Dialectic of Enlightenment*. Horkheimer and Adorno write of Odysseus who, having escaped the Cyclops, cannot hold his tongue and fails to resist the temptation to reveal his identity through a linguistic trick—Udeis, Odysseus: "Speech, though it deludes physical force, is incapable of restraint. Its flow is a parody accompanying the stream of consciousness, thought itself, whose unswerving autonomy acquires an aspect of foolishness—manic foolishness—once it enters reality in the form of discourse, as if thinking corresponded with reality, when in fact the former is superior to the latter merely by virtue of its distance" (*DE* 68; *GS* 3:87). The metaphorical affinity between flow of speech and stream of consciousness underscores that all thought, in order to be thought, must enter into the world of discourse. But at the moment in which "discourse enters into reality," it is forced to treat both reality and thought as if they were language, as if they had the same name. The terrible identification of the world with the world of thought betrays their distinction, because language suppresses their difference. Language forgets this difference because it has already forgotten the difference between what is language and what is not. But the flow of speech accompanies thought not as its parody, but only "as parody." To the extent that discourse always speaks of something else, lets something else speak along with it, the knowledge that discourse has forgotten (namely, that it is neither reality nor thought) can also be heard. Discourse is haunted by what it must forget if it is to enter reality as discourse. But this knowledge exists only "as" parody, as something other, an aside. That discourse accompanies thought as parody lets an older semantic layer of the word resonate. "Ado" means "I sing"; the prefix "para," which is responsible for the ambivalence of parody, can be taken either adversarially or authoritatively, in the sense either of a strike against something or of an imitation of something.[28]

If parody is understood in this vein, negation and affirmation are momentarily in balance and volatile agreement.[29] What had been described as the logic of process and afterthought always leads away from the end of art and points toward the subterranean flow of a latent theory of language that—as parody—accompanies Adorno's thinking.

Whenever Adorno begins to talk of discourse, things start to flow. The image of the stream of speech and flow of discourse that contrasts starkly with the reductionist economization in the Beckett essay appears most frequently in texts about authors who cannot be subsumed beneath the heroic "il faut être absolument moderne" of the *Aesthetic Theory*. The obvious explanation—that Adorno in his encounters with latecomers such Mörike, Eichendorff, Borchardt, or George gives free reign to his elitist or nostalgic longings—falls short. Much more decisive is the fact that these are authors who, on account of their anachronistically restorative ambitions, move inadvertently into the vicinity of a parody of what they never were—that is, modern. It is no accident that in the center of Adorno's interpretations in the essay "On Lyric Poetry and Society" lies the anachronistic citational character of the texts, in Mörike's "On a Walk" for instance, the antiquated overtones of the free rhythms and the isolated word "Muse" (*NL* 1:48; *GS* 11:61). In a poem of Stefan George's, Adorno exposes the medieval tone of the verse: "Nun muss ich gar / Um dein aug und haar / Alle tage / In sehnen leben" (Now must I so / For your eyes and hair / Every day / Live in yearning) (*NL* 1:51; *GS* 11:64). Adorno's reading emphasizes the reference to medieval German Minnesang. "The four lines [. . .], which I consider some of the most irresistible lines in German poetry, are like a quotation, but a quotation not from another poet but from something language has irrevocably failed to achieve: the medieval German poetry of the *Minnesang* would have succeeded in achieving it if it, if a tradition of the German language—if the German language itself, one is tempted to say—had succeeded" (*NL* 1:53; *GS* 11:66). Such an irretrievability is no longer an historical mistake, but denotes a failure (as in Benjamin, a German failure) that no poetry and no language could ever make right.

In the essay "In Memory of Eichendorff," the subterranean stream of Adorno's latent philosophy of language, which crosses his theoretical constructions like a countercurrent, comes closest to the surface and simultaneously overflows its banks. The loosening of philosophical-discursive stringency affects Adorno's own prose so deeply that it surrenders unconditionally to the image of flowing and streaming, the stream of language. Adorno's reading of Eichendorff celebrates such dissolution and devotion to the linguistic impulse: "Eichendorff's poetry confidently lets itself be borne along by the stream of language, without fear that it will drown in it. For this generosity, which is not stingy with its own resources, the genius of language thanks him" (*NL* 1:64; *GS* 11:78). But however moved and moving Adorno's reading may be, here, too, one encounters eventually a dead end similar to that of the chapter on the culture industry and the essay on Beckett. As if, like Odysseus, he could not stop himself from speaking, Adorno surrenders to the temptation to hypostasize the purification of language in the excess of its self-expenditure and gives it a religious tinge. Language is not a "second-order convention," as in Beckett. Rather, Eichendorff's "law of form" is that "the law of language as a second nature, in which the objectified nature that has been lost to the subject returns as an animated nature" (*NL* 1:69; *GS* 11:84). "The reconciliation of things through language" takes place. At the point where, in the *Dialectic of Enlightenment*, apocalypse, and in the Beckett essay the existentialism of death, appeared, we find here a good end of art, its apotheosis as language. That gives Eichendorff too much credit, however, and falls below the level of insight of Adorno's own theory of the negativity of language as parody. In another passage of the same essay, Adorno recants the apotheosis and admits that Eichendorff's language is no language of nature, neither first nor second order. It is as if he were writing not only of Eichendorff, but about his own excesses with the metaphysical tact of the subjunctive, "as though nature had become a meaningful language for this melancholy man. But in Eichendorff's writing the allegorical intention is borne not so much by nature, to which he ascribes it in this passage, as by his language in its distance from meaning" (*NL* 1:69; *GS* 11:83). "Distance from meaning" and distant meanings are not the same as the total collapse of meaning, nor are they identical to full meaning. In Adorno, as well, the end of art withdraws into an allegorical distance. The false end of the culture industry, the ambivalent end in the Beckett essay, and the good end in the Eichendorff essay are passionate parodies of this end of art.

CHAPTER 6

The Same End and the Other
Beginning: Heidegger

The reference to Hegel is obvious.

—MARTIN HEIDEGGER

I

With Heidegger, the chronological order of the preceding chapters comes to an end. Indeed, Heidegger relates the notion of an end of art so explicitly to the entire aesthetic tradition, and in particular to Hegel's *Aesthetics*, that here indeed the (provisionally) *last* reflection on this figure and all that goes along with it has been reached. But because Heidegger's reflections on art cannot be severed from his political decision in favor of national socialism, they also represent the fatal apex of that tradition, and render it transparent. A situation so extreme and extremely critical is made all the more difficult by the fact that Heidegger's texts have systematically thwarted interpretive methods. Put a bit more directly: Readings either fall all too easily into Heideggereze and thus understand nothing; or they resolutely resist his terminology, and also understand nothing. Given this heightened risk of misinterpretation, it is advisable to approach Heidegger's texts from the periphery and begin where the philosopher of the question of Being struggles with the literary critic over a poem.

"Ein Kunstbild der echten Art. Wer achtet sein? / Was aber schön ist, selig scheint es in ihm selbst" (A work of art of the true kind. Who notices it? / Yet what is beautiful seems blissful within itself). So run the final verses of Mörike's poem "To a Lamp."[1] The correspondence between Emil

Staiger and Martin Heidegger on these lines from the fall of 1950 is not only a textbook example of hermeneutical intricacy, but is also and even more emphatically a debate on the end of art, or more exactly, a debate that is performed under the discursive conditions of this topos. It is not a matter of the *Art of Interpretation*,[2] but of the interpretation of art—in terms of its end.

   Staiger imagines that he can read the problematic verb form *scheint* (seems) in the verse in question as *videtur* rather than *lucet* because as a literary critic, he hears here an echo of the verse "Das Schöne bleibt sich selber selig" (the beautiful stays blessed to itself) from Goethe's *Faust*. This connects the poem for Staiger with "Mörike's epigonic situation and his melancholy recollection of the literary-historical Age of Goethe" (418; *GA* 13:94). The philosopher answers the literary-historical reminiscence as one might expect a philosopher to do. Instead of Goethe, he hears Hegel: "The two verses express Hegel's aesthetics *in nuce*" (421; *GA* 13:95); and: "In this connection, compare Hegel's *Lectures on Aesthetics* from 1835" (421; *GA* 13:96). Staiger initially counters this philosophical pedantry by recalling that Mörike's familiarity with the Hegelian system left something to be desired, in order then to insist emphatically on the literary qualities of the poem: "He, the late-comer, can only suppose and conjecture as possible; the nature of things remains half concealed for him. Would you sacrifice this precious, highly individual color of the poet and the verses in question for a single sentence that would be only one more summation of Hegel's aesthetics?" (422–23; *GA* 13:99). Up to this point, everything is proceeding as might be expected in a contest between philosophy and literary studies. But the displacements and irritations that will interrupt the familiar course of this dialogue have already begun, and they demonstrate again that at the juncture of the end of art the strands get tangled and the positions confused. To the extent, namely, that Staiger insists on Mörike's post-Goethean belatedness, he himself has already reduced the poem to a literary echo of the Hegelian philosopheme of the end of art. By the same token, the philosopher Heidegger proves to be the better reader of lyric in what follows, because he is able to gain the very insight into the specific literary achievement of the poem as a linguistic artifact that Staiger postulates but fails to deliver in his thematically bound reading. "The art form of the beautiful lamp has entered the poem so beautifully and fittingly in lines 1–8 that only the utterance of the poem itself illuminates the beautiful lamp in its beauty. The poem does not light the lamp, but it lights the beautiful lamp" (425; *GA* 13:104).

Such inversion of their respective positions as literary historian and philosopher, respectively, is made possible by their common recourse to Hegel's *Aesthetics.* Its poles—Aesthetic Ideal on the one hand and the End of Art on the other—have been apportioned between the antagonists. Thus Staiger neglects to mention Hegel by name, but presupposes the validity of his thesis of the end of art, with no concern for the rest of Hegelian aesthetics. Heidegger, in turn, does cite Hegel as the legitimate authority in matters of artistic forms, but eclipses the thesis of the end of art, to which he himself had devoted an extended addendum in "The Origin of the Work of Art," by declaring the "aphorism" of Hegel's notion of an end of art valid as long as the decision about art has not yet fallen.[3] Both Heidegger and Staiger make reference to an "end of art," but their differently abbreviated recourses to Hegel result in differing interpretations of that end.

It is not that Heidegger refuses to recognize Mörike's epigonal status, but as opposed to Staiger, he understands the end of art not as a simple fact that can only be sadly regretted; rather, he hopes to reap philosophical profit from its past character and perhaps even the promise of a return to a beginning. Heidegger assumes that Mörike "as an epigone [. . .] has evidently seen more and borne more than his predecessors have" (426; *GA* 13:107). With this poem, "something arrives as a latecomer in the vicinity of what existed in the early stages of Western art" (426; *GA* 13:107). The initial verse of the poem, explicitly considered by neither of the disputants, supports either reading. When the poem says "Noch unverrücket, o schöne Lampe, schmückest du / [. . .] / Die Decke des nun fast vergeßnen Lustgemachs" (Not yet displaced, O beautiful lamp, you still adorn / [. . .] / The ceiling of the now almost forgotten pleasure chamber), Staiger understands the temporal adverb *noch* (still) in the sense of "but soon *no longer.*" For Heidegger, artistic images and art are "even still," and their essence resides in that pastness. "The lamp, already extinguished, still shines; it illuminates as a beautiful lamp. Showing itself (*scheinend*), it brings its world (the pleasure chamber) to illumination" (426; *GA* 13:107). Behind the question of whether the measure of art is half empty or half full, there admittedly lies the distinction between Heidegger's understanding of historicity and Staiger's historicism. It leads to differing but secretly complicit interpretations of the end. Paradoxically, Staiger can support his reading of appearance as *videtur* only by presupposing the end of art as a matter of fact. It not only *appears* to be at an end, it *is* at an end. For Heidegger, by contrast, beauty remains objectively what it is, independently of how the question "who notices it?" might be answered: "The mood of melancholy affects the art object when the art object is no longer given the notice due it. The artwork cannot compel the fulfillment of this obligation, nor can it save itself without impairment" (426; *GA* 13:107). Where Staiger has to assert the end of the age of Goethe, Heidegger in turn has to assert an uninterrupted existence of art in order to render the poem the occasion for a decision facing us, human beings, with regard to our relation to language: "Because something more is at stake here than only the single interpretation of a verse. That other issue may be decided perhaps sooner, perhaps later—but foremost and even entirely, it certainly involves the relation of language to us, to mortal beings" (423; *GA* 13:100).

Under the pressure of Staiger's positing of an end of art that has already occurred and its no less apodictic postponement in Heidegger to a future time of decision, the positions of literature and philosophy shift once again. Although Staiger is firmly grounded in the Hegelian aesthetic tradition of the end of art, this foundation leads him to interpret the poem as the rejection of all aesthetics and all art to the extent that they are concerned with expressions of beauty. Goethe could still say in *Faust*: "the beautiful remains blessed in itself," but, Staiger writes, "Mörike does not go that far. He no longer dares to know completely how beauty feels" (418; *GA* 13:94). The epigone thus renounces the aesthetics that determines his status as epigone. Heidegger, for whom, as is well known, everything depends on the overcoming of traditional aesthetics, because it is compromised by western metaphysics,[4] is nonetheless not reticent about attributing to the poet philosophical claims about art: Mörike "*knows* that the true kind of an art object, the beauty of the beautiful, does not depend on the grace of human beings—on whether or not they notice the artwork, on whether or not they take pleasure in what is beautiful. Beauty remains what it is, independent of the answer to the question 'who notices it?'" (425; *GA* 13:105; emphasis added). This reflects an initially surprising affinity in Heidegger to the tradition of aesthetics, for a claim about the irrevocable validity of beauty remains a (Hegelian) philosophical proposition. The proximity to the aesthetic tradition of its sharpest critic—owed to the paradox that an antiaesthetic posture cannot help but perpetuate aesthetic theorems—is apparent in Heidegger's unexpectedly devout reference to Hegel. Although Heidegger thereby signals that the attempt to free oneself from (Hegel's) aesthetics seals its validity, Staiger confronts the problem in a more naïve way and seems not to recognize that he can read a renunciation of aesthetics into the poem only at the cost of presupposing in an unreflected way Hegel's topos of an end of art.[5] For Heidegger, by contrast, the structural imbrication of aesthetics with all attempts to leave it behind is itself thematized, although qualified by any number of ontological-philosophical conditions that cannot simply be ignored.

To the extent that the extremely ambivalent and necessarily divided relationship to the Idealist tradition of philosophical aesthetics, and in particular to Hegel,[6] is the decisive motif that a reconstruction of his end of art must keep in view, the official ontological-philosophical background requires some consideration. One must confront one difficulty in particular, never quite resolved even in Heidegger's thinking on art: the question of the relation of human beings to art, the "creating" and the "preserving" relations to the work and its truth, as they are called in the "Origin of the Work of Art."[7] In the artwork essay, this question had so troubled Heidegger that he later devoted a "supplement" to it. If Beauty is independent of "the grace of human beings," how do things then stand with the event of truth in the beautiful work of art? What happens when no one looks? On the basis of the correspondence with Staiger, one might want to conclude that for Heidegger there can be no end of art, only the failure of human beings to enter the realm illuminated by art. The lamp awaits human beings to the same extent that, in the artwork essay, the Germans have yet to measure up to the work of Hölderlin. Yet since, after Heidegger's "turn" (*Kehre*), concealment (*Verbergung*), withdrawal (*Entzug*), and distortion (*Verstellung*) necessarily belong to the essence of truth, this disregard of art cannot simply be a neglect or deficiency on the part of human beings. In the space of this ambivalence, which Heidegger links to Hegel as the instance of a decision, thinking therefore enters as mediator; of course, this thoughtful preparation is necessarily exposed to the suspicion of being itself "aesthetics." Thus Heidegger emerges at the close of the artwork essay: "this reflective knowledge is the preliminary and therefore indispensable preparation for the becoming of art. Only such knowledge prepares its space for art, their way for the creators, their location for the preservers" (187; *UK* 66). It seems that Hegel's end is reinterpreted by Heidegger as a beginning. Philosophical reflection does not leap over art, but on the contrary helps it to a (different) beginning. In the *Contributions to Philosophy*, written at the same time as the artwork essay and sometimes considered Heidegger's other major work, thinking retains its preparatory function.[8] Although he writes in a posthumously published fragment rather desperately: "We have no art (we don't know, whether we have or don't have— appearance [*Schein*]!) we don't know what art 'is'—we don't know whether art can be again—we don't know if it has to be,"[9] with reference to the other beginning, he states emphatically, "future art, thoughtful grounding to prepare this time through thoughtful knowledge!"[10]

As critical as Heidegger is of all aesthetics, he must at the same time exalt it for reasons that are entwined both with the complex discourse of the end of art since Hegel and with unsolved problems in his own thought. Where these two converge, Heidegger appears as the (re)discoverer of the end of art as discourse. Imputing (or granting) him this role is not without its risks, because it requires a rather intensive submission to Heidegger's own discourse, which is not primarily interested in the end of art, but rather is concerned with the question of Being. Heidegger's relation to aesthetics is ambivalent for an officially ontological reason: all aesthetics is itself ambivalent, because in it resides—as in the metaphysical tradition of ontological forgetfulness in general after the turn—the potential for its overcoming, or, as he later writes, its "torsion" (*Verwindung*). This ambivalence of aesthetics is expressed above all in the tendency toward self-destruction and self-transgression that has been attributed to it repeatedly. According to Heidegger, aesthetics possesses an autodestructive potential—a deconstructive disposition, if you will. This notion determines Heidegger's lectures on Nietzsche, whom Heidegger casts as the last metaphyician on account of the absolute priority he accords to art. Because this concept of aesthetic art is thoroughly informed by the logic of production and productivity, Heidegger believes it to be bound to metaphysics.[11] "In that way Nietzsche's interrogation of art is aesthetics driven to the extreme, an aesthetics, so to speak, that somersaults beyond itself" (77; *N* 92). And: "Hence such aesthetics, within itself, is led beyond itself" (129–30; *N* 152). Heidegger even claims that every true aesthetic "explodes itself."[12]

How one interprets these symptoms of Heidegger's ambivalent relation to the tradition of philosophical aesthetics determines the position one assumes vis-à-vis Heidegger's thinking of art, above all with respect to the question of whether Heidegger himself belongs to the tradition of idealist aesthetics or whether, by breaking with it, he overcomes it. To venture into this debate means also to continue in the tracks of a discussion that is not only genetically and systematically a discussion of the end of art, but is also dominated by its rhetorical and discursive presuppositions. With Heidegger, the question of the end of art has been explicitly transformed into the question of the possibility of ending aesthetics. But that by no means signifies an end to the end of art. What ties (philosophical) aesthetics to art is, in Heidegger's view, nothing other than the end of an art, "for, in truth, the fact whether and how an era is committed to an aesthetics, whether and how it adopts a stance toward art of an aesthetic character, is decisive for the way art shapes the history of that era—or remains irrelevant for it" (79; *N* 94). For Heidegger, too, the end of art converges with the rise of aesthetics: "Aesthetics begins with the Greeks only at that moment when their great art and also the great philosophy that flourished along with it comes to an end" (80; *N* 95). Aesthetics presupposes the end of (great) art in the (Hegelian) sense, in that it enters as heir and disciple by saying what the art that once was can no longer say. At the same time, however, Heidegger is familiar with the antiaesthetically inspired radicalization of this connection. In this context aesthetics figures as the medium in which art "dies" (*UK* 67). "At the historical moment when aesthetics achieves its greatest possible height, breadth, and rigor of form, great art comes to an end" (84; *N* 100). This variant, as well, in which aesthetics not only balances the end of art, but by cognizing art first posits and makes an end of art, is indebted to Hegel. And just this: to have articulated the interpretively underdetermined but nonetheless binding nexus between the end of art and aesthetics, and thus to have recognized the decisive significance of the end of art not only for aesthetic discourse but also for any attempt to evade it—this is, according to Heidegger, Hegel's greatness, the greatness of his aesthetics. "The achievement of aesthetics derives its greatness from the fact that it recognizes and gives utterance to the end of great art *as such*. The final and greatest aesthetics in the Western tradition is that of Hegel" (84; *N* 100; emphasis added).[13]

That Hegel's great *Aesthetics* is able to do this and yet remains aesthetics suggests that every overcoming of aesthetics, every attempt to bring aesthetics to an end, is exposed to the suspicion of still being aesthetics. On the other hand, the particularity of Hegel's aesthetics rests for Heidegger in the fact that here the self-destructive law of aesthetics is itself recognized. The self-overcoming and the characteristic self-transgression of aesthetics is recognizable precisely in the self-limitation of the "slogan" of the end of art. Although Heidegger understands Nietzsche's philosophy, as well, as completion and thereby transition, this is only on account of the immeasurableness with which Nietzsche's aesthetics encompasses the entire tradition. "If in Nietzsche's thinking the prior tradition of Western thought is gathered and completed in a decisive respect, then the confrontation with Nietzsche becomes one with all Western thought hitherto" (4; *N* 13). By contrast, the Hegelian *Aesthetics* is an aesthetics of aesthetics, which revokes and limits itself in the topos of the end of art. Hegel ends aesthetics with the end of art, and precisely with this end simultaneously ensures that every turn away from aesthetics remains bound to it. This is Heidegger's insight into Hegel's "greatness" and the source of all the discomfiture that exudes from Hegel's aesthetics into Heidegger's philosophy of art. The following sections pursue this discomfiture through a reading of the artwork essay. Anticipating its results, one may say that Heidegger betrays his insight into Hegel's aesthetics everywhere he construes art as a beginning that opens the destiny of a people. At these points, he colludes in what he reproaches Nietzsche with: a regression into metaphysics. The opportunity provided by the recognition in Hegel's aesthetics of the connection between self-transgression and self-limitation in the end of art is squandered. What Heidegger says in the *Contributions* about the last God, however, should hold true as well for the last aesthetics: It is "not the end but the other beginning of immeasurable possibilities."[14] There is, in fact, for Heidegger such an other beginning of immeasurable possibilities, but not in Hegel. It is Hölderlin alone who testifies to an other beginning. The consequences for the discourse on the end of art of this turn to Hölderlin in and after Heidegger are briefly considered in the fourth and last section.

2

> Now when in the afterword to my essay I cite Hegel approvingly [. . .], then that
> is neither an agreement with Hegel's understanding of art nor the claim that art is
> at an end.
>
> —MARTIN HEIDEGGER, LETTER OF 25 APRIL 1950 TO KRÄMER-BADONI

In the artwork essay of 1936, Heidegger was apparently as blind to the "greatness" of Hegel's aesthetics as he was to the fact that his own thinking, despite its antiaesthetic program, continued a tradition that imputed truth to art and did not hesitate to make (philosophical) claims about it.[15] "An essential way in which truth inhabits the beings it opens is the setting-itself-in-the-work of truth" (*UK* 49). The formulation is paradoxical, because truth apparently inhabits the work that truth first opens. This is, of course, the hermeneutic circle, and like all of Heidegger's philosophy after *Being and Time*, it governs the artwork essay as well: "every separate step that we attempt circles in this circle" (150; *UK* 2). But the hermeneutic aspect of truth is not yet sufficient reason to accord Heidegger's text a place outside or beyond the tradition of aesthetics; after all, he still assumes a reciprocal relation between art and truth.

If Heidegger's essay is interpreted accordingly as a failed attempt to escape aesthetics, as a regression into an essentialism of art prejudiced by the idealist tradition, then the afterword (which unfortunately cannot be exactly dated),[16] where the unambiguous Hegel passages on the end of art are introduced, appears as a correction and an attempt at distancing that results from Heidegger's deeper insight into his own complicities, including what he now recognized as his ontological imbrication in the tradition of aesthetics. With one and the same gesture of reverence toward Hegel, Heidegger pays this tradition the respect owed it in a being-historical sense, and manages to uncouple it from art. That Heidegger at the latest in the 1950s distanced himself from the hopes he had placed in art is confirmed by the essay "The Question Concerning Technology" (1953), where art is spoken of in the imperfect tense and more cautiously. "What was art? Perhaps only for that brief but magnificent age?"[17] Art is at this point neither as essential nor as pressing as it was in the essay on the "Origin of the Work of Art" twenty years earlier. In the supplement from 1956,

Heidegger explicitly precludes every attempt to misunderstand his reflections as claims about art: "What art is, is one of those questions to which the essay gives no answer. What appears as such are indications toward the question. (See the first sentences of the Afterword)" (*UK* 73). The more emphatically Heidegger denies it, the more clearly the traditional dimension of his essay appears, and together with it his newly altered stance. By 1956, but also already in the undated afterword, art is no longer the possible site of a decision about truth, but, quite the contrary, "the beautiful belongs in the taking place of truth" (*UK* 69). The priorities are set even more clearly in the supplement: "The consideration of what *art* is is thoroughly and decisively determined through the question of *Being*" (*UK* 73). But in the text itself, it seemed as if it was art that first enabled a relation to Being. It was certainly only one of the ways that truth establishes itself, alongside the "state-founding deed," the "essential sacrifice," and the "question of the thinker" (*UK* 49). But art was "a distinctive way" (187; *UK* 65). One could even argue that these other ways in which truth occurs follow the primacy of art. For ultimately it is art that opens to a people its destiny, enabling something like the founding of a state.

For reasons that can only be speculated upon, Heidegger does not want to understand the supplemental corrections in his addenda as denials, but as profiles of latently extant ambivalences. Although this appears plausible with regard to the supplement, it is much harder to accept for the afterword concerned with Hegel. What presents itself as clarifying summation masks a massive difference. The essay itself had ended with a rhetorical question: "Are we in our existence historically at the origin? [. . .] Or, in our relation to art, do we merely make appeal to a cultivated acquaintance with the past?" (187; *UK* 85). That the question is rhetorical, and that Heidegger indeed imagines that "we," unambiguously "we Germans" in 1936, are at the origin, is confirmed by the final sentence: "For this either-or and its decision there is an infallible sign. Hölderlin, the poet—whose work still confronts the Germans as a test to be stood— named it in saying: 'Schwer verläßt / Was nahe dem Ursprung wohnt, den Ort.' [Reluctantly / that which dwells near its origin departs]" (187; *UK* 65). Everything thus points toward an (other) beginning. In the afterword, however, Hölderlin is replaced by Hegel and the origin by the end. The question is no longer: are we already or again at the origin, but "is art still an essential and necessary way in which the truth that is decisive for our historical *Dasein* occurs, or is art no longer this? [. . .] The decision on Hegel's claim has not yet been made; for behind this claim stands Western thinking since the Greeks, a thinking that corresponds to a truth of beings that has already occurred" (*UK* 68). The question whether art was or was not an origin and a beginning must be distinguished from the question whether it is at an end or not. If it is a beginning, art can point both forward and backward. If it is not, art remains caught in the past, can still point backward but no longer forward.

The surprise and the riddle of this shift from Hölderlin to Hegel consists in the fact that in the face of a decision suspended until further notice, Hegel's claim itself is not suspended, but confirmed. "The decision about this claim is reached, when it is reached, from this truth of beings and about beings. Until then the claim maintains its validity" (*UK* 68). Why does Heidegger here affirm the claim? Why does he take what until this point had always been Hegel's yet-to-be-decided "thesis" as claim and judgment? In the essay itself, Heidegger had written: "The beginning already contains the end hidden within itself" (*UK* 64); in the anticipation of the project, the end is already overcome. Now, however, *the very* Hegel is cited and endorsed in whose thinking the end contains the beginning and sublates it into itself as result.[18]

There are various ways to justify this surprising confirmation of the Hegelian judgment as conclusive for the time being. From the perspective of Heidegger's interpretation of metaphysics, it follows that art is a component of metaphysics, and remains so, despite the precipitous hopes of the artwork essay. Art cannot be an origin, cannot become a beginning, as long as metaphysics rules. Therefore Hegel correctly says that art is at an end. But this interpretation imputes an insight to Hegel, and one could add, Hegel of all people, that Heidegger should want to reserve for himself and for his own thinking. But if the decision on the truth of beings is reached (and whether it is reached at all is left open by the conjunction "if," which introduces a hesitation that is absent from the urgent pathos of the essay), and an other beginning occurs, then art is no longer what it was, to the extent that its essential transformation had up until now always corresponded to the "essential transformation of truth" (*UK* 69–70).[19] A nonmetaphysical art would no longer be art. (And this is in fact the case for Heidegger with respect to Hölderlin's poetry.)

But this does not yet explain the fact that Heidegger adopts here an interpretation from Hegel, or how he does so. In taking on the claim with just the equivocation that Hegel had already given it with respect to philosophy, and which finds expression in the paradox that art must be at an end before it can be thought but that where art can be thought it is at an end, Heidegger simultaneously hides and reveals the ambivalence of an entire tradition that is not to be rejected or overcome, but, he claims, is to be appropriated as the history of Being. That Heidegger confirms Hegel is thus from this perspective merely a necessary and preliminary appearance, because the difference between Hegel's and Heidegger's end cannot be perceived[20] as long as the beginning is lacking. (One could invoke here the last sentence of the supplement of 1956, as well, where Heidegger objects to the necessary condition that as an author he must "at the various stations of the path speak in the way appropriate to that stage" [*UK* 74]. Precisely on account of the ambivalence that Hegel's claim already evinces, Heidegger's language would be predestined to display the equivocations of the entire metaphysical tradition.)

At the same time, it is important to recognize what any justification for the authoritative Hegel citation necessarily excludes. Such justification prevents, namely, just the interpretation dominant in Heidegger research, whereby the culture-critical resentment that sounds in Heidegger's grim references to the fatal culture industry is now radicalized, and so an idealistic optimism must give way to a realistic pessimism. But it is more than ironic to instrumentalize *the* end and to submit oneself precisely to *that* end that is a constitutive factor of the very tradition of aesthetics in which art "dies" (*UK* 67). But because here we are primarily concerned with neither the official ontological-philosophical structure of Heidegger's thought, nor with its developmental trajectory, Hegel's presence in the afterword must be considered as a symptom of the peculiar status of the Hegelian aesthetic and its end of art, a status Heidegger acknowledges.

However one interprets the Hegel citation, and however it is chronologically to be located, a tension remains between text and afterword, Hölderlin and Hegel, art and aesthetics, origin and end. This tension exists, however, only to the extent that Heidegger's essay indeed partakes unproblematically in the tradition. But under the assumption that this appropriation of Hegel's end in the afterword retrospectively modifies that tradition, that Heidegger does not simply distance himself from this tradition but justifies his sojourn in it by complicating it in a way that makes its straightforward rejection impossible, then the essay must be read differently and can no longer be dismissed as an idealistic indulgence. And what the essay says about art and its end must be read differently as well. The puzzling afterword, even if it actually is contemporaneous with the essay, offers the opportunity to reread the essay—from its end.

3

Seen from the end, from Hegel's end, beyond and beneath the end of Heidegger's text, the artwork essay appears familiar from the start with Hegel's *Aesthetics*.[21] The same contradiction that emerges in a first Hegel reading of the *Aesthetics*—between the proclaimed end of art and its continued existence—shows up also in Heidegger. There one finds at first: "Art, that is only just a word to which nothing real corresponds any longer" (*UK* 2). And yet art occurs and with it truth before van Gogh's painting of the shoes, which discovers the truth of the equipmental character in reliability (163; *UK* 20). This is initially just a "small" truth, but in the course of the essay, it reveals astonishing consequences. Doubtless art continues to uncover truth and essence.

But this apparent contradiction quickly dissolves in light of what Heidegger says about preservation and the preservers of artworks. The innovation of the artwork essay consists above all in Heidegger's demotion of the production of art, in congruence with his Nietzsche critique, in favor of its preservation. The privileged preservation assumes the prerogatives previously accorded to works of creativity. With this change, what Heidegger understands by art as (other) beginning becomes extremely complex, for beginning turns out to be a modality of preservation. In the third part of the essay, where Heidegger determines the essence of art as poetry, he states: "Founding, however, is actual only in preserving" (186; *UK* 63). True, the work first creates the preservers along with itself, but "it is only for such preserving that the work yields itself in its createdness as actual, i.e., now: present in the manner of a work" (183; *UK* 54). A work is only really a work when it is held in preserving. And this reveals the intentional equivocation in the concept of reality at work in the sentence: "Art, that is only just a word to which nothing real corresponds any longer" (*UK* 2).

Reality here can be understood as Hegel's *actualitas* and metaphysically as *adequatio*, but it can just as well be understood on the basis of the essay's own concept of reality. So understood, the sentence does not mean an end to art but rather the fact that the preserving created along with the artwork has not yet entered the realm of truth opened by the artwork and thus does not correspond to the continuing reality of the artwork. Not only is there no contradiction between the end of art and the occurrence of truth, but there is also no end of art as long as there are works, whether they exist in memory or in some other deficient way. Even the lack of a preserving that corresponds to the work is owed to the artwork: "If a work then does not find its preserver, does not immediately encounter it in a way that corresponds to the truth occurring in the artwork, this by no means signifies that the work is a work even without the preserving" (*UK* 54). The following sentence shows that this does *not* mean that the work is no longer a work when no one notices it, rather that the work has already created the preserving and remains related to it, even when the preserving does not heed the work: "It always remains, as long as it is a work, dependent on the preserving even if and *particularly if* it only awaits the preserving and courts and anticipates its return to the truth it reveals. Even the forgetfulness into which the work may fall is not nothing; it is still a preserving. It lives off of the work" (*UK* 54; emphasis added).

Admittedly not all the modalities of preserving have the same status, and they correspond to the reality of the work in varying degrees: "Preserving occurs at different levels of knowledge with correspondingly different scopes, permanence and illumination" (*UK* 56). Thus recollection can also "offer the work a site from which it can contribute to forming history. The ownmost reality of the work by contrast only comes to bear where the work through the truth of its own occurring is preserved" (*UK* 56).[22] Recollection, forgery, art history, museum organizations, and "experience" are still forms of preservation; even the forgetting and decay of an artwork can do nothing else but confirm its unbroken reality, for they are still effects of the work. In other words, the priority of the preserver and the potential extent of preservation (which Heidegger would nonetheless immediately like to restrict to its "ownmost" modalities) preserves art— from its end. For the fact that a work has no genuine correspondent, that it is placed in a museum, forgotten or reduced to the occasion for an experience, guarantees that works are real and that in this sense there is art. If one wishes to call the forms of preserving that Heidegger denounces as derivative and inauthentic—or, stated positively, the infinite possibilities of distorted and alienated art preservation—an "end of art," then one must also say: there is an end of art only to the extent that there are art and artworks. This inversion, that the end of art not only testifies to the reality of art but even presupposes and continues it, is not Heidegger's insight alone, if one can even speak here of insight (particularly because everything for Heidegger depends upon the possibility of limiting the free play of preservation in a hierarchical way), but the consequences of this emphatically perceived condition are radical. It means that Heidegger—the Heidegger of 1936, who showed himself so reluctant in matters of modern art, much to the chagrin of his exegetes—exposes modernity by showing that until now, no conception of it has been able to recognize its own preservational character—or its unsuspected possibilities. The problem with all conceptions of modernity so far, including any reflexive, second modernity, is that in the face of their inevitable disillusion about their own powers of innovation, they seem condemned either to confess in melancholy or embarrassed tones their own derivativeness or, in the conservative version, to invoke that derivativeness as a restoration. To the extent that Heidegger's modalities of preserving neutralize the innovative and derivative alternatives, whose intersection is remarked by the end of art, both art and its end are provided with infinite possibilities of preservation. In order to liberate this insight that Heidegger suggests but immediately restricts, it must be removed from the context in which it occurs—if need be, torn from it. Heidegger's beginning is namely schizophrenic in a very precise sense. On the one hand, it means that foundation is only possible in preserving, while on the other hand, it implies that there is a dimension of the beginning that means just the opposite. Because Heidegger insists at all costs on art as a beginning, particularly in the second and third sections of the essay, he ends up in the paradoxical situation of having to invoke the end of art, and must unreflectedly instrumentalize the old topos once again. This familiar end of art appears on the horizon wherever Heidegger commits art to beginning, founding, and anchoring history.

The lurch into "the unopened plenitude of the monstrous" (*UK* 64) is the event of the truth of art as the foundation of history. "Whenever being as a whole as being itself demands an anchor in openness, art achieves its historical essence as founding" (*UK* 64). For Heidegger, this first took place in antiquity: "Each time a new and essential world emerged. [. . .] Every time disclosure of being took place. It posits itself in the work, and this positing is the achievement of art" (*UK* 64–65). Heidegger insists unmistakably that *each time* and "*whenever* art occurs, that is, when it is a beginning, a lurch enters into history, history begins or starts over" (*UK* 65; emphasis added). What Heidegger means here by history is, unfortunately, unambiguous: "History is the displacement of a people [*Volk*] in what it surrenders as the placement into what is given with it" (*UK* 65). Heidegger certainly acknowledges that art is also historical "in the external sense that it occurs in changing time along with many other things and in so doing changes and passes away" (*UK* 65), but art can pass away only where it is a beginning: "Art is history in the essential sense that it grounds history" (*UK* 65). Because art has always and everywhere grounded history newly, it can and must also guarantee the beginning in the sense that Heidegger has in mind, the so-called other beginning. Because he is committed so unconditionally to beginning, Heidegger has no choice but to submit to the discursive rules of the end of art and to reduce everything to the alternative: is art a beginning or is it at an end? Where art is burdened with the beginning, the end is always in sight.

"The Origin of the Work of Art" can also be read in such a way that traces remain of a doubt Heidegger may have harbored about the foundational myth of art with its end as the necessary counterpart. Heidegger leaves open the question of whether art is simply *able* to ground history or whether it *must* ground history.[23] "What is truth, when it *can or even must occur* as art?" (*UK* 44; emphasis added). He writes cautiously at one point: "What is truth itself, that it *sometimes* comes to pass as art?" (166; *UK* 24; emphasis added). At another point, as ambivalently as decisively: "But what is truth, that it *has* to happen in *such a thing as* something created?" (180; *UK* 48; emphasis added). The claim that "in the essence of truth lies *a pull toward the work*" (*UK* 50) describes a tendency and a possibility but not a necessity. But already on the following page the pull has become a will: "Truth wills to be established in the work as this strife of world and earth" (181; *UK* 50). The justification for this will lies, as is well known, in the essence of earth and world, for the world demands what is opened and earth wants closure. But why does the truth will the work? Whenever art occurs, a lurch enters into history. But when a lurch enters history, does this always occur as art? Such hesitation delays the end of art as well, because if the beginning and the foundation of history as art are only possible but not necessary, then the end of art is also a possibility but no necessity. Only when in the afterword necessity is being discussed does the end of art become authoritative: "Is art still an essential and necessary way in which the decisive truth for our historical *Dasein* occurs, or is art this no longer?" (*UK* 68).

The question whether art grounds history necessarily or only under certain conditions arises from the competition of thinking with art, a competition that would not have become so urgent had Heidegger taken up the possibilities inherent in his theory of preservation. He did not do so, and as a consequence the competition and aporetic connection between thinking and art subsists in his artwork essay, the connection inscribed into the end of art as discourse and activated by every instrumentalization of the topos. If art is a beginning, then this beginning is preceded by a thinking determination of the question of art. Certainly such thinking is not able to "force art and its coming-to-be. But this reflective knowledge is the preliminary and therefore indispensable preparation for the becoming of art" (187; *UK* 66). It is not art that pushes history open and closed but the (philosophical) question of art. Not in art, but "in such knowledge [. . .] the question is decided whether art can be an origin and then must be a forward spring, or whether it is to remain a mere appendix" (187; *UK* 66). But—and this is the paradox of the situation—if thinking can prepare for art, then art is no longer a beginning, because before its innovative lurch, there lies the prior intervention of the thinker to which art for its part can only correspond. Then there is no more beginning of art; it is always only an appendix; it must ultimately be at an end.

But Heidegger's essay allows for another reading, one that brings the end of art into play once more in a different way. The alternative implicit in the question whether art is a possible or a necessary occurrence of truth and foundation of history has a second, corresponding alternative that remains legible despite the fact that Heidegger nowhere formulates it explicitly. This concerns the end of art in the sense of an irrecoverable disappearance of its world, that event that permits the priority of preservation and whose potential is simultaneously restricted by the hierarchical structure of preservation.

The Aegina sculptures in the Munich collection, Sophocles' Antigone in the best critical edition, are as the works they are, torn out of their own native sphere. However high their quality and power of impression, however good their state of preservation, however certain their interpretation, placing them in a collection has withdrawn them from their own world. But even when we make an effort to cancel or avoid such displacement of works—when, for instance, we visit the temple in Paestum at its own site or the Bamberg cathedral on its own square—the world of the work that stands there has perished. (167; *UK* 26)

As unambiguous as this end is, the genesis of the perishing of the world is all the more ambivalent, for there is a difference between the cultural-critical thesis that by being placed in a collection the works have been torn from their world, and the melancholy recognition that the world of the works has disintegrated. It is the same difference between "world-with-drawal and world-decay" as that which exists between the fatal flight of the Gods from the temple (*UK* 29) and the murderous aesthetic in which art "dies" (*UK* 67). In the afterword, as well, this dual significance persists, for Heidegger appears at first to make aesthetics responsible for the dying out of art, only then to formulate neutrally, "great art together with its essence" has "retreated" from human being (*UK* 68).

This indecisiveness may be explained by two different features of the artwork essay. On the one hand, the essence of the artwork itself is responsible for this ambivalence. The conflict between world and earth, between what opens itself and what closes itself, is a conflict of truth in the sense of *aletheia* as interplay and resistance between concealment and discovery. Concealment, however, Heidegger explains, occurs in two ways, as refusal and as dissembling. "Concealment can be a refusal or merely a dissembling. We are never fully certain whether it is the one or the other. Concealment conceals and dissembles itself" (176; *UK* 41). It is implicit in the essence of truth, then, that we can never finally decide whether the world of true works has retreated and refused itself or whether it is dissembling. That is the one, as it were, official, horizon of justification, because it concerns truth and the manner of its showing itself and occurring. The other context concerns the relation of human beings to art, which Heidegger discussed with uncommon clarity in the supplement of 1956. The question whether world withdrawal or world decay reigns, whether we have prepared an end of art or whether it has withdrawn from us, depends upon how the relation of human beings to the truth occurring in the work turns out. "In the title: Setting-into-the-Work of Truth, in which who or what in whichever manner 'sets' remains undetermined but determinable, lies hidden the reference to Being and the human essence, a reference that in this version is already inappropriately thought through,—a pressing difficulty that has become clear to me since 'Being and Time' and which I have discussed in many versions" (*UK* 74).[24]

If world withdrawal and world decay are not merely undecidable right now, but can never be decided at all, then the alternative between the possibility and the necessity of art, as well, is not only provisionally but principally undecidable. Then this question, the question of the beginning, poses itself only to the extent that the world of the work has disintegrated.[25] Then it holds that with the indeterminate and underdetermined end of art as the disappearance of the world—as puzzling and underdetermined as Nietzsche's reputure in tradition—the decision between the possibility and necessary of art is not only provisionally but in principle impossible.

Under these conditions, the question of art moves into the background and the problem of the work takes precedence.[26] The question is no longer: is art a beginning or an end, but are works? Are there works at all, and are works works when their world has been destroyed and/or has retreated? This is where the preservers enter the picture, and together with them the privileged preservation, "where the work is preserved in the truth occurring through it" (*UK* 56). But at one point in the text Heidegger risks a question that undermines this hierarchy of preserving: "Yet is the work *ever* accessible in itself?" (*UK* 26; emphasis added). Heidegger answers with the passage on world withdrawal and world decay. His answer is thus, works are *no longer* what they once were. But the question also has another answer—namely, that works were never accessible, nor are they now. Their "former self-subsistence" (168; *UK* 27) has not fled; rather, what is called a work was never accessible in itself.[27] Viewed in terms of this possibility, the sentence with which Heidegger elucidates the claim that "the works are no longer the same as they once were" reveals another potential reading: "It is they themselves, to be sure, that we encounter there, but they themselves are gone by" (167; *UK* 26–27). This *can* imply an idealistic fiction of the end of great art, but it does not have to be read this way if being a work means never being "itself" and therefore never being "accessible," and so anachronistic in a Hegelian sense.

Isolating the conception of preserving and removing from its context, the question of whether a work is *ever* itself seems justified to the extent that individualization, displacement, and decontextualization belong, according to Heidegger, to the essence of the work of art. In front of Van Gogh's painting "we were suddenly somewhere else than we usually tend to be" (164; *UK* 21). The work is not accessible and no longer itself not because its world has disintegrated, but because the work of art has no predetermined site and belongs in no predetermined place. The site of art is not a place, but a no-place or an un-place, because the work lurches, pushes aside, pushes away. Equipment truly shows itself to be the reliability it is only in the abandoned, empty, and unlocalized shoes: "There is nothing surrounding this pair of peasant shoes in or to which they might belong—only an undefined space" (163; *UK* 18–19).[28] Heidegger claims that artworks belong in the domain that they open; but how can something whose essence consists in displacement and dislocation belong anywhere at all? If one takes seriously the spatial dimension that Heidegger attributes to art, then there is no place for a temporal end of art; it has neither occurred nor is it in the offing. If art is from the start exiled and exiles itself, then it is at home nowhere but in the mode of nonbelonging. Because it can displace other places, art itself is without a place. That art, in order to render us siteless and to dislocate us, must itself be without a site can be argued in analogy with Heidegger's suggestion that art is produced because it produces (earth), that it is displayed because it displays (world). Art displaces and dislocates, it follows, because it is itself displaced and without a proper place. This means not only that its displacement is not strictly predictable, least of all that it must be directed toward a people [*Volk*] and its destiny, but also has the consequence that the qualitative differences between the exile of art in a museum collection and the space that the temple prepares for a God collapse. A work is never itself and has never been itself, because it is always already at another site and displaced onto another site. Art sets aside. It exiles and dislocates the preservers. It neutralizes the references and exposes itself thereby to its own nonbelonging.

Heidegger's treatise discovers the possibility of an understanding of art that resists just those services to which the text would like to bind it, that struggles against the site at which Heidegger would like to situate it. With the reference to Hegel, his essay moves in the direction of a theory of the end of art that it discovers as discourse. But Heidegger also posits the end where he locates art as beginning in the sense of a foundation of history. The old and the new end; the same and the other end lie in the closest proximity. And at least in one respect the new end that Heidegger discovers is the same as the old end: no end without Hegel. Heidegger was right to give him the last word on the end of art in his afterword. The artwork essay not only presupposes and deploys the old end in an instrumentalizing way, but poses it as well. At the same time this equivocation is sealed by Heidegger's return to Hegel. For, as the first chapter attempted to demonstrate, it is Hegel's end of art that discovers, grounds, and establishes the unlocalizability of art in the discourse of its end. What Hegel founded was, strictly speaking, not a thing but an empty place, an indeterminacy, an unclarity, an absence. It has proven endlessly productive. The end of art has continually been filled in again, reinterpreted differently. Nietzsche, Benjamin, Adorno, and Heidegger, each in his own way, have succumbed and have had to succumb to this empty site of the end. They have their prominence here because in different ways but in contact with one another, they all did not attempt to end the end of art, but to open it in new ways and to leave it open, by rediscovering in it an under- or overdetermined empty space, as parody or allegory, and with Heidegger finally as the possibility of preservation. Heidegger goes first and last in this respect, and yet at the same time the potential of his thought is so contaminated by the context in which it occurs that one has no other choice but to tear it from that context and replant it in another.

One of the most striking moments in Heidegger's artwork essay is no doubt the passage in which the artwork as created being is described in a way that radically departs from all models of creativity that privilege inventive imagination. "It is not the N. N. fecit that must be made known, but the simple 'factum est' must be held open in the work [. . .]. There, where the artist and process and the circumstances of the development of the work remain unknown, this lurch, this 'that' of having been made emerges most purely from the work" (*UK* 52–53). By breaking the accustomed unity of work and author, Heidegger breaks with a fundamental ordering principle. "At issue is an opening into which the writing subject endlessly disappears."[29] These are not Heidegger's words in 1936 but those of Michel Foucault in his essay on the function of the author in 1969. What Heidegger says about the work can also be described as "the disappearance of the author—since Mallarmé, an event of our time."[30] In this context, it is clear how immanently modern Heidegger's conception of the work might have been, even if this relevance must be wrested from his text. What Heidegger discovers in the possibility of preservation in place of creation can be rediscovered in what Foucault says about the recourse to the text of founders of discursivity. "It is always a return to the text in itself, specifically, to a primary and unadorned text with particular attention to those things registered in the interstices of the text, its gaps and absences. We return to those empty spaces that have been masked by omission or concealed in a false and misleading plenitude."[31] In this text, which beneath the Beckett motto "What matter who's speaking?"[32] presents Foucault as the discursive founder of discourse theory, what Foucault cannot say but only practice is: that the past whose forgetting and repressing, whose gaps and empty spaces must be rediscovered, that this past must first be founded. Modernity does not suffer from a repressed, oppressed, or lost past— quite the contrary: there is in modernity a genuine obsession with all forms of return. Every effort is made to establish the repressed, latent, or forgotten past in such a way that rediscovery of the hidden, forgotten, or repressed is and remains possible. What must be rediscovered must first be invented. And what is presented as invention is always only rediscovered. The possibilities of this game, whose rules Hegel inaugurated for the end of art, are perhaps exhausted, but what emerges in the course of playing it is a shift from temporal to spatial relationships. The new obsession is the spaces, and indeed such spaces in which time is produced, for example the museum or the archive, the cemetery, the crypt, the clearing, the border, the installation, the network.[33] "What can be done when we can go neither forwards nor backwards? We can shift our attention. We have never moved forward or fallen back. We have always selected and chosen active elements that belonged to different times. We can always continue to select. *It is this selecting that makes the times, not the times that make the selection.*"[34]

If in the discourse on the end of art its rule also emerges—namely, that the assertion of what was once the case is always also an assertion of what should have been the case, and that every such saying can be revealed to have been a rediscovery—then at this point a confession is appropriate: Hegel did not inaugurate anything, did not establish an empty site, did not initiate the discourse of the end of art. "Hegel" is a selection, a prop, a role that Hegel can fill well, a stage, just as tragedy was for Nietzsche, Trauerspiel was for Benjamin, apocalypse for Adorno, the symbolic protoart for Hegel, and Hegel's "slogan" for Heidegger. This insight is not the end of the rumor about the end, but a condition of its different possibilities and the condition for its interpretation as discourse.

4

It thus seems as if the discourse on the end of art, which since Hegel has been uttered with two voices and has rested on two foundations, is recognized and comes to itself in Heidegger's reflections on Hegel's *Aesthetics*—provided these reflections are appropriately decontextualized and carefully selected, and that Heidegger's insights into the aesthetic tradition are separated from his own philosophical-political involvement in that tradition. But is it legitimate and even possible to separate the "old" end from the "new" insights into the discursive structures of the end? If it was true of the other philosophers we have considered that they continually modified the discourse on the end of art, then this also holds for Heidegger's insights into this discourse—that with them the principally problematic implications of this discourse on the end of art, in particular the hypostatization of art, have by no means been abolished. In other words, insight into the functioning of the discourse "end of art" and the interpretation of its structure do not protect against the potentially disastrous consequences that can attend the instrumentalization of this discourse, consequences that clearly come to light in Heidegger's politics of the 1930s. If Heidegger understood like no other post-Hegelian thinker the functioning of the aesthetic tradition—and the recourse to Hegel's end of art emphatically be-

longs to that tradition—he is also the thinker in whom the political ambitions of this (German) aesthetic and antiaesthetic tradition reach their
culmination: in the name of Hölderlin's poetry, Heidegger announced an
end of art that was to have guaranteed "the Germans" a return to their
own destiny. Beyond particular limitations (such as, for instance, the hierarchical order of preservational possibilities in the artwork essay), it is
finally Heidegger's identification of political and aesthetic structures that
signifies his falling short of Hegel's insight into the constitutive connection between the self-overcoming and self-restriction of art. Heidegger's
Hölderlin lectures are a two-edged documentation of this shortcoming;
the unmistakable sign of a catastrophic overestimation of art is, once again,
the end of art that Hölderlin's poetry signals for Heidegger, an end that
seems to have nothing more to do with Hegel's "slogan" or with the aesthetic tradition at all. For Heidegger, Hölderlin is he "who falls out of all
metaphysics."[35] Because all art until now has only been thought metaphysically, Hölderlin's poetry is no longer art but lies "outside the essential domain of western art" (Ister, 21).

Admittedly: In the preceding section what was rather laboriously extracted and reformulated in repeated readings of the artwork essay—the
discovery of the preserving possibilities and the insight (already latent in
Hegel and explicitly formulated by Heidegger) that what the (art)work
means has no proper place—all this can be found much more extensive-
ly and explicitly in Heidegger's Hölderlin lectures, in particular those on
Hölderlin's poems to rivers, from 1942. Because a detailed reading of these
lectures cannot be offered here, at least some of the reasons why it is lacking should be presented.

The uncanny and monstrous aspect of these lectures, whose central section is devoted to a reading of the *deinon* from the first choral song
of *Antigone*, consists in the experience that here a philosopher rewrites a
poem in an unprecedented and perhaps unique way, and how he does so.
As opposed to the usual criticism of Heidegger's hermeneutically and philologically violent reinterpretation, his readings of Hölderlin raise a very
different question: what does it mean when a philosopher gives up phi-
losophizing in order to become the mouthpiece or medium of a poet? In
the tradition of the end of art this is unprecedented. In the popular in-

terpretation of Hegel's philosophically decreed end, it was always a matter of art's self-assertion against this dictum; at stake was the legitimacy of modern art. But the more emphatically autonomy was insisted upon and Hegel opposed, all the more clearly the heteronomy inscribed in this gesture showed itself, because in the modern announcements of an end of art one was always thrown back to Hegel. Insofar as the choice of authors considered here was determined by the criterion to what extent they managed to do justice to the constitutive connection between autonomy and heteronomy that finds its expression in, among other things, the mutual implication of philosophy and art in modernity, Heidegger had his rightful place here. But his Hölderlin lectures invert this pattern, for now philosophy abdicates in favor of poetry. Whereas before art saw itself thrown back on the decrees of a philosopher, in Heidegger, the philosopher subjects himself to the poet. Now the poet dictates an end of art to the philosopher that puts the latter under pressure to legitimate and assert this stance.

Hölderlin, who has fallen out of metaphysics and therefore out of the essential domain of western art, confronts, according to Heidegger, the continual domination of metaphysical thinking of art. If Hölderlin's poetry is not art, "all the usual readings and interpretations of these poems would be futile, because all interpretation imperceptibly draws its tools and its efforts from metaphysics and the metaphysical doctrine of art, that is, aesthetics" (Ister, 21). Heidegger is far from excluding himself and his discussions, however idiosyncratic and different they may be, from "the usual readings and interpretations of these poems." Quite the contrary, the central problem of this lecture, its hermeneutical crux and its presentational difficulty is precisely the fact that thinking continues to move in the spell of metaphysics and yet Hölderlin is no longer or not yet art in the metaphysical sense. In the attempt to think together the end and the non-end of art (and of metaphysics in toto), what must first be recognized are the enormous distance and the incompatibility that separate Hölderlin from metaphysically conceived art: "Insofar now as Hölderlin's hymns fall out of all metaphysics, while nonetheless in versifying the rivers the historicity of human beings and thus place and time are necessarily written, metaphysics cannot immediately help us illuminate location and wandering and their unity" (Ister, 66). Yet already in this sentence, which appears to deny philosophy its competence, there are signs that although Hölderlin is the "other" (Ister, 58), in this alterity, he remains conditioned by our—that is,

metaphysical—thinking, and that consequently perhaps not immediately, but mediatedly, this thinking can indeed help. The Hölderlin who has fallen out of metaphysics is still and at the same time also the poet of historicity and the poet of place and time. The turn of phrase "while nonetheless" indicates that this is a countermove, through which this poetry, although no longer contained by metaphysics, still, if contradictorily, thematizes the categories of space and time that play a decisive role in metaphysics. In fact Heidegger clings to the necessity of "thinking [Hölderlin] from our thinking" (Ister, 67). "Because, therefore, our thinking is still thoroughly and more decisively than ever metaphysical, we must also keep the metaphysical space-time determination in view" (Ister, 66–67). What has here, from an eccentric position, been brought into the unity of a dialectical interplay, is the end of (metaphysical) art and the unbroken domination of metaphysical (that is, aesthetic) thinking. Within this dialectic Hölderlin assumes the role of the alien and "other" that has yet to be recognized as its own, in contrast to "our thinking." This relation between one's own and the alien is patterned on the "conversation" that the German Hölderlin entertains with the Greek Sophocles, whose choral song in Heidegger's view already is concerned with the relation between the domestic and the alien in Greek thought. The extent to which this dialectic of proper and alien is finally Hegelian: what role Hölderlin's reflections in the famous Böhlendorff letter played for Hegel, how and whether Hölderlin's relation to Hegel is related to Heidegger's relation to Hölderlin, what role Hölderlin plays in idealism and what role idealism plays in Heidegger— all of these are technical questions of philosophy and literary history that have long since given rise to their own field of research.[36] Not only their complexity prevents us from delving more deeply into them here; to do so would also mean beginning all over again and writing a different history of the end of art. Within the framework we have established here, it remains undecided whether Heidegger's curious inversion of Hegel's end of art is a Heideggerian turn or a Hegelian dialectic. But it must be said in all clarity: If Heidegger (alongside of and after Hegel) unfolded most radically the riven structure of the end, he is also the thinker in whom the political problematic of the discourse of the end of art is most clearly discernible. Its characteristic symptom is the politically dubious overestimation of art, even if the art at issue is Hölderlin's the no-longer-art poetry.

Whether the modern discourse on the end of art can be freed from these political implications, whether something like a rediscovery and a new reading of the Hegelian *Aesthetics* would achieve this or whether Heidegger's reading of the rumor of the end of art, the last reading so far, indicates that this topos remains politically dangerous—these are questions that the preliminary discussions here assembled do not pretend to decide. They thus close open-endedly, and so do not really close, but remain, for the time being, without conclusion and closure.

The following epilogue instead avails itself of the opportunity of recollecting a beginning of a different sort, one that allows, or even requires, that the different motives of the discourse of the end of art, including the question of its political implications, be played out a second time but in a different tone and at another site. The guiding word is provided by Heidegger himself, who cites Hölderlin's ode "Stimme des Volkes" ("Voice of the People") in connection with the river hymns, although only in the short first version.

Um unsre Weisheit unbekümmert
Rauschen die Ströme doch auch, und dennoch

Wer liebt sie nicht? und immer bewegen sie
Das Herz mir, hör ich ferne die Schwindenden
Die Ahnungsvollen, meine Bahn nicht
Aber gewisser ins Meer hin eilen.

[No less indifferent to our wisdom
Likewise the rivers yet rush on, but who does

Not love them? Always too my own heart is moved
When far away I hear those foreknowing ones
The fleeting, by a route not mine but
Surer than mine, and more swift, roar seaward.][37] (Ister, 32)

Heidegger cites the text above all to indicate "that the rivers themselves in their streaming are doubly directed" (Ister, 33), that what has been, and what is coming, the past and the future "once" accommodated in a way that emerges in "foreknowing." He cites only these verses and remarks, "The poem itself we leave resting in itself" (Ister, 36).

There are reasons not to do so. Above all, because in this text with the resonant title "Voice of the People" the relation of art to politics is addressed quite directly, as is the problematic relation of the poet to the people. The poem is moreover concerned with a violent, self-destructive and immediately "political" end of art:

Das Ungebundne reizet und Völker auch
Ergreift die Todeslust und kühne
Städte, nachdem sie versucht das Beste,

Von Jahr zu Jahr forttreibend das Werk, sie hat
Ein heilig Ende troffen [. . .] er selbst,
Der Mensch, mit eigner Hand zerbrach, die
Hohen zu ehren, sein Werk, der Künstler.

[Chaotic deeps attract, and whole peoples too
May come to long for death, and valiant
Towns that have striven to do the best thing,

Year in, year out pursuing their task—these too
A holy end has stricken; [. . .] he himself,
The man, the artist with his own two
Hands broke his work for their sake, in homage.]

The poem explores the possibilities of the end, between tragic renewing sacrifice—"Like firstfruits of the harvest" (a verse that anticipates Benjamin's notion in the Trauerspiel book of the first examples of the new human harvest in tragedy)—and chaotically senseless suicide: "All were beside themselves." In its second part, the poem introduces a narrative that tells of two particular cases of such suicidal self-sacrifice, whereby the collective in the second case seems only to be anachronistically imitating an historical precedent. Thus it is not simply a matter of the end, but of different possible interpretations of the end, including the question of the connection between distanced interpretations of a tradition and their restaging or instrumentalization and thus a matter of just the problematic that lends the claims about the end of art their oddly riven character: " . . . no doubt such lore / Is good, because it serves to remind us of / The Highest; yet there's also need of / One to interpret these holy legends." A decade before Hegel's *Aesthetics: Lectures on Fine Art* spelled out the end of art, and a full thirty years before it became common knowledge after Hotho's publication, Hölderlin wrote this lyrical instruction about the treacherousness of traditions, and in so doing made reference to rumors and lore that have to do with the end.

CHAPTER 7

Epilogue: "That Mysterious Yearning Toward the Chasm"

Deceiving many: beginning and end.

—FRIEDRICH HÖLDERLIN

Stimme des Volks
(Zweite Fassung)

Du seiest Gottes Stimme, so glaubt ich sonst
In heilger Jugend; ja, und ich sag es noch!
Um unsre Weisheit unbekümmert
Rauschen die Ströme doch auch, und dennoch

Wer liebt sie nicht? und immer bewegen sie
Das Herz mir, hör ich ferne die Schwindenden,
Die Ahnungsvollen meine Bahn nicht,
Aber gewisser ins Meer hin eilen.

Denn selbstvergessen, allzubereit, den Wunsch
Der Götter zu erfüllen, ergreift zu gern,
Was sterblich ist, wenn offnen Augs auf
Eigenen Pfaden es einmal wandelt,

Ins All zurück die kürzeste Bahn; so stürzt
Der Strom hinab, er suchet die Ruh, es reißt,
Es ziehet wider Willen ihn, von
Klippe zu Klippe, den Steuerlosen,

Das wunderbare Sehnen dem Abgrund zu;
Das Ungebundne reizet und Völker auch
Ergreift die Todeslust und kühne
Städte, nachdem sie versucht das Beste,

Von Jahr zu Jahr forttreibend das Werk, sie hat
Ein heilig Ende troffen; die Erde grünt
Und stille vor den Sternen liegt, den
Betenden gleich, in den Sand geworfen,

Freiwillig überwunden die lange Kunst
Vor jenen Unnachahmbaren da; er selbst,
Der Mensch, mit eigner Hand zerbrach, die
Hohen zu ehren, sein Werk, der Künstler.

Doch minder nicht sind jene den Menschen hold,
Sie lieben wieder, so wie geliebt sie sind,
Und hemmen öfters, daß er lang im
Lichte sich freue, die Bahn des Menschen.

Und, nicht des Adlers Jungen allein, sie wirft
Der Vater aus dem Neste, damit sie nicht
Zu lang ihm bleiben, uns auch treibt mit
Richtigem Stachel hinaus der Herrscher.

Wohl jenen, die zur Ruhe gegangen sind,
Und vor der Zeit gefallen, auch die, auch die
Geopfert, gleich den Erstlingen der
Ernte, sie haben ein Teil gefunden.

Am Xanthos lag, in griechischer Zeit, die Stadt,
Jetzt aber, gleich den größeren, die dort ruhn,
Ist durch ein Schicksal sie dem heilgen
Lichte des Tages hinweggekommen.

Sie kamen aber, nicht in der offnen Schlacht,
Durch eigne Hand um. Fürchterlich ist davon,
Was dort geschehn, die wunderbare
Sage von Osten zu uns gelanget.

Es reizte sie die Güte von Brutus. Denn
Als Feuer ausgegangen, so bot er sich,
Zu helfen ihnen, ob er gleich, als Feldherr,
Stand in Belagerung vor den Toren.

Doch von den Mauern warfen die Diener sie,
Die er gesandt. Lebendiger ward darauf
Das Feuer und sie freuten sich und ihnen
Strecket' entgegen die Hände Brutus.

Und alle waren außer sich selbst. Geschrei
Entstand und Jauchzen. Drauf in die Flamme warf
Sich Mann und Weib, von den Knaben stürzt' auch
Der von dem Dach, in der Väter Schwert der.

Nicht räthlich ist es, Helden zu trotzen. Längst
Wars aber vorbereitet. Die Väter auch,
Da sie ergriffen waren, einst, und
Heftig die persischen Feinde drängten,

Entzündeten, ergreifend des Stromes Rohr,
Daß sie das Freie fänden, die Stadt. Und Haus
Und Tempel nahm, zum heilgen Aether
Fliegend, und Menschen hinweg die Flamme.

So hatten es die Kinder gehört, und wohl
Sind gut die Sagen, denn ein Gedächtnis sind
Dem Höchsten sie, doch auch bedarf es
Eines, die heiligen auszulegen.

[Voice of the People
(Second Version)

The voice of God I called you and thought you once,
In holy youth; and I say it still!
No less indifferent to our wisdom
Likewise the rivers yet rush on, but who does

Not love them? Always too my own heart is moved
When far away I hear those foreknowing ones,
The fleeting, by a route not mine but
Surer than mine, and more swift, roar seaward,

For once they travel down their allotted paths
With open eyes, self-oblivious, too ready to
Comply with what the gods have wished them,
Only too gladly will mortal beings

Speed back into the All by the shortest way;
So the river plunges—not movement, but rest it seeks—
Drawn on, pulled down against their will from
Boulder to boulder—abandoned, helmless—

By that mysterious yearning toward the chasm;
Chaotic deeps attract, and whole peoples too
May come to long for death, and valiant
Towns that have striven to do the best thing,

Year in, year out pursuing their task—these too
A holy end has stricken; the earth grows green,
And there beneath the stars, like mortals
Deep in their prayers, quite still, prostrated

On sand, outgrown, and willingly, lies long art
Flung down before the Matchless; and he himself,
The man, the artist with his own two
Hands broke his work for their sake, in homage.

Yet they, the Heavenly, to men remain well-disposed,
As we love them so they will return our love
And lest too briefly he enjoy the
Light, will obstruct a man's course to ruin.

And not the eagle's fledglings alone their sire
Throws out of eyries, knowing that else too long
They'd idle—us the Ruler also
Goads into flight with a prong that's fitting.

Those men I praise who early lay down to rest,
Who fell before their time, and those also, those
Like firstfruits of the harvest offered
Up—they were granted a part, a portion.

By Xanthos once, in Grecian times, there stood
The town, but how, like greater ones resting there,
Because a destiny ordained it
Xanthos is lost to our holy daylight.

But not in open battle, by their own hands
Her people perished. Dreadful and marvelous
The legend of that town's destruction,
Traveling on from the East, has reached us.

The kindliness of Brutus provoked them. For
When fire broke out, most nobly he offered them
His help, although he led those troops which
Stood at their gates to besiege the township.

Yet from the walls they threw all the servants down
Whom he had sent. Much livelier then at once
The fire flared up, and they rejoiced, and
Brutus extended his arms towards them,

All were beside themselves. And great crying there,
Great jubilation sounded. Then into flames
Leapt man and woman; boys came hurtling
Down from the roofs or their fathers stabbed them.

It is not wise to fight against heroes. But
Events long past prepared it. Their ancestors
When they were quite encircled once and
Strongly the Persian forces pressed them,

Took rushes from the rivers and, that their foes
Might find a desert there, set ablaze their town;
And house and temple—breathed to holy
Aether—and men did the flame carry off there.

So their descendants heard, and no doubt such lore
Is good, because it serves to remind us of
The Highest; yet there's also need of
One to interpret these holy legends.]

Although individual verses from Hölderlin's "Voice of the People," in particular that "mysterious yearning toward the chasm," have often been cited, there are few interpretations of this enigmatic poem,[1] and in particular almost no commentary on stanzas 5 and 6, which strangely interrupt its lyrical flow:

Towns that have striven to do the best thing,

Year in, year out pursuing their task—these too
A holy end has stricken; the earth grows green,
And there beneath the stars, like mortals
Deep in their prayers, quite still, prostrated

On sand, outgrown, and willingly, lies long art
Flung down before the Matchless; and he himself,
The man, the artist with his own two
Hands broke his work for their sake, in homage.

Stanzas 9 through 18 render the allegorical scene more concrete through the legend of the fate of the residents of the city on the river Xanthos "in Grecian times": "But not in open battle, by their own hands / Her people perished. Dreadful and marvelous / The legend of that town's destruction, / Traveling on from the East, has reached us" (12.1–4). The legend of the self-inflicted end of the city, however, turns out to be, in the course of the poem, the legend of the long-term effects of a legend, because those who died at their own hands acted as if under the spell of a repetition compulsion. Just as the later generation had heard the legend of the heroic suicide of their ancestors, so the reader in turn now hears of this event as legend: "Dreadful and marvelous / The legend of that town's destruction, / Traveling on from the East, has reached us." In this twofold doubling—of the event within the narrative intrusion and the repeating illustration of the allegory in the form of the historical anecdote—this particular end's overdetermination finds thematic and formal expression. Moreover, the poem's own ambivalence vis-à-vis the many meanings of an end comes to the fore.

Conceived in 1798 as an epigrammatic short ode, Hölderlin rewrote and expanded "Voice of the People" over the next three years. Chronologically and thematically, the ode is situated between "Dichterberuf" ("The Poet's Vocation"), which explores the poet's need to participate in the world of conflict and revolution, and "Wie wenn am Feiertage . . . " ("As on a Holiday . . . "), where the vision of an isolated and distanced poet collapses for reasons that Peter Szondi's reading has elucidated.[2] Although the older long version of "Voice of the People" unambiguously urged action— "Drum weil sie fromm ist, ehr ich den Himmlischen / Zu lieb des Volkes Stimme, die ruhige, / Doch um der Götter und der Menschen / Willen, sie ruhe zu gern nicht immer!"[3] (Because it is pious, I honor the heavenly / For the sake of the people's voice, the peaceful, / Yet for the sake of Gods and men / let them not rest too easily forever!)—the second version, augmented by the story of the nameless city by Xanthos, ends with the necessity of interpretation: "So their descendants heard, and no doubt such lore / Is good, because it serves to remind us of / The Highest; yet there's also need of / One to interpret these holy legends" (18.1–4).

This gesture toward interpretation, which completes the narrative excursus and concludes the poem, is not simply a *fabula docet* that could be drawn from the story of the city's inhabitants, but is as well the ex post facto affirmation of the interpretation that has already occurred in the course of the poem and its presentation of these events. That the "marvelous legend" (12) is not merely the object of interpretation but is simultaneously the result of interpretation, is apparent from the inversion of the chronological sequence of the events the poem depicts. The later event precedes the earlier. That the suicide of the city's residents in the face of the Roman besiegement under Brutus constitutes a repetition of what an earlier generation had already done when "strongly the Persian forces pressed them" (15.4) reveals itself only in the final stanzas. The intervention of interpretation is also indicated by the apodictic advice: "It is not wise to fight against heroes" (16.1) that disrupts the regular progression of the narrative. The numerous differences between the first and second events culminate in the fact that the later generation merely imitated what the earlier generation had done on its own initiative. "But / Events long past prepared it" (16.1–2) and "So their descendants heard" (18.1). The later generation repeats and restages its own prehistory handed down as legend. The second destruction of the city might then be considered an example of what Hölderlin had identified elsewhere as the reason for the destruction of all peoples and societies: a tradition grown static and postivitistic. "And what more generally is the reason for the collapse of all peoples, namely, that their originality, their proper living nature was submerged by the positive forms, by the luxury their forefathers had produced, that seems to be our fate as well, only to a greater extent, since an almost limitless prior world that we learn of either through instruction or experience works and presses upon us."[4]

Drawing on Hölderlin's reflections about the relation between antiquity and modernity in his letter to Böhlendorff from 4 December 1802,[5] one could interpret the difference between an original act and its parasitic repetition as an echo of the distinction that separates the more recent, modern reception of the legends of antiquity from the Greeks themselves. Hölderlin's ode would then be an allegorical lesson on how the legend of the end of antiquity was instrumentalized to form modern self-consciousness—and a lesson on the rather catastrophic consequences this can have. Considering the earlier chapters, in particular the previous discussion of Heidegger, it is difficult not to notice in the lyrically presented impulse to repeat a warning against the unreflected appropriation of the legend of the end. After all, the first destructive conflagration was a divinely sanctioned sacrifice on the path to "holy / Aether" (17.3–4); the second destruction is a hypertropic act against the generous opponent Brutus.

But this pious reading must presuppose that the text itself and its own legend stands outside of what it narrates. Yet it offers no position, no safe site from whence a warning could be uttered. Precisely its own collusion in the logic it denounces renders Hölderlin's poem pertinent to the discourse on the end of art. What appears to be a rejection of the fatal fascination with the end is itself not free of this fascination. This ambivalence determines the linguistic gesture of the entire poem. It has difficulty and little interest in distancing itself from the story it tells. At least the wise appeal at the close, despite its systematic reference to legend and childhood and youth in the first stanza, seems strangely abstract and curiously powerless in the face of the so vividly demonstrated seductiveness of legends. Who could resist the "Chaotic deeps," who does not want to surrender to the "mysterious yearning toward the chasm"? The emphatic reference in the second stanza to "a route not mine" (2.3) testifies also to the immediate jeopardy facing the poetic voice.

The closing verses—"and no doubt such lore / Is good [. . .]; yet there's also need of / One to interpret these holy legends"—suggest that the later generation has committed an error in responding to a similar crisis situation by reverting to a legend in order to restage the event of which the legend tells. In contrast to hasty identifications of legends as God's voice, desire, and command, Hölderlin's text insists on interpretation. And to whom could this task of interpretation be entrusted if not the poet, whose relation to the world of history is ultimately the subject of this poem and the others of this time? But to the extent that the poem as legend and recounting of the event already exhibits traces of an interpretive intervention, any attempts to distinguish among event, legend, and interpretation must falter. This also calls into question the interpretive role of the poet as mediator. Because the text takes on the form of a narrative intervention and tells how the event becomes a legend that in turn motivates action and brings about an event that, together with its legendary precedent, becomes for us a legend about the effects of legends, a reading of the poem must concern itself above all with the relation of event and narration, act and legend, legend and what it recounts, and with both their unity and their disjunction.

The poem begins disjunctively. The two sides of the equation in the old saying "vox populi, vox dei" are split into the title and the opening verse of the poem. Then there is the temporal disjunction between past and present as well as the semantic distinction between credence and assertion: "The voice of God I called you and thought you once, / In holy youth; and I say it still!" (1.1–2). Although "Wie wenn am Feiertage . . ." ("As on a Holiday . . . ") ends in a rupture and falls mute, the "Voice of the People" begins as a rupture. The text addresses the voice of the people as something past and in the mode of indirect speech as something once said. The voice of the poem's beginning is not God's voice and not the voice of the people, but neither is it the voice of the poet; they lend him a voice that is no longer God's voice or the people's. With a forked tongue, the voice speaks of and to a past that no longer survives except as legend: "and I say it still!"

What is said is itself nothing more than a saying, because the famous "vox populi, vox dei" is saying and discourse, word and slogan, open to many interpretations and appropriations. At the time the poem was written, this saying was given one of its most enduring reinterpretations, because "people" (*Volk*) was nobilitated by Herder and others who launched the term as a competitor to the French "nation."[6] The tumultuous history of this saying[7] shows that discourse, legend, and saying not only document events, but provoke them and can bring them about.

But there is another sense in which the first verses are merely legend, word, and discourse, because the saying, the act of speech, is split off from what is said. The affirmative saying—"and I say it still!"—is nothing more than saying. Nothing is said but the saying itself, which is in the first verse event and act. If saying, even the mere saying of a saying, can be an action that here in the first verses establishes the present of the poem with reference to past saying, then the seemingly vast gulf separating poetic subjectivity from the people and their path has narrowed. The error of the later generation has become more understandable, more likely, so to speak more possible. Their mistaken action and their active transformation of the legend into the act and the event of which it speaks was possible because saying, even that saying that only says and says no more than a saying, is already divided into act and meaning, split into the act of saying and what is said. The same poem that in the end demands the supplemental interpre-

tation of the legend creates in its first verse the conditions that make interpretation necessary and possible.

The difference between the way that the first verse deals with saying
and the way that the later generation handles the legends handed down
to them consists in the fact that the latter believe in the identity between
God's voice and the voice of the people, while the lyrical no longer does.
But that this faith has past and lingers only in the form of legend does
nothing to mitigate the effectiveness of the legend. It nonetheless has effects and brings about events. Saying, even the saying that emphatically
reduces itself to mere saying, is always exposed to the possibility of the
event.

This particular saying brings about an event long before any mention
has been made of the actual legend of the city on Xanthos. The following
verse demonstrates in a quasi-performative fashion that legends are never
only speech, because the intoxication of discourse, the flow of the legend
takes another course:

No less indifferent to our wisdom
Likewise the rivers rush on, but who does

Not love them? Always too my own heart is moved
When far away I hear those foreknowing ones,
The fleeting, by a route not mine but
Surer than mine, and more swift, roar seaward. (1.3–2.4)

This flow that sweeps over the ends of verse and stanza has consistently
been interpreted as the path of the people, distinct from the lonely path of
the poetic subject,[8] although only in the fourth stanza does the stream appear in contrast and in the singular: "So the river plunges" (4.2). Even later,
in the fifth stanza, an identification of stream and people is justified: "Chaotic deeps attract, and whole peoples too / May come to long for death"
(5.2–3). But since Lawrence Ryan's reading, the interpretational model of
the curved and the straight paths has become so engrained that one tends
to misread the text. That the shortest path back into the cosmos is also a
straight path, as Ryan takes it to be, seems questionable when rivers are at
issue. The notion of the path reduces the complexity of the river image as
it appears in the poem, which, like actual rivers, changes as the poem pro-
gresses, from plural into singular, from a mere image to a metaphor for the

people, in order finally to achieve a geographically and historically concrete location in the city on the river Xanthos.

The earliest rivers in this poem refer initially to the first distich, upon which they comment and which they reflect. How else can one explain the connective "likewise" (*auch*) in "Likewise the rivers yet rush on"? The "likewise" and the "yet" (*doch*) as faint echo of "and I say it still [*noch*]!" refer to the flow of legend and discourse that leaves behind the rupture between saying and believing, speech and what is said. The poet—if it is a poet who is speaking—listens to his own words. First invoked and said as mere saying, speech rushes along and only for that reason can it return as premonition. There is no more substantial connection, no explicit or implicit comparison between the first verse and the ones that follow, than that the flow of discourse continues like rivers. Rivers rush and speech says. Where saying occurs, what is said takes its own course. Saying and legend follow a different path from that taken by the discursive subject, and this difference is in every respect prior to the difference between poet and people.[9]

But precisely because the words flow forth from the speaking subject, who owes his voice and his speech to others, the Latin slogan "vox populi, vox dei" for instance, the rivers can signify something other than peoples and their histories. Emerging from an other and taking a different direction, rivers can return as premonitions. In Hölderlin's work, there is one word that denotes systematically the double movement of language that, coming from the past, names the past and, because every saying goes beyond what it says, opens possible futures. That word is the word for saying: *Sage* (legend). With *Sage* Hölderlin designates that which is no longer present but which just for this reason keeps the future open. Thus in "Diotima" we read: "Ach! Und da wie eine Sage, / Mir des Lebens Schöne schwand" (O! And there like a legend / life's beauty vanished from me). And in "Am Quell der Donau" ("At the Source of the Danube"): "Jetzt aber endiget, seligweinend, / Wie eine Sage der Liebe, / Mir der Gesang" (But now, like a legend of love, / Blissfully weeping, my song / Comes to its end).[10] In "Germanien" the *Sage* remains during the interim of the absent gods: "Nur als von Grabesflammen, ziehet dann / Ein goldner Rauch, die Sage, drob hinüber" (Only as from a funeral pyre henceforth / A golden smoke, the legend of it, drifts / And glimmers on around our doubting heads).[11] A very late, short poem with the title "Herbst" ("Autumn") laconically retraces the double movement of legend and all speech: "Die Sagen, die der Erde sich entfernen, / Vom Geiste der gewesen ist und wiederkehret, / Sie kehren zu der Menschheit sich, und vieles lernen / Wir aus der Zeit, die eilends sich verzehrt" (The legends that depart from the earth / Were from its spirit and return, / They return to mankind and we learn much / From the time that rapidly consumes itself).[12]

This reference to history, the initial verse suggests, results from the fact that saying always says something else as well. Only what comes from elsewhere and streams away from any speaking subject has a voice. We have a voice and can say "we" only because what we say is not our voice, but something else lends us a voice. For this reason the possessive pronoun "our" in the verse "No less indifferent to *our* wisdom" (1.3) can only be spoken once the poem has evoked and experienced as slippage the disjunction between saying and what is said: "No less indifferent to our wisdom / Likewise the rivers yet rush on."[13] This "our," which returns later in the personal pronoun "us," who are reached by the legend from the East, is based on nothing but the rupture that separates the flowing legend from what an I or a God or a people say. What belongs to us and what renders something into our possession is the fact that language is not ours; the riven, shared, and lonely experience that we have no language, no voice that would be ours and ours alone. In contrast to the divine voice, the voice of a people, the voice of mortal human beings, is always distorted by the gap between saying and what is said, act and discourse. On account of its ruptures and its fragility, human language is essentially historical, for the space of the historical is only opened by this gap between narrative and event, discourse and occurrence. Only because human language is essentially historical can saying and legend in Hölderlin's poem become a recollection of the Most High.

The distorted and distorting structure of human language, however, at the same time exposes mortals to the danger of being all too moved by the flow of language. The danger of surrendering entirely and uncontrollably to language and to saying, this danger inherent in every language and all saying, is named by the third verse:

For once they travel down their allotted paths
With open eyes, self-oblivious, too ready to

Comply with what the gods have wished them,
Only too gladly will mortal beings

Speed back into the All by the shortest way. (3.1–4.1)

Mortals are in jeopardy when they take their own path. Just then, when a poet insists that the path of rivers, the course of the legend is not this own way, mortals and the mortal poet are in the greatest danger, for they are threatened by the collapse of the difference that separates saying from acting, and hence run the risk of hypostatizing the divine. That would mean the sublation and the end of the historicity that opened as a gap. This danger is absolutely unavoidable even where mediating interpretation is emphatically insisted upon, for the interpretation of a saying is also saying.

And how could this poem, an Alcaic ode with an undulating rhythmic flow, evade this danger? The interpretation that it demands is possible for the poet and the poem only because of this danger. Interpretation would have to learn to distinguish between one way of submitting to the flow of discourse and a different sort of self-interpretation that sounds in the verse "And there beneath the stars [. . .] lies long art" (6.3, 7.1). Only here, once the presuppositions of the poem and their dangers have been recognized, could an interpretation of the text and a reading of its end begin. It would have to consider above all the relations entertained by the fifth and sixth stanzas to the events recounted in the narrative excursus, for the nonviolent calm of the earlier stanza is connected to and yet also contrasts with the tumult of the later stanza.

Hölderlin's poem is also a legend about the self-destructive involvement with sayings and traditions, in particular those legends centered around the end. But his own poetic articulation of the legend is not free of the idealist-aesthetic logic of immanent self-transcendence in the figure of the end. The text cannot emancipate itself from this logic, because according to the text, this logic is always possible where speaking and saying occur. Because the potential of this logic is localized in speaking itself, Hölderlin's critical impulse lies neither in his ambivalent posture toward the end nor in the imperative of interpretation. Decisive are rather the conditions that the text creates by speaking and the premises under which it first brings itself into poetic existence, that saying comes from elsewhere, from Latin, from the past or from the East. Saying comes from the other and takes a different path. Because saying always says something else and gives voice to something other than what is meant, it is always exposed to the possibility that it will bring about effects, give rise to events. This possibility is all the more likely when one or many lay claim to the saying that claims them. This is the case, for example, where Heidegger understands as an exclusively German-Greek dialogue Hölderlin's multilingual sayings, or when the unity of autonomy and heteronomy of all speech has been forgotten.

By critically warning against the hasty appropriation of saying, Hölderlin shows just as emphatically why a complete renunciation of this sort of saying must remain impossible; in so doing he implicitly restores the oldest level of meaning in "vox populi, vox dei." It shows up, already a cliché, in AD 798 in a letter by Alcuin to Charlemagne, in which the ruler is advised to pay this saying no mind.[14] But it had been prepared long before. In much older Greek verses from Hesiod's *Works and Days* (verses 763–64), "vox populi, vox dei" signifies the divine power of sayings and rumors: "A rumor that many peoples have repeatedly spoken will never / Entirely disappear, for a rumor itself is also a god."[15] Thus Hölderlin's poem about sayings and traditions itself returns to tradition. But in this return, the poem also opens another perspective on tradition, and on the problematic tradition of the notorious end, as well.

The center and balancing point of the volatile "Voice of the People" lies in that "holy end" (6.2) of stanzas 6 and 7. It does not reveal the end, but the rupture—"with his own two / Hands"—that is, the suicidal logic that the poem describes. But the calm emphasis on the rupture remains enclosed in the process of the poem. The desire to extract this opening by breaking out of the process that alone constitutes it as an open site, this is the "mysterious yearning," an early sign of the promise that accounts for the seductive power of the discourse of the end of art since Hegel. This discourse can be renounced or absolutized, celebrated or mourned, only until the next end. In the meantime, what remains is to go on.

Notes

CHAPTER I

1. Gottfried Benn, "Kommt," in *Gedichte in der Fassung der Erstdrucke*, ed. Bruno Hillebrand (Frankfurt a. M.: Fischer, 1982), 467.

2. On this prehistory from a literary-historical perspective, compare the concept-historical reconstruction by Hans Robert Jauß, "Das Ende der Kunstperiode—Aspekte der literarischen Revolution bei Heine, Hugo und Stendhal," in *Literaturgeschichte als Provokation* (Frankfurt a. M.: Suhrkamp, 1979), 107–43. The most convincing philosophical-historical reconstruction of the role of the end of art in Schelling and Hegel is by Odo Marquard, "Gesamtkunstwerk und Identitätssystem: Überlegungen im Anschluß an Hegels Schellingkritik," in *Aesthetica und Anaesthetica: Philosophische Überlegungen* (Paderborn: Ferdinand Schöningh, 1989), 100–112.

3. Niklas Luhmann, *Die Kunst der Gesellschaft* (Frankfurt a. M.: Suhrkamp, 1995. Translated as *Art as a Social System*, trans. Eva M. Knodt. Stanford, Calif.: Stanford University Press, 2000). On the end of art in particular, see the chapter "Self-Description," 244–315. He himself provides an example of the continuing irritation provoked by the end of art, for Luhmann cannot exclude the possibility that the end of art, inasmuch as it means the "system can also contain a self-negation of the system" (292) has not itself arrived at its end, its liminal possibilities being "by now exhausted as well" (296). Admittedly, few have seen as clearly as he that in the history of self-descriptions of the artistic system it is always a matter of the same thing. "The history of modern self-descriptions of the artistic system from romanticism via the avant-garde up to postmodernism can be subsumed under one perspective, as a variation on a single theme. What is at stake in all of them is the question of how to relate to the past within a system that has become autonomous" (303; 489). Indeed. The present study presumes to read these variations, because the system-theoretical machine deprives us of the differences that are, finally for Luhmann himself, the important thing. On the attempt to recuperate the history of aesthetics in system-theoretical terms, see Gerhard Plumpe, *Ästhetische Kommunikation der Moderne*, vol. 1, *Von Kant zu Hegel* (Opladen: Westdeutscher Verlag, 1993). On Hegel's end of art in particular, see 300–355.

4. Karl Marx, "Der 18: Brumaire des Louis Napoleon," in Karl Marx and Friedrich Engels, *Historisch-Kritische Gesamtausgabe* (Berlin, 1975), 8:115 (Marx, *Selected Writings*, ed. David McLellan [Oxford: Oxford University Press, 1977], 300).

5. Bruno Latour, *Wir sind nie modern gewesen: Versuch einer symmetrischen Anthropologie* (Frankfurt a. M.: Fischer, 1998).

6. Carl Einstein, *Die Fabrikation der Fiktionen*, ed. Sybille Penkert (Reinbek b. Hamburg: Rowohlt, 1972), 21.

7. Francis M. Nauman, *Marcel Duchamp: The Art of Making Art in the Age of Mechanical Reproduction* (Ghent: Ludion Press, 1999). In a strict sense, Duchamp's urinal is available only in its reproductions. On this, see the excellent book by Thierry de Duve, for whom Duchamp's urinal is anything but a break with tradition: *Kant After Duchamp* (Cambridge, Mass.: MIT Press, 1999). On the contrary, Duchamp validates tradition by making it visible for the first time. I am grateful to Sina Najafi for bringing this book to my attention.

8. Paul de Man, "Literary History and Literary Modernity," in *Blindness and Insight: Essays in the Rhetoric of Contemporary Criticism* (Minneapolis: University of Minnesota Press, 1983), 142–65, here 158.

9. Ibid., 161.

10. Ibid., 162. That, despite the recourse to psychoanalysis, this provides no model of literary history, as Harold Bloom's *Anxiety of Influence* would like, is demonstrated by de Man's critique of Bloom in *Blindness and Insight* (267–76). In a reflection on the role of "failure" in modern self-understanding, Werner H. Hamacher radicalizes de Man's insight by accusing the theoreticians of modernity of making themselves comfortable with the idea that disintegration is a survival mode: "In terms of its self-definition, modernity cannot be entirely serious about failure. Modernity is not serious about failure as long as it subjects itself to the principle of knowledge and links the experience of failure with the law of representational cognition." *Premises: Essays on Philosophy and Literature from Kant to Celan*, trans. Peter Fenves (Stanford, Calif.: Stanford University Press, 1996), 295. Hamacher emphatically contrasts the cognitively available dialectic of end and beginning, old and new, success and failure in the theories of modernity with the "practitioners." Not entirely surprisingly, it is up to Kafka (and Benjamin) to radicalize failure as the failure of failure.

11. "The avant-garde of 1967 repeats the deeds and gestures of the one from 1917. We are experiencing the end of the idea of modern art." Octavio Paz, "Baudelaire als Kunstkritiker," in *Essays II* (Frankfurt a. M.: Suhrkamp, 1984), 329. On the end of art in 1968, see Karl Markus Michel, "Ein Kranz für die Literatur," *Kursbuch* 15 (1968): 169–86; and in the same issue, Hans Magnus Enzensberger, "Gemeinplätze, die Neueste Literatur betreffend," 187–97.

12. For instance, by Wolfgang Welsch, "Ach, unsere Finaldiskurse . . . Wider die endlosen Reden vom Ende," in *Zukunft oder Ende: Standpunkte, Analysen,*

Entwürfe, ed. Rudolf Maresch (Munich: Klaus Boer Verlag, 1993), 23–28. In the field of art history, see Rosalind E. Krauss, *The Originality of the Avant-Garde and Other Modernist Myths* (Cambridge, Mass.: MIT Press, 1985). Long before Peter Bürger and others descried the aging of the modern, there were conservative reflections in this direction: Harold Rosenberg, *The Tradition of the New* (New York: Horizon Press, 1959); Wyndham Lewis, *The Demon of Progress in the Arts* (London: Methuen, 1954); Hans Sedlmayer, *Verlust der Mitte: Die bildende Kunst des 19. und 20. Jahrhunderts als Symptom und Symbol der Zeit* (Salzburg, 1948).

13. *Spiegel*, Kultur Extra, vol. 7, July 1997.

14. Peter Bürger, *Theorie der Avantgarde* (Frankfurt a. M.: Suhrkamp, 1974); translated as *Theory of the Avant-Garde* (Minneapolis: University of Minnesota Press, 1984).

15. Similarly Henning Ritter, "Immergleiches Spiel der Überraschungen: Die erschöpfte Freiheit der Kunst," in the *Frankfurter Allgemeine Zeitung* of 17 January 1998. In Boris Groys's attempt to conceptualize the logic of innovation of modernity as cultural economy, banalization is not a late, but rather the only, logic. Groys counters the ecological perspective that confronts us with the profaning of the logic of profanation, and therefore with the end of innovation, with the argument presupposed by this picture: "between culture and profane space, which is understood as life, nature, spontaneous folk culture, etc., firm boundaries are given, so that the entire profane space of culture can be occupied [. . .]. But the difference between valorized culture and profane space is bound to distinct positions and is constantly changing." *Über das Neue: Versuch einer Kulturökonomie* (Munich: Carl Hanser Verlag, 1992), 115. Dieter Heinrich, who considers the end of art together with the end of subjectivity, has recently attempted to describe the changes in the history of modern art so that "the evidence on which both theses of the end are based is eliminated." *Versuch über Kunst und Lesen: Subjektivität— Weltverstehen—Kunst* (Munich: Carl Hanser Verlag, 2000), 231.

16. Georg Wilhelm Friedrich Hegel, *Aesthetics: Lectures on Fine Art*, trans. T. M. Knox, 2 vols. (Oxford: Clarendon Press, 1975). All Hegel citations are from this translation, with volume and page number given in the text. Here, 1:605.

17. Werner Hamacher has exposed and pursued to its ultimate consequences, not only for art but for the problem of self-consciousness and its linguistic constitution, this sense of dramatization in general and comedy in particular in his essay "Das Ende der Kunst mit der Maske," in *Sprachen der Ironie—Sprachen des Ernstes*, ed. Karl Heinz Bohrer (Frankfurt a. M.: Suhrkamp, 1999), 121–56. Compare also Christoph Menke's *Tragödie im Sittlichen: Gerechtigkeit und Freiheit nach Hegel* (Frankfurt a. M.: Suhrkamp, 1996).

18. Hegel, *Aesthetics*, 1:607.

19. Ibid., 1:605.

20. Ibid., 1:608.

21. With direct reference to Hegel, and following Odo Marquard's compensation theorem, Wolf Lepenies similarly writes: "Art, that for so long had to compensate for the disenchantment of the world, must now come to terms with the possible end of the world. Art must surprise us, present us with alternatives, it must remind us of what has come to pass and make us believe that there is still a future." "Das Ende der Kunst und das Ende der Geschichte," in *Aufstieg und Fall der Intellektuellen in Europa* (Frankfurt a. M.: Campus Verlag, 1992), 73–95, here 94.

22. Although laden with pathos, essentially the same figure appears in the book, successful in the early 1960s, by Wladimir Weidlé, *Die Sterblichkeit der Musen: Betrachtungen über Dichtung und Kunst in unserer Zeit* (Stuttgart: Deutsche Verlagsanstalt, 1958). And even as astounding a book as Giorgio Agamben's *The Man Without Content* (Stanford, Calif.: Stanford University Press, 1994) concludes its idiosyncratic analysis of aesthetic judgment with a related figure borrowed from Heidegger; once again, the origin emerges at the end: "According to the principle by which it is only in the burning house that the fundamental architectural problem becomes visible for the first time, art, at the furthest point of its destiny, makes visible its original project" (115).

23. Thus Günther Seubold derives the conceptual monstrosity of a "generative-destructive aesthetics" from a dual reading of Adorno and Heidegger in *Das Ende der Kunst und der Paradigmenwechsel in der Ästhetik: Philosophische Untersuchungen zu Adorno, Heidegger und Gehlen in systematischer Absicht* (Freiburg: Verlag Karl Alber, 1997). More convincing by contrast are J. M. Bernstein's reflections on alienation in *The Fate of Art: Aesthetic Alienation from Kant to Derrida and Adorno* (Cambridge: Polity Press, 1992).

24. Maurice Blanchot, "Der Literaturschwund," in *Der Gesang der Sirenen: Essays zur modernen Literatur* (Munich: Carl Hanser Verlag, 1962), 265–74, here 265.

25. Thus, for instance, Karl Heinz Bohrer's emphatic plea for the modern aesthetics of suddenness in *Plötzlichkeit: Zum Augenblick des ästhetischen Scheins* (Frankfurt a. M.: Suhrkamp, 1981). He writes heroically there: "Let us not allow philosophy to legitimize the beautiful. Above all let us not allow every better discussion to freeze up before Hegel's verdict on the end of art" (86). On the other hand, Bohrer insists emphatically on the liminal character of specifically modern appearance, which he would like to defend against philosophical attacks or ideology critiques. If aesthetic appearance is a boundary experience, then heteronomy is essential to it. On ending and interruption, see Hans Jost Frey, *Der unendliche Text* (Frankfurt a. M.: Suhrkamp, 1990).

26. Christine Pries, ed., *Das Erhabene: Zwischen Grenzerfahrung und Größenwahn* (Weinheim: VCH Humaniora, 1989); Hans-Thies Lehmann, "Das Erhabene ist das Unheimliche: Zur Theorie einer Kunst des Ereignisses," in *Merkur* 487–88 (September–October 1989): 751–64. On the relation of the avant-garde to

the sublime, see Jean-François Lyotard, "Das Erhabene und die Avantgarde," in *Merkur* 424 (1984): 151 ff.

27. Marianne Schuller, "Versuch zum Abschied," in *Moderne: Verluste* (Frankfurt a. M.: Stroemfeld, 1997); Reinhard Baumgart, *Addio: Abschied von der Literatur: Variationen über ein altes Thema* (Munich: Carl Hanser Verlag, 1995), which is admittedly haunted by a phantasmatic fear of a genuinely threatening death of literature. Incomparably more elegant, by contrast, is Karl Heinz Bohrer, *Der Abschied: Theorie der Trauer* (Frankfurt a. M.: Suhrkamp, 1996). In terms of precision and radicality, little can contend with the reflections on literature as taking leave (Abschied) in the essay by Werner Hamacher, "Über einige Unterschiede zwischen der Geschichte literarischer und der Geschichte phänomenaler Ereignisse," in *Kontroversen, alte und neue, IX: Historische und aktuelle Konzepte der Literaturgeschichtsschreibung; Zwei Königskinder? Zum Verhältnis von Literatur und Literaturwissenschaft*, ed. Albrecht Schöne et al. (Tübingen: Niemeyer, 1985), 5–15.

28. Already in 1980, in his famous Adorno Prize acceptance speech, Jürgen Habermas pursued this option and confronted all attempts to sublate art with this dilemma. Jürgen Habermas, "Die Moderne—ein unvollendetes Projekt," in *Kleine philosophische Schriften 1–4* (Frankfurt a. M.: Suhrkamp, 1981), 444–64. That his plea for a therapeutic dosage of art and literature, as he formulates it at the close of the essay on the occasion of Peter Weiss's novel *The Aesthetic of Resistance*, intersects with the conservative version of the same model in Odo Marquard's understanding of art as "exile in cheerfulness" may suffice to indicate that the discourse on the end of art can be censored only at a very high price. Odo Marquard, "Exile der Heiterkeit," in *Aesthetica und Anaesthetica*, 47–63. Critical objections to the radicalization and finalization strategies with regard to the end of art are raised by Thierry de Duve. The ironic highlights of his archeology of modernity organized around a single artwork is that his decision to ignore all radicalization strategies (represented by all conceptual art) releases art and returns the aesthetic tradition—not only Hegel's, but also Kant's—to its jurisdiction.

29. Having recognized this dilemma, various reactions are possible. With Düttmann and following Adorno, one can justify and unfold the end philosophically. *Entkunstung: Überlegungen zum Ende* (Frankfurt a. M.: Suhrkamp, 2000). But once philosophy has determined the contradiction and nonidentity of any end, there can be no other history of the end, past or future, than the same old story of its contradictions, the unfolding of its constitutive contradiction. But can one really exclude the possibility that in the meantime, among the stories that are told about the end, the rumors that swirl around it, the experiences it gives rise to, something might have changed? On the other hand, one can try to extend the efforts to radicalize the end, as for instance Jean-Luc Nancy and Werner Hamacher have, with varying accents, attempted to do. See in this regard the chapter "Hegel Without End."

30. Rodolphe Gasché in *L'esprit createur* 35 (Fall 1995): 3–4, here 4 (special issue, "Beyond Aesthetics?," ed. Rodolphe Gasché).

31. Thus Elaine Scarry, famous for her book *The Body in Pain*, has published a Neoplatonic apology for beauty with the revealing pre-Kantian title *On Beauty and Being Just* (Princeton, N.J.: Princeton University Press, 1999).

32. Matei Calinescu, *Five Faces of Modernity: Modernism, Avantgarde, Decadence, Kitsch, Postmodernism* (Durham, N.C.: Duke University Press, 1987).

33. Frank Kermode, *The Sense of an Ending: Studies in the Theory of Fiction* (New York: Oxford University Press, 1967); special issue of *Yale French Studies*, "Concepts of Closure" (1986), ed. David Hult; Christiaan Hart Nibbrig, *Ästhetik der letzten Dinge* (Frankfurt a. M.: Suhrkamp, 1989).

34. See Karlheinz Stierle, "Die Wiederkehr des Endes: Zur Anthropologie der Anschauungsformen," in *Das Ende: Figuren einer Denkform*, ed. Karlheinz Stierle and Rainer Warning (Munich: Wilhelm Fink Verlag, 1996); and Reinhart Herzog, "Vom Aufhören: Darstellungsformen menschlicher Dauer im Ende," in *Das Ende*, 578–99, 283–349.

35. On this issue, see Dieter Thomä, *Erzähle dich selbst: Lebensgeschichte als philosophisches Problem* (Munich: C. H. Beck Verlag, 1998).

36. In his book *Humor als dichterische Einbildungskraft: Studien zur Erzählkunst des Poetischen Realismus* (Munich: Fink, 1976), the literary critic and historian of literary form Wolfgang Preisendanz has ventured the claim "that Hegel's *Aesthetics* likely remains the most reliable foundation for a justification of all subsequent 'constructions and forms'" (122), for it is the "greatest attempt at a history of forms" (122). I consider the relation between history of form and the end of art in more detail in "'Wiederholte Spiegelungen': Formgeschichte und Moderne bei Kommerell und Preiendanz," *Deutsche Vierteljahresschrift* 2 (June 2002).

37. Michel Foucault, *Wahnsinn und Gesellschaft* (Frankfurt a. M.: Suhrkamp, 1969), translated as *Madness and Civilization: A History of Insanity in the Age of Reason*, trans. Richard Howard (New York: Vintage, 1973).

38. In addition to de Duve, Clemens Pornschlegel has also anchored the end of art in the juridical problematic of sovereignty (*Der literarische Souverän: Zur politischen Funktion der deutschen Dichtung bei Goethe, Heidegger, Kafka und im George-Kreis* [Freiburg i. Brsg.: Rombach, 1994]). But whereas de Duve insists on the inevitability of aesthetic judgments, Pornschlegel instrumentalizes the end of art relatively unquestioningly. Having shown that poetry and literature are related to the theological-juridical disposition of the state and its sovereignty, he affirms the end of art in Goethe and Hegel as corresponding to an end of the older concept of sovereignty that cedes to new individualization and disciplinary techniques. Hegel's "prosaic reality" is the end of art in these modern techniques, which Pornschlegel finds exemplified in the "Society of the Tower" in Goethe's *Wilhelm Meisters Lehrjahre*. According to him, attempts to reanimate the poet

as sovereign in the late nineteenth and early twentieth centuries (for instance by Heidegger) all turned into political disasters because the old notion of sovereignty had long since been abdicated. In light of recent discussions of the *longue durée* of sovereignty (in Giorgio Agamben, among others), this is no longer credible. And in a narrower sense, in terms of the end of art, there can be no doubt that the end of art is a sovereign, perhaps *the* sovereign, gesture. Compare Giorgio Agamben, *Homo Sacer: Sovereignty and Bare Life*, trans. Daniel Heller-Roazen (Stanford, Calif.: Stanford University Press, 1998).

39. See Thierry de Duve, *Kant After Duchamp*, 301ff.

40. In Adorno's words: "Art needs something heterogeneous to it, in order to become art." "Kunst und Künste," in *Gesammelte Schriften*, ed. Rolf Tiedemann (Frankfurt a. M.: Suhrkamp, 1997), 1, 10, 439.

41. On rumors, see Avital Ronell, "Street-Talk," in *Finitude's Score: Essays for the End of the Millennium* (Lincoln: University of Nebraska Press, 1994), 83–104.

42. Before Heine proclaimed the end of the artistic period, its still-living incarnation warned of a threatening end of art in global communication: "Wealth and velocity is what the world admires, what everyone strives for; the railway, rapid postal systems, steamships and all possible facilitation of communication are what the educated world wants, to outbid itself, to transform itself and thereby to get stuck in mediocrity," Goethe writes to Zelter on 7 June 1825, and adds stoically, "Let us remain as much as possible in the attitude in which we arrived; we will be, with perhaps a few others, the last of an epoch that will not soon return." Cited in Karl Viëtor, *Goethe—Dichtung. Wissenschaft. Weltbild* (Bern: Francke, 1975), 561.

43. The literature on the end of art in Hegel is simply endless. Annemarie Gethmann-Siefert and Otto Pöggeler, eds., *Welt und Wirkung von Hegels Ästhetik* (Bonn: Bouvier, 1986; *Hegel-Studien*, supplemental issue 27), provide a useful survey; Willi Oelmüller, "Hegels Satz vom Ende der Kunst und das Problem der Philosophie der Kunst nach Hegel," *Philosophisches Jahrbuch* 73 (1965): 75–94; Dieter Henrich, "Kunst und Kunstphilosophie der Gegenwart (Überlegungen mit Rücksicht auf Hegel)," in *Immanente Ästhetik und Ästhetische Reflexion*, ed. Wolfgang Iser (Munich: Wilhelm Fink Verlag, 1966), 11–32; Hans-Georg Gadamer, "Ende der Kunst? Von Hegels Lehre vom Vergangenheitscharakter der Kunst bis zur Anti-Kunst von heute," in *Ende der Kunst—Zukunft der Kunst* (Munich: Deutscher Kunstverlag, 1985), 16–33.

44. Hegel, *Aesthetics*, 1:11.

45. On this and other contradictions, see Thomas M. Knox, "The Puzzle of Hegel's Aesthetics," in *Selected Essays on G. W. F. Hegel*, ed. Lawrence S. Stepelevich (Atlantic Highlands, N.J.: Humanities Press International, 1993), 2–10.

46. For a critical appraisal, see Peter Szondi, "Hegels Lehre von der Dichtung," in *Poetik und Geschichtsphilosophie I*, ed. Jean Bollack et al. (Frankfurt a. M.: Suhrkamp Verlag, 1974), 267–511.

47. Compare the close reading by Timothy Bahti, "Mournful Anthropomorphism and Its Passing: Hegel's *Aesthetics*," in *Allegories of History: Literary Historiography After Hegel* (Baltimore, Md.: Johns Hopkins University Press, 1992), 95–133.

48. The view of Hegel's thesis as his "prognosis," as one reads, for example, in the closing chapter of Peter Bürger's *Theorie der Avantgarde*, follows the same pattern, for only under these conditions can one continue to discuss whether Hegel's prognosis has or has not been fulfilled.

49. On the definition of founders of discourse or establishers of discursivity, Michel Foucault writes that authors of this sort—his examples are Freud, Marx, and by implication himself as the founder of the discourse of discourse theory— "not only made possible a certain number of analogies that could be adopted by future texts, but, as importantly, they also made possible a certain number of differences. They cleared a space for the introduction of elements other than their own, which, nevertheless, remain within the field of discourse they initiated." "What Is an Author?," in *Language, Counter-Memory, Practice: Selected Essays and Interviews*, ed. Donald F. Bouchard (Ithaca, N.Y.: Cornell University Press, 1977), 113–38, here 132.

50. Although this is the view of Peter Bürger, and following him, David Roberts as well, in *Art and Enlightenment: Aesthetic Theory After Adorno* (Lincoln: University of Nebraska Press), 1988.

51. Werner Hamacher gives a detailed discussion of this in "Pleroma—zu Genesis und Strukur einer dialektischen Hermeneutik bei Hegel," in *Georg Wilhelm Friedrich Hegel, "Der Geist des Christentums": Schriften, 1796–1800*, ed. Werner Hamacher (Frankfurt a. M.: Ullstein Verlag, 1978), 9–333. Translated as: *Pleroma—Reading in Hegel*, trans. Nicholas Walker and Simon Jarvis (Stanford, Calif.: Stanford University Press, 1998).

52. That this sort of return is still possible has been recently demonstrated by Brigitte Hilmer, whose impressive reconstruction of an antiaesthetic in Hegel's *Aesthetics: Lectures on Fine Art* neutralizes the anti-Hegelian effect. *Das Scheinen des Begriffs: Hegels Logik der Kunst* (Hegel-Deutungen, vol. 3) (Hamburg: Felix Meiner Verlag, 1998).

53. Michel Foucault, *The Archeology of Knowledge*, trans. A. M. Sheridan Smith (New York: Pantheon Books, 1972), 183: "Archeological territories may extend to 'literary' or 'philosophical' texts, as well as scientific ones."

54. Since Gadamer's great, and for good reason unsuccessful, attempt to rehabilitate the concept of tradition in *Wahrheit und Methode* (Tübingen: Mohr, 1984), theorizations of the concept of tradition have been sparse. There are, however, models, above all in the area of research on rhetoric, that have recourse, if indirectly, to the concept of tradition. And the concept appears in the context of postmodern reflective appropriations of tradition. Postmodernity distinguishes it-

self from an older concept of tradition, which it takes to be related to the concept of inheritance, whereas its contemporary tradition—that is, postmodern tradition—admits it is "invented." See Charles Jencks, "Postmodern vs. Late-Modern" in *Zeitgeist in Babylon: The Postmodernist Controversy*, ed. Ingeborg Hoesterey (Bloomington: University of Indiana Press, 1991), 4–21. That finding and inventing are not in opposition is a fact one can read already in Hegel. Acknowledging recognition that tradition is always invented and constructed does not excuse its examination. Moreover, that traditions are constructed makes them no less binding. On the construction of tradition, compare Eric Hobsbawm and Terence Ranger, eds., *The Invention of Tradition* (Cambridge: Cambridge University Press, 1992); David Gross, *The Past in Ruins: Tradition and the Critique of Modernity* (Amherst: University of Massachussetts Press, 1992); Benedict Anderson, *Imagined Communities: Reflections on the Origin and Spread of Nationalism* (London: Verso, 1991). On the role of tradition in modernity, see Thierry de Duve, *Kant After Duchamp*, 67ff.

55. See in this regard Arthur Danto, *The Philosophical Disenfranchisement of Art* (New York: Columbia University Press, 1986). In "Schwerpunkt: Arthur C. Danto and 'das Ende der Kunst,'" Alexander García Düttmann, reviewing Danto's book *Deutsche Zeitschrift für Philosophie* (1997), sharply criticizes Danto in *Kunstende: Drei ästhetische Studien* (Frankfurt a. M.: Suhrkamp, 2000), 64–70.

56. The fact that this study is concerned exclusively with texts of aesthetic philosophy does not mean that the end of art is an exclusively theoretical affair. On the contrary, it is just the discussion of the end of art that permits the mutual dependency between aesthetic theory and practice. An investigation of the end of art in art would have to examine a whole series of canonized artworks—in painting, for example, Malewitsch on the one hand and Duchamp on the other. Compare Werner Haftmann, *Malerei im 20: Jahrhundert* (Munich: Prestel-Verlag, 1954). In the field of literature, such names as Kleist and Hölderlin, Beckett and Kafka stand for a literature concerned in one way or another with the end. There are even individual works that can make the claim to be texts about the end of art, for instance Balzac's tale "The Unknown Masterpiece"; compare Hans Belting, "Das unsichtbare Meisterwerk," *DU* 12 (1997). But the propositional character of talk about the end of art can be, first, more easily elucidated in a text that has not itself already been canonized as a work of art; and second, this study hopes to demonstrate that art has nothing to fear from Hegel's so-called thesis of the end of art, except to the extent that modern art, when it brings into play the end of art, finds itself in the gravitational field of philosophy. These relations change dramatically when a philosopher assigns the end of art to an artist. This perhaps unique inversion occurs in Heidegger. See Chapter 6 of this volume, "The Same End and the Other Beginning: Heidegger."

57. Compare Philippe Lacoue-Labarthe, *La fiction du politique* (Paris: Christian Bourgois, 1987).

58. Compare Odo Marquard, "Gesamtkunstwerk und Identitätssystem."

59. Paul de Man, *Aesthetic Ideology*, ed. Andrzej Warminski (Minneapolis: University of Minnesota Press, 1996).

60. This is what Christoph Menke claims in *Die Souveränität der Kunst: Ästhetische Erfahrung nach Adorno und Derrida* (Frankfurt a. M.: Suhrkamp, 1991). He proceeds from Derrida's collapse of the boundary between art and text, and contrasts this universalized concept of text with Adorno's aesthetic self-limitation.

61. Menke's contrast of Adorno and Derrida in *Die Souveränität der Kunst* misses this asymmetry. An attempt at reconstructing the relation between art (in particular literature) and philosophy in Derrida, against the background of a specifically American Derrida reception, appears in Rodolpe Gasché, *Inventions of Difference: On Jacques Derrida* (Cambridge, Mass.: Harvard University Press, 1994).

CHAPTER 2

1. Georg Wilhelm Friedrich Hegel, *Aesthetics: Lectures on Fine Art*, 2 vols., trans. T. M. Knox (Oxford: Clarendon Press, 1975). All Hegel citations are based on this translation, with occasional minor emendations for the sake of terminological consistency. Volume and page numbers are given in the text. Here, 1:2.

2. See Jacques Derrida, "From Restricted to General Economy: A Hegelianism Without Reserve," in *Writing and Difference*, trans. Alan Bass (Chicago: University of Chicago Press, 1978), 251–77.

3. Werner Hamacher, "Das Ende der Kunst mit der Maske," 121–55; Jean-Luc Nancy, *The Muses*, trans. Peggy Kamuf (Stanford, Calif.: Stanford University Press, 1996).

4. [The "wonderful power" that makes the German word *Erinnerung* dialectical in the Hegelian sense is its positioning of memory as the transition of a past external to the present into processes internal to present awareness. *Erinnerung*, the ordinary German word for remembering, thus means literally "bringing [back] into awareness," across an implicit boundary (neither exclusively spatial nor temporal, i.e., dialectical) between outside and inside. This wonderful power does not of course survive the translation into English "remembering." Although no English word simultaneously conveys the meanings of remembering and interiorizing, "recollection," which Knox has chosen, seems closest. J.M.]

5. Jean-Luc Nancy, *La Remarque Speculative* (Paris: Galilée, 1973).

6. On digestion and eating in Hegel's early religious-philosophical writings, see Werner Hamacher, *Pleroma—Reading in Hegel*, trans. Nicholas Walker and Simon Jarvis (Stanford, Calif.: Stanford University Press, 1998); Timothy Bahti, "Mournful Anthropomorphism," 109ff.

7. Peter Szondi, "Hegels Lehre von der Dichtung."

8. Jacques Derrida provides a detailed analysis in "The Pit and the Pyramid: Introduction to Hegel's Semiology," in *Margins of Philosophy*, trans. Alan Bass (Chicago: University of Chicago Press, 1982), 69–108.

9. On the problem of the example in Hegel, see Andrezej Warminski, *Readings in Interpretation: Hölderlin, Hegel, Heidegger* (Minneapolis: University of Minnesota Press, 1987), 163–79.

10. Paul de Man, "Sign and Symbol in Hegel's *Aesthetics*," in *Aesthetic Ideology*, 91–104, here 100ff.

11. Ibid., 101.

12. Ibid., 102.

13. Ibid.

14. Ibid.

15. Hegel, *Phenomenology of Spirit*, trans. A. V. Miller (Oxford: Oxford University Press, 1977), 455, hereafter *PS*. [Although the Miller translation of the *Phänomenologie des Geistes* has gained widespread acceptance, it is by no means as accurate or elegant as Knox's translation of the *Aesthetics*, and has had to be modified considerably in light of Hegel's German and the context of the author's argument. The references in the text indicate where Miller's version of these passages can be found. J.M.]

16. Giorgio Agamben's reflections move in a similar direction, when he writes of Hegel's end of art: "His is in no way a simple eulogy but is rather a meditation on the problem of art at the outer limit of its destiny, when art loosens itself from itself and moves in pure nothingness, suspended in a kind of diaphanous limbo between no longer being and not yet being." *Man Without Content*, 53.

17. Nancy, *Muses*, 1. Further references are indicated in the text.

18. This recalls again Dieter Henrich's important interpretation of Hegel's end of art as the beginning of art as partiality in "Kunst und Philosophie der Gegenwart (Überlegungen mit Rücksicht auf Hegel)," in *Immanente Ästhetik*, 11–32.

19. That it is in fact possible to link together the heterogeneous strands of aesthetic experience (Kant) and Hegel's presentational aesthetics, and that perhaps their coarticulation was already accomplished by Hegel, has been shown in a lucid reading by Jacques Taminiaux. See "Between the Aesthetic Attitude and the Death of Art," in *Poetics, Speculation, and Judgment: The Shadow of the Work of Art from Kant to Phenomenology* (Stony Brook, N.Y.: SUNY Press, 1995), 55–72, here 69ff.

20. Werner Hamacher, "Das Ende der Kunst mit der Maske," 145.

21. Ibid.

22. Compare Christoph Menke, *Tragödie im Sittlichen*, 50ff.

23. This is apparent in the fact that Hegel invokes Goethe's epic "Hermann and Dorothea" in order to demonstrate that not only in Homer is everything domestic (1:262), but that a nonalienated existence is also possible under modern conditions: "In the cool of the day they drink a local growth, 1783, in the local

glasses which alone are suitable for Rhine wine" (1:263).

24. This is only an indication of the anticlassical features of classical art. See Peter Szondi's discussion of the mourning of the Greek gods in "Hegels Lehre von der Dichtung," 407ff.

25. Perhaps the most convincing example of anachronism in art is Hegel's anachronistic description of a contemporary Goethe bust by Rauch. The Greek gods are "raised above their own corporeality" in their beauty, Hegel writes, and continues: "In this connection the Greek gods produce an impression, despite all difference, similar to that made on me by Rauch's bust of Goethe when I first saw it" (1:483–84). The first part of the description of the regal poet that follows proceeds in an expected classical way: "this lofty brow, this powerful command-ing nose, the free eye, the round chin, [. . .] and in all the vitality of the bust, the peace, stillness, and majesty of an elderly man." But then, "and now along with this the leanness of the lips which retreat into a toothless mouth, the looseness of the neck and cheeks whereby the bridge of the nose appears still greater and the sides of the forehead still higher.—The power of this fixed shape which at bot-tom suggests immutability especially looks, in its loosely hanging mantle, like the raised head and the shape of the Oriental in his wide turban but loose outer gar-ments and shuffling slippers; it is the firm, powerful, and timeless spirit which, in the mask of encircling mortality, is on the point of letting this veil fall away and still lets it just hang freely around itself" (1:484). Where one expects a young Greek god, one finds instead a doddering old man, bedecked with the props of the sub-lime and oriental, which come from the realm of symbolic art and which don't gesture ahead to the emancipation from corporeality but back to the symbolic era. See Beat Wyss, "Klassizismus und Geschichtsphilosophie im Konflikt," in *Kun-sterfahrung und Kunstpraxis im Berlin Hegels*, ed. Annemarie Gethmann-Siefert and Otto Pöggeler (*Hegel-Studien*, supplement 22) (Bonn: Bouvier, 1983).

26. Boris Groys, *Logik der Sammlung: Am Ende des musealen Zeitalters* (Mu-nich: Carl Hanser Verlag, 1997), 10.

27. Ibid., 13.

28. Ibid. Compare Henri Pierre Jeudy, *Die Welt als Museum* (Berlin: Merve Verlag, 1987).

29. Groys, *Logik der Sammlung*, 14.

CHAPTER 3

1. References to Nietzsche in the text are given to the following translations: *The Birth of Tragedy*, in *The Birth of Tragedy and The Case of Wagner*, trans. Walter Kaufmann (New York: Vintage, 1967), hereafter *BT*; *Unfashionable Observations*, trans. Richard T. Gray (Stanford, Calif.: Stanford University Press, 1995), hereaf-ter *UO*; *Human, All Too Human*, trans. R. J. Hollingdale (Cambridge: Cambridge

University Press, 1986), hereafter *HA*; *The Gay Science*, trans. Walter Kaufmann (New York: Vintage, 1974), hereafter *GS*; *The Case of Wagner*, in *The Birth of Tragedy and The Case of Wagner*, hereafter *CW*; and *Ecce Homo*, in *On the Genealogy of Morals and Ecce Homo*, trans. Walter Kaufmann (New York: Vintage, 1989), hereafter *EH*. For the convenience of the reader with German, these references are followed by references to the German *Kritische Studienausgabe* of Niezsche's work edited by Giorgio Colli and Mazzino Montinari (15 vols.; Berlin: Walter de Gruyter, 1988), indicated as *KSA* with volume and page number. The epigraph can be found at *GS* 168; *KSA* 3:468.

2. Jürgen Habermas, "Introduction to Postmodernity: Nietzsche as Turning Point," in *The Philosophical Discourse of Modernity*, trans. Frederick G. Lawrence (Cambridge, Mass.: MIT Press, 1987), 93–107.

3. Karl Löwith, *From Hegel to Nietzsche: the Revolution in Nineteenth Century Thought*, trans. David E. Green (London: Constable, 1965). On Nietzsche's overcoming of the dialectic, see Gilles Deleuze, *Nietzsche and Philosophy*, trans. Hugh Tomlinson (New York: Columbia University Press, 1983), a translation of *Nietzsche et la philosophie* (Paris: Presse Universitaires de France, 1962).

4. Michel Foucault, "Nietzsche, Genealogy, History," in *Language, Counter-Memory, Practice*.

5. See Werner Hamacher, "Echolos," in *Nietzsche aus Frankreich*, ed. Werner Hamacher (Berlin: Ullstein, 1985), 5–14.

6. Volker Gerhardt, "Artistenmetaphysik: Zu Nietzsches frühem Programm einer ästhetischen Rechtfertigung der Welt," in *Pathos und Distanz: Studien zur Philosophie Nietzsches* (Stuttgart: Reclam, 1988), 46–72; and also see the contributions by Friedrich Kaulbach and Diana Behler in *Kunst und Wissenschaft bei Nietzsche*, ed. Mihailo Djuriac and Josef Simon (Würzburg: Königshausen & Neumann, 1986); Helmut Pfotenhauer, *Die Kunst als Physiologie: Nietzsches ästhetische Theorie und literarische Produktion* (Stuttgart: Metzler, 1985); Alexander Nehamas, *Nietzsche: Life as Literature* (Cambridge, Mass.: Harvard University Press, 1985); Eric Blondel, "Nietzsche: Life as Metaphor," in *The New Nietzsche: Contemporary Styles of Interpretation*, ed. David B. Allison (New York: Dell, 1977), 150–75.

7. De Man has shown that this delimitation and destruction of aesthetics is at bottom a rehabilitation of rhetoric in the essays "Rhetoric of Tropes (Nietzsche)" and "Rhetoric of Persuasion (Nietzsche)," both in *Allegories of Reading: Figural Language in Rousseau, Nietzsche, Rilke and Proust* (New Haven, Conn.: Yale University Press, 1979), 103–34. In this regard, see the first chapter of Anselm Haverkamp, *Figura Cryptica* (Frankfurt a. M.: Suhrkamp, 2003).

8. Werner Hamacher, "The Promise of Interpretation: Remarks on the Hermeneutic Imperative in Kant and Nietzsche," in *Premises*, 81–142.

9. Siegfried Blasche, "Hegelianismen im Umfeld von Nietzsches Geburt der Tragödie," *Nietzsche-Studien: Internationales Jahrbuch für die Nietzscheforschung* 15 (1986): 59–71.

10. Paul Valéry, "Die Krise des Geistes," in *Gesammelte Schriften* (Frankfurt a. M.: Insel Verlag, 1971), 7:98.

11. To give a further example: "From now on there is no longer any immanent evolution of the arts. All logically coherent art histories are over; absurdities no longer have any consequences: the evolution is over and what comes now already exists: syncretism and a hodge-podge of all styles and all possibilities: the post-histoire." Arnold Gehlen, *Zeit-Bilder zur Soziologie und Ästhetik der modernen Malerei* (Frankfurt: Athenäum, 1965), 206.

12. Jacques Derrida, *Spurs: Nietzsche's Styles*, trans. Barbara Harlow (Chicago: University of Chicago Press, 1978).

13. Erich Menthen, "Pathos der Distanz: Zur Struktur der ironischen Rede bei Nietzsche," in *Nietzsche oder "Die Sprache ist Rhetorik,"* ed. Josef Kopperschmidt and Helmut Schanze (Munich: Fink Verlag, 1994).

14. See Dieter Borchmeyer, ed., *Vom Nutzen und Nachteil der Historie für das Leben: Nietzsche und die Erinnerung in der Moderne* (Frankfurt a. M.: Suhrkamp, 1996).

15. This melancholy motif, which may derive from the mourning gods in Hegel's *Aesthetics*, returns much later in Walter Benjamin's artwork essay: "In the cult of remembrance of dead or absent loved ones, the cult value of the image finds its last refuge. In the fleeting expression of a human face, the aura beckons from early photographs for the last time." "The Work of Art in the Age of its Technological Reproducibility (Third Version)," trans. Harry Zohn and Edmund Jephcott, in *Selected Writings Vol. 4. 1938-1940.* ed. Michael Jennings (Cambridge: Belknap, 2003), p. 258. In German, "Das Kunstwerk im Zeitalter seiner technischen Reproduzierbarkeit," in *Gesammelte Schriften in 7 Bänden*, ed. Rolf Tiedemann et al. (Frankfurt a. M.: Suhrkamp, 1991), 1:471–508, here 1:485. Benjamin's essay, to which we will return, shows surprising parallels to Nietzsche in another respect, above all as a construction from a still-unrevealed—and for Benjamin decisively undecideable—future. See also Karl Heinz Bohrer, *Der Abschied*, 417–88.

16. On the role of rhetoric in these detours, see Philippe Lacoue-Labarthe, "The Detour," in *The Subject of Philosophy*, trans. Thomas Trezise et al. (Minneapolis: University of Minnesota Press, 1993), 14–36.

17. See Siegfried Blasche, "Hegelianismen."

18. In a reading of *The Birth of Tragedy* that follows Lacoue-Labarthe, which could well be seen as exemplary for how de Man understands deconstruction, de Man has described this common ground as a "genetic pattern," whose dilemma consists in "leading to insights that destroy the claims on which the genetic continuity was founded, but that could not have been formulated if the fallacy had not been allowed to unfold." In *Allegories of Reading*, 79–102, here 101–2. On Hegel above all, see 79–80.

19. On transposition, see also Philippe Lacoue-Labarthe, "Detour," 23–24.

20. On the deconstruction of the primacy of the Dionysian, see Paul de Man, who concedes that this insight hardly needs a deconstructive operation, because "the deconstruction of the Dionysian authority finds its arguments within the text itself." Paul de Man, "Genesis and Genealogy," in *Allegories of Reading*, 98.

21. This image, too, returns in Benjamin; at the close of Benjamin's essay on "Surrealism," one finds a reference to a "nearness [that] looks at itself through its own eyes." In *Reflections*, ed. Peter Demetz, trans. Edmund Jephcott (New York: Harcourt Brace Jovanovich, 1978), 192. Translation modified. German in *Gesammelte Schriften*, 2:309.

22. Christoph Menke, "Distanz und Experiment: Zu zwei Aspekten ästhetischer Freiheit bei Nietzsche," *Deutsche Zeitschrift für Philosophie* 41 (1993): 61–77.

23. Thus the notion of the terror of tragic knowledge, "which, merely to be endured, needs art as a protection and remedy" (*BT* 98; *KSA* 1:101), is a collateral effect and not an axiom of *The Birth of Tragedy*.

CHAPTER 4

1. Thus Gianni Vattimo, for example, claims that Benjamin's text accomplishes the "transition from utopian-revolutionary to the technological significance of the end" of art. "Tod oder Untergang der Kunst," in *Das Ende der Moderne*, trans. and ed. Rafael Capurro (Stuttgart: Reclam, 1990), 55–70, here 59.

2. Walter Benjamin, *Das Kunstwerk im Zeitalter seiner technischen Reproduzierbarkeit*, translated as "The Work of Art in the Age of Mechanical Reproduction," in *Illuminations*. This translation has been modified throughout for the present essay; for the reader's convenience, page references are nonetheless given to it (marked *I* and page number) as well as to the original German text in the seven-volume *Gesammelte Schriften* (marked *GS* with volume and page number). Here, *GS* 1:508; *I* 242.

3. Thus Samuel Weber in "Genealogy of Modernity: History, Myth and Allegory in Benjamin's *Origin of the German Mourning Play*," *Modern Language Notes* 106 (April 1991): 465–500, esp. 476. In this context, see also Peter Fenves, "Tragedy and Prophecy in Benjamin's *Origin of the German Mourning Play*," in *Arresting Language: From Leibniz to Benjamin* (Stanford, Calif.: Stanford University Press, 2000), 227–48.

4. Walter Benjamin, *Origin of German Tragic Drama*, trans. John Osborne (London: Verso, 1977), 103 (*GS* 1:281). Further references are given to this translation in the text (marked *O* and page number), together with references to the German edition in the *Gesammelte Schriften*.

5. With regard to this double criticism of Schopenhauer and Nietzsche, however, one must add that there are passages in Benjamin's book that operate in quite

the same way. Nietzsche resounds in the very diction of a passage such as the following on Protestantism: "Life itself protested against this. It feels deeply that it is not there merely to be devalued by faith" (*GS* 1:318; *O* 139).

6. As is well known, Christian Florens Rang plays an important role here, which Uwe Steiner reconstructed in *Die Geburt der Kritik aus dem Geist der Kunst: Untersuchungen zum Begriff der Kunstkritik in den frühen Schriften Walter Benjamins* (Würzburg: Könighausen & Neumann, 1989).

7. See Peter Fenves, "Tragedy and Prophecy."

8. If this failure of German Trauerspiel amounts to a tragic fate that founds a new community, then Benjamin's rivalry with Nietzsche appears as an *agon* for the dominant position in a certain tradition of German philosophy, a struggle over the right to write German (art) history, and thus finally a struggle as well over who gets to enunciate the end of art or the end of this end.

9. "Whereas phenomena determine the scope and content of the concepts which encompass them, by their existence, by what they have in common, and by their differences, their relationship to ideas is the opposite of this inasmuch as the idea, the objective interpretation of phenomena—or rather their elements—determines their relationship to each other." *GS* 1:214–15; *O* 34.

10. Nietzsche, *Unfashionable Observations*, 126 (*KSA* 1:290).

11. In this context, Benjamin as well refers to the proximity of art to science: "[T]he philosopher [. . .] occupies an elevated position between that of the scientist and the artist. [. . .] [The scientist] shares the philosopher's interest in the elimination of the merely empirical; while the artist shares with the philosopher the task of presentation [*Darstellung*]" (*GS* 1:212; *O* 32; translation modified).

12. Compare Samuel Weber, "Genealogy of Modernity."

13. "The Platonic dialogue was, as it were, the barge on which the shipwrecked ancient poetry saved itself with all her children: crowded into a narrow space and timidly submitting to the single pilot, Socrates, they now sailed into a new world." *BT* 90–91; *KSA* 1:93–94.

14. Samuel Weber has given this paradoxical passage a careful interpretation in his essay.

15. "Belief in the indestructibility of the work [. . .] was a basic mystical conviction of early Romanticism. [. . .] Formal irony [. . .] presents a paradoxical venture: through demolition to continue building on the formation, to demonstrate in the work itself its relationship to the idea." Benjamin, "The Concept of Criticism in German Romanticism," in *Selected Writings 1: 1913–1926*, ed. Marcus Bullock and Michael W. Jennings (Cambridge, Mass.: Harvard University Press, 2000), 165; *GS* 1:87.

16. On the possibility of an interpretation of Hamlet as the end of Trauerspiel, see Peter Fenves, "Marx, Mourning, Messianicity," in *Violence, Identity, and Self-Determination*, ed. Hent de Vries and Samuel Weber (Stanford, Calif.: Stanford

University Press, 1997), 253–70, esp. 264–70. Compare also Anselm Haverkamp in *Hamlet: Hypothek der Macht* (Berlin: Kadmos, 2000).

17. Weber, "Genealogy of Modernity," 500.

18. For an overview of the concept of allegory in Benjamin, see Bettine Menke, *Sprachfiguren: Name, Allegorie, Bild nach Benjamin* (Munich: Fink Verlag, 1991).

19. A retrospective consideration of the history of this canonical text appears in Hans Ulrich Gumbrecht and Michael Marrinan, eds., *Mapping Benjamin: The Work of Art in the Digital Age* (Stanford, Calif.: Stanford University Press, 2003).

20. The opening contribution by Dirk Baecker in Gumbrecht et al. is helpful in this context.

21. Jürgen Habermas and Susan Buck-Morss represent the classical positions in this debate. See Susan Buck-Morss, "Benjamin's Passagenwerk: Redeeming Mass Culture," *New German Critique* 29 (1983): 211–40; Jürgen Habermas, "Walter Benjamin: Consciousness-Raising or Rescuing Critique," in *On Walter Benjamin: Critical Essays and Recollections*, ed. Gary Smith (Cambridge, Mass.: MIT Press, 1988), 90–128.

22. Burkhardt Lindner, "Technische Reproduzierbarkeit und Kulturindustrie, Benjamins 'positives Barbarentum' im Kontext," in *Walter Benjamin im Kontext*, 2nd ed., ed. Burkhardt Lindner (Königstein/Ts: Athenäum, 1985), 180–223, here 189.

23. Theodor W. Adorno, "Einleitung zu Benjamins Schriften," in *Gesammelte Schriften*, 2:567–82, here 2:579.

24. In his notes to the *Arcades Project*, Benjamin had emphasized that in materialist works, a "precipitous close" is preferable to a refined conclusion (*GS* 5:592).

25. The objection that "fundamental relations" are independent from temporal-qualitative changes, so that capitalism as structure has remained the same from its beginnings, is refuted by Benjamin's own text, because the "fundamental relations" of reproductive technology do not in fact remain the same: "Quantity has been transmuted into quality" (*GS* 1:503; *I* 239). That holds not only for the masses to whom Benjamin is here referring, but also for the technologies of reproduction whose development in the way Benjamin presents it would be unthinkable without the masses.

26. Under such conditions, Adorno's critical regret that the reality of the culture industry appeared less positive to him than it did to Benjamin is surely insufficient; Benjamin does not even pretend that his primary concern is to describe contemporary reality. Adorno's wish for "more dialectic" (*GS* 1:1004) misses the point entirely. Benjamin could better be reproached with "too much" dialectic, for he has made his text not only the organon, but the stage of an historical-philosophical dialectic. Thus Benjamin could react calmly to Adorno's request for more dialectic in his response: "In general it seems to me that our investigations [the

artwork essay and Adorno's study "On Jazz"; E.G.] are like two spotlights directed from opposite sides on an object, rendering the contours and dimension of contemporary art recognizable in an entirely new and much more productive way than has heretofore been done" (*GS* 1:1022).

27. This is the only place in the essay where Benjamin uses the future tense. That may signify that he holds out the most hope for this development while believing in it the least. Perhaps the future tense also marks Benjamin's own uncertainty as to whether his investigation is yet science or still art. Benjamin had already thematized the connection between art and science under the aspect of the problem of presentation in the Trauerspiel book. The philosopher gains "the raised middle point between the researcher and the artist." The researcher "is linked to the philosopher through his interest in extinguishing mere empiricism, to the artist by the task of presentation" (*GS* 1:212; *O* 32).

28. Compare Rolf Tiedemann, *Dialektik im Stillstand: Versuche zum Spätwerk Walter Benjamins* (Frankfurt a. M.: Suhrkamp, 1983).

29. On the problem of pure immediacy, see Werner Hamacher, "Afformative, Strike: Benjamin's 'Critique of Violence,'" in *Walter Benjamin's Philosophy: Destruction and Experience*, ed. Andrew Benjamin and Peter Osborne (London: Routledge, 1994), 110–38.

30. As the ideal type of this mode of reception, architecture in this text is something of an exception, excluded from the quasi-typological structure of reference—quasi, because produced only through the presentation. Architecture appears immune to the historical change in function that effects all other arts: "Architecture has always represented the prototype of a work of art the reception of which is consummated by a collectivity in a state of distraction. [. . .] The human need for shelter is lasting" (*GS* 1:504; *I* 239–40). Architecture, like film in its own way, belongs to the motifs in Benjamin's thinking in which the convergence of presentation, method, and object can be manifestly demonstrated. Thresholds and of course the *Arcades* function in similar ways. See Winfried Menninghaus, *Schwellenkunde: Walter Benjamins Passage des Mythos* (Frankfurt a. M.: Suhrkamp, 1986).

31. One can consider Benjamin's essay on the storyteller as a counterexample. Its unambiguous lament over the loss of experience revealed by the degeneration of storytelling might appear to contradict the claim that loss is the mode of production of the aura. But first, storytelling, although an art "that is coming to an end" (*GS* 2:439; *I* 83), is not identical to auratic, aesthetic art; and second, there are also passages in the storyteller essay that reveal the constitutive connection between loss and maintenance: "To present someone like Leskov as a storyteller does not mean bringing him closer to us but, rather, increasing our distance from him" (*GS* 2:438; *I* 83).

32. Jürgen Habermas remarks: "Benjamin does not explain this deritualization

of art," and for lack of anything better, he turns to Max Weber's concept of disenchantment for help—a mistake, for the problem of reproduction is not the loss of enchantment, but rather the fact that it persists in the "phony enchantment of a commodity" (*GS* 1:492; *I* 231). Habermas, "Walter Benjamin: Consciousness-Raising or Rescuing Critique," in *On Walter Benjamin: Critical Essays and Recollections*, ed. Gary Smith (Cambridge, Mass.: MIT Press, 1991), 102.

33. Düttmann has drawn attention to the dialectic of tradition that Benjamin's artwork essay as a whole carries out. Düttmann is moreover one of the few critics to have recognized that the decay of the aura is not the end of art, but the end of a form of historicity tied in with it, and that the truly central theme of the essay is not art, but tradition. Alexander García Düttmann, in "Tradition and Destruction: Benjamin's Politics of Language," *Modern Language Notes* 106 (April 1991): 32–58.

CHAPTER 5

1. This has been taken to be evidence of its historical limitations. So, for instance, Burkhardt Lindner: "As far as its principle of construction is concerned, Adorno's aesthetics is a historical-philosophical ideological-critical reflection from the perspective of a (threatening) end of art." "Il faut être absolument moderne: Adornos Ästhetik: Ihr Konstruktionsprinzip und ihre Historizität," in *Materialien zur Ästhetischen Theorie: Theodor W. Adornos Konstruktion der Moderne*, ed. Burkhardt Lindner and W. Martin Lüdke (Frankfurt a. M.: Suhrkamp, 1979), 262; see also 301ff.

2. Max Horkheimer and Theodor W. Adorno, *The Dialectic of Enlightenment*, trans. John Cumming (New York: Continuum, 1972), 59. Hereafter cited as *DE*. For the reader's convenience, references are also provided throughout to the German edition of Adorno's twenty-volume *Gesammelte Schriften*, indicated as *GS* with volume number and page, here *GS* 3:78.

3. Jürgen Habermas, "Die Verschlingung von Mythos und Aufklärung: Horkheimer und Adorno," in *Der philosophische Diskurs der Moderne* (Frankfurt a. M.: Suhrkamp, 2001), 104–29. The contributions by Bolz, Seel, Reijen, and Lethen in *Vierzig Jahre Flaschenpost*, ed. Wilhelm van Reijen and Gunzelin Schmit-Noerr (Frankfurt a. M.: Fischer Verlag, 1987), are also for the most part critical. Hauke Brunkhorst offers an apologetic reading in *Theodor W. Adorno: Dialektik der Moderne* (Munich: Piper, 1990). One of the few who has taken the presentational logic of the *Dialectic of Enlightenment* into account is Fredric Jameson in *Late Marxism: Adorno, or, The Persistence of the Dialectic* (London: Verso, 1990). See also Sven Kramer, "'Wahr sind Sätze als Impuls . . .': Begriffsarbeit und sprachliche Darstellung in Adornos Reflexion auf Auschwitz," *Deutsche Vierteljaturesschrift* 2 (1996): 501–23; and Alexander García Düttmann, *Kunstende*. Only after this manuscript

had gone to press did works appear by Britta Scholze, *Kunst als Kritik: Adornos Weg aus der Dialektik* (Würzburg: Könighausen & Neumann, 2000); and Eric Krakauer, *The Disposition of the Subject: Reading Adorno's Dialectic of Technology* (Evanston, Ill.: Northwestern University Press, 1998). On the debate, see my collective review "Adorno macht's möglich: Neue Lektüren," in *Monatshefte* 94 (2002), ed. Gerhard Richter; here *GS* 3:78.

4. Compare Düttmann, *Kunstende*.

5. In an interpretation of *Minima Moralia*, I have tried to expose this dimension in the context of a different problematic. "Mega Melancholia: Adorno's *Minima Moralia*," in *Critical Theory: Current State and Future Prospects*, ed. Peter Uwe Hohendahl and Jaimey Fisher (New York: Berghahn Books, 2001), 49–68.

6. Theodor W. Adorno, *Kierkegaard: Construction of the Aesthetic*, trans. Robert Hullot-Kentor (Minneapolis: University of Minnesota Press, 1989), 6 (*GS* 2:13). All further references are to this edition and will be given in the text as *K* and page number, followed by the German reference. This is the decisive objection to any attempt to subsume Adorno's prose entirely in art. See Bernd Bräutigam, *Reflexion des Schönen—Schöne Reflexion: Überlegungen zur Prosa ästhetischer Theorie—Hamann, Nietzsche, Adorno* (Bonn: Bouvier, 1975).

7. Compare Britta Scholze, *Kunst als Kritik*, 356ff.

8. Adorno, *Aesthetic Theory*, trans. Robert Hullot-Kentor (Minneapolis: University of Minnesota Press 1997), 251 (*GS* 7:373). All further references to the English edition of this book are given in the text as *AT* with page number followed by the reference to the German edition.

9. Theodor W. Adorno, *Prisms*, trans. Samuel and Shierry Weber (Cambridge, Mass.: MIT Press, 1982), 34 (*GS* 10:30). All further references to the English edition are given in the text as *P* with page number, followed by the German reference.

10. The argument admittedly presupposes a considerably one-sided understanding of Adorno's aesthetic theory. Christoph Menke has offered an alternate reading in *Die Souveränität der Kunst*. But the dictatorial "il faut être absoluement moderne" is at least one side of Adorno's aesthetic theory, as can be seen in the following remark: "The relation to tradition is transplanted into a canon of the forbidden." Theodor W. Adorno, "Über Tradition," *GS* 10:313–14.

11. Theodor W. Adorno, *Negative Dialectics*, trans. E. B. Ashton (New York: Continuum, 1973), 362–63 (*GS* 6:355–56). All further references to the English edition are given in the text as *ND* and page number followed by the German reference.

12. A systematic exegesis of these sentences and the concept of *Versäumnis* ("neglect") in Düttmann, *Kunstende*.

13. The opening sentence of *Aesthetic Theory* is quite similar: "It is self-evident that nothing concerning art is self-evident anymore, not its inner life, not its relation to the world, not even its right to exist" (*AT* 1; *GS* 7:9).

14. Adorno's arrest of history before and after Auschwitz has its own reception history. A critical analysis of the discourse on the end of art after Auschwitz and its history in Germany (and not only in Germany) after 1945 remains to be written. But one can at least indicate at this point that the debate on artistic presentation of the Holocaust after 1989 has returned with an intensity that also has to do with the fact that the survivors and perpetrators are dying. That the debate on the appropriateness, or lack thereof, of this or that representation—first it was Spielberg's film *Schindler's List* (1993) and then Roberto Benigni's film *Life Is Beautiful* (1997) and the memoirs of Binjamin Wilkomirski (aka Bruno Grosjean Dossekker)—coincides historically with an unprecedented extension of commercialized publicity of the Holocaust in new and old media, ought to be taken into account. There has been, particularly since 1989, a tendency to use Auschwitz to ensure not the impossibility, but conversely the possibility and necessity, of an aesthetic normativity. Geoffrey Hartmann's contribution, "The Book of Destruction," in the volume *Probing the Limits of Representation: Nazism and the Final Solution*, ed. Saul Friedlander (Cambridge, Mass.: Harvard University Press, 1992), 318–34. The intensive discussion of the notion of "witness" in which Hartmann, as a co-founder of Yale University's video archive of survivors' testimony, has participated suggests a latent need to mobilize Auschwitz as a factual end of art in the service of a yet-to-be-determined, ethically imperative normative aesthetics, even if it is an aesthetics of the no longer beautiful. On this discussion, compare *"Niemand zeugt für den Zeugen": Erinnerungskultur nach der Shoah*, ed. Ulrich Baer (Frankfurt a. M.: Suhrkamp, 2000). A critical counterposition to the attempt to salvage witnessing for the sake of a potential art is argued by Giorgio Agamben in *Remnants of Auschwitz: The Witness and the Archive*, trans. Daniel Heller-Roazen (New York: Zone Books, 1999), 35ff.

15. Theodor W. Adorno, *Minima Moralia: Reflections from Damaged Life*, trans. E. F. N. Jephcott (London: Verso, 1985), 75 (*GS* 4:84). All further references to the English edition are given in the text as *MM* with the page number, followed by the German reference.

16. Compare Alexander García Düttmann, "Entkunstung," *L'esprit createur* 35 (Fall 1995): 53–65 (special issue, "Beyond Aesthetics?," ed. Rodolphe Gasché).

17. Theodor W. Adorno, *Notes to Literature*, 2 vols., trans. Shierry Weber Nicholsen (New York: Columbia University Press, 1991), 1:274–75 (*GS* 11:321). All further references to the English edition are given in the text as *NL* with volume and page number, followed by the German reference.

18. On the relation between apocalypse and mystery see Jacques Derrida's "On a Newly Arisen Apocalyptic Tone in Philosophy," as well as the excellent preface and English translation by Peter Fenves in *Raising the Tone of Philosophy* (Baltimore, Md.: Johns Hopkins University Press, 1993).

19. The role of the name was first illuminated by Alexander García Düttmann in *Das Gedächtnis des Denkens: Versuch über Heidegger und Adorno* (Frankfurt a. M.: Suhrkamp, 1991).

20. A contrary view, however, can be found in Schmitt-Noerr's contribution in *Neue Versuche, Becketts Endspiel zu verstehen: Sozialwissenschaftliches Interpretieren nach Adorno*, ed. Hans-Dieter König (Frankfurt a. M.: Suhrkamp, 1998).

21. Compare Martin Seel, "Dialektik des Erhabenen: Kommentare zur 'ästhetischen Barbarei von heute,'" in *Vierzig Jahre Flaschenpost*, ed. Wilhelm van Reijen and Gunzelin Schmid-Noerr (Frankfurt a. M.: Fischer, 1987), 11–40.

22. [This appendix to the *Dialectic of Enlightenment* is not included in the English translation—JM]

23. That the disappearance of the reciprocal and mutually conditioning domains of kitsch and avant-garde do indeed present a problem, particularly today, has been argued by Boris Groys. In a provocative essay, he has located the contemporary currents of fundamentalism in the attempt to close the divide between kitsch and art, a divide that constitutes each of them and is in principle infinite. Boris Groys, "Fundamentalismus als Mittelweg zwischen Hoch- und Massenkultur," in *Logik der Sammlung*, 63–80.

24. Michael Theunissen has said everything relevant and justifiably criticizable in this regard in "Negativität bei Adorno," in *Adorno-Konferenz 1983*, ed. Ludger von Friedeburg and Jürgen Habermas (Frankfurt a. M.: Suhrkamp, 1983), 41–64.

25. Herbert Schnädelbach, "Dialektik als Vernunftkritik: Zur Konstruktion des Rationalen bei Adorno," in *Adorno-Konferenz 1983*, 66–93.

26. Referring to Nietzsche, Jacques Derrida remarks: "No, somewhere parody always supposes a naivety withdrawing into an unconscious, a vertiginous nonmastery. Parody supposes a loss of consciousness, for were it to be absolutely calculated, it would become a confession or a law table." Jacques Derrida, *Spurs*, 101. See also Samuel Weber, "Upping the Ante: Deconstruction as Parodic Practice," in *Deconstruction is/in America: A New Sense of the Political*, ed. Anselm Haverkamp (New York: New York University Press, 1995), 60–78.

27. In an elegant interpretation, Britta Scholze has managed, however, to translate Adorno's theory of mimesis into his theory of language in the chapter "Mimesis und Ausdruck," in *Kunst als Kritik*, 136–83.

28. Compare the entry on "Parodie" in *Historisches Wörterbuch der Philosophie*, ed. Joachim Ritter et al. (Basel: Schwabe, 1971).

29. The passage on parody and discourse has a correlate and opposite in the final sentences of the excursus on Odysseus, where what is at stake is not the flow of discourse but a caesura that interrupts the narrative flow of the *Odyssey*. It concerns the Homeric description of the bloodbath that Odysseus commits among the suitors and maids. The executed maids, Homer says, "kicked out for a short while, but not for long" (*DE* 79; *GS* 3:98). Adorno and Horkheimer then remark: "But after the 'not for long' the inner flow of the narrative is arrested. Not for long? The device poses the question, and belies the author's composure. By cutting short the account, Homer prevents us from forgetting the victims, and re-

veals the unutterable eternal agony of the few seconds in which the women strug-gle with death" (*DE* 79–80; *GS* 3:99). Like parody, caesura speaks silently along with discourse, and like parody, caesura also distorts discourse at the threshold of what is no longer language and yet still belongs to it. Without saying anything, parody and caesura say what can no longer be subsumed in language. Only in this way language maintains a relation to the thought but also the nameless suffering of the dying maids.

CHAPTER 6

1. Eduard Mörike, *Sämtliche Werke*, ed. Herbert G. Göpfert (Munich: Carl Hanser Verlag, 1964), 85. The English translation follows, with slight variations, that included in the published translation of the Heidegger/Staiger exchange, identified below.

2. This was the title Staiger gave to correspondence when he published it in a collection of his essays. It is also included in Martin Heidegger, "Zu einem Vers von Mörike: Ein Briefwechsel mit Martin Heidegger und Emil Staiger," in *Gesamtausgabe* (Frankfurt a. M.: Vittorio Klostermann, 1983), vol. 13. In English, the exchange of letters appears as Berel Lang and Christine Ebel, trans., "A 1951 Dialogue on Interpretation: Emil Staiger, Martin Heidegger, Leo Spitzer," *PMLA* 105 (1990): 409–35. References in the text are to this translation, followed by the reference to the German edition in the *Gesamtausgabe* (hereafter abbreviated *GA*) of Heidegger's works, vol. 13.

3. Martin Heidegger, "The Origin of the Work of Art," in *Basic Writings*, ed. David Farrell Krell (New York: Harper & Row, 1977), 143–87. This translation is heavily abridged and does not include either the afterword or the supplement that follows the German edition, "Der Ursprung des Kunstwerks," in Martin Heidegger, *Holzwege*, 7th ed. (Frankfurt a. M.: Vittorio Klostermann, 1994), 1–74. References in the text are to this English translation where possible, followed by the reference to this edition of the German, marked as *UK* and page number. Where the cited passage is not included in Krell's translation, the present translator has rendered them and given the reference only to the German. Here, *UK* 66.

4. On this, see the chapter on Heidegger in Jay M. Bernstein's *Fate of Art*, 66–135.

5. Staiger's final letter reveals that this point escapes him when he intuitively reduces the debate to the opposition between the classical philosopher and the literary historian. "You read the poem as attesting to the poetic and the beautiful in its unchanging simplicity. I read it more as witness to the distinctive, irretrievable nature of the poetic and the beautiful realized by Mörike at the middle of the last century" (427; 13:109). That with the concept of the "particular, unrepeatable

type" he finds himself securely on the terrain of Hegel's *Aesthetics* is something that Staiger misses. Certainly he is blind to what Heidegger means by historicity, but he is not entirely mistaken in accusing Heidegger of an ahistorical classicism, as is well known. Because art for Heidegger is historical insofar as it grounds history, it is not itself historical transformation. In the same vein, Heidegger cannot perceive the poem's undecidability, for which Staiger at least retains some sensibility. Because the poem poses the decision for Heidegger, it cannot itself be indecisive in a way that might not be recuperable by philosophy.

6. In the scholarship on Heidegger, opinions differ as to whether there is even a Heideggerian philosophy of art, or if such a thing is subordinated to the entire philosophical project. See Otto Pöggeler, *Die Frage nach der Kunst: Von Hegel zu Heidegger* (Freiburg i. Brsg.: Alber, 1984); or the same author's "Kunst und Politik im Zeitalter der Technik," in *Heideggers These vom Ende der Philosophie: Verhandlungen des Leidener Heidegger-Symposions im April 1984*, ed. Marcel F. Fresco et al. (Bonn: Bouvier, 1989), 93–114; Peter Trawny, "Über die ontologische Differenz in der Kunst: Ein Rekonstruktionsversuch der Überwindung der Ästhetik bei Martin Heidegger," *Heidegger-Studien* 10 (1994): 207–21; and Christoph Jamme and Karsten Harries, ed., *Martin Heidegger: Kunst—Politik—Technik* (Munich: Wilhelm Fink Verlag, 1992). On the difference between Hegel's and Heidegger's end of art, see David Couzens Hoy, "The Owl and the Poet: Heidegger's Critique of Hegel," in *Martin Heidegger and the Question of Literature: Towards a Postmodern Literary Hermeneutics*, ed. William V. Spanos (Bloomington: Indiana University Press, 1979), 53–70.

7. On this, see Christopher Fynsk, *Heidegger: Thought and Historicity* (Ithaca, N.Y.: Cornell University Press, 1986); and Dieter Thomä, *Die Zeit des Selbst und die Zeit danach: Zur Kritik der Textgeschichte Martin Heideggers, 1910–1976* (Frankfurt a. M.: Suhrkamp, 1990).

8. Otto Pöggler, *Neue Wege mit Heidegger* (Freiburg i. Brsg.: Alber, 1992); Günter Seubold, *Kunst als Enteignis: Heideggers Weg zu einer nicht mehr metaphysischen Kunst* (Bonn: Bouvier, 1992).

9. Martin Heidegger, "Die Unmöglichkeit des Da-seins (<Die Not>) und die Kunst in der Notwendigkeit (<Die Bewinkende Be-Sinnung>)," *Heidegger-Studien* 8 (1992): 6–12, here 8.

10. Ibid., 12. The high esteem in which Heideggerians hold the *Contributions* is perhaps due to the apologetic needs of the exegetes, who see here a chance to redeem Heidegger from the reproach of classicism (and its political implications). The mythologizing of Heidegger's encounter with Cezanne and Klee, as in Pöggeler and Seubold, is also suspicious. If one can accept their insights into Heidegger's notes on Klee, then the turn to Klee, if it is in fact as Seubold describes it, would be highly problematic. That late Heidegger would be so naïve as to bury the ontic-ontological difference in a painting would truly be a regression into pure

idealism. The opposing position, that Heidegger continued to identify with the artwork essay to the end, is held by Joseph J. Kockelmann in *Heidegger on Art and Artworks* (Dordrecht: Martinus Nijhoff, 1985), 81.

11. "According to the expanded concept of artist, art is the basic occurrence of all beings; to the extent that they are, beings are self-created, created." Heidegger, *Nietzsche* (Pfullingen: Neske, 1961), 85; trans. David Farrell Krell (New York: Harper & Row, 1979). Further references are to this translation and will be given parenthetically in the text, along with the German reference marked *N*. Here, 72; *N* 85. On Heidegger's critique of Nietzsche, see David Farrell Krell, "Art and Truth in Raging Discord: Heidegger and Nietzsche on the Will to Power," in *Martin Heidegger and the Question of Literature: Towards a Postmodern Literary Hermeneutics*, ed. William V. Spanos (Bloomington: Indiana University Press, 1979), 39–52.

12. In a fragment from the early 1930s with the title "Overcoming Aesthetics," Heidegger writes of aesthetics: "The original interest in art cannot survive in it, and nonetheless it asserts itself again and again and no overcoming is reached." *Heidegger-Studien* 6 (1990): 5–7, here 6.

13. This can be trumped only by the "End of Philosophy." See Martin Heidegger, "Das Ende der Philosophie und die Aufgabe des Denkens," in *Zur Sache des Denkens* (Tübingen: Niemeyer, 1969). For a discussion of this theme, see Marcel F. Fresco et al., *Heideggers These vom Ende der Philosophie*.

14. Martin Heidegger, *Contributions to Philosophy (From En-owning)*, trans. Parvis Emad and Kenneth Maly (Bloomington: Indiana University Press, 1998), a translation of *Beiträge zur Philosophie (vom Ereignis)*, ed. Friedrich-Wilhelm Hermann (Frankfurt a. M.: Vittorio Klostermann, 1989), vol. 65 of the Heidegger *Gesamtausgabe*. References in the text will be given to the translation and the original, marked *C* and *B*, respectively. The epigraph is from *C* 289; *B* 411.

15. Already Gadamer can write, for reasons that have to do with the Hegelian heritage of hermeneutics, and so involve his own thought: "Heidegger thus renews not only a speculative aesthetics that defines the work of art as the sensible appearance of the Idea. This Hegelian definition of the Beautiful shares with Heidegger's own thinking the fundamental overcoming of the opposition between subject and object, Ego and Object, and does not describe the Being of the artwork from the standpoint of subjectivity. And yet it describes the artwork in its direction." "Nachwort," in Martin Heidegger, *Der Ursprung des Kunstwerkes*, ed. Hans Georg Gadamer (1960; Stuttgart: Reclam Verlag, 1997), 107.

16. The afterword cannot be dated. Heidegger himself writes puzzlingly in the foreword to the new edition of the text that it was "in part written later"; yet the supplement is precisely dated to the year 1956. On the editorial history of the text and the early draft published in 1989 in *Heidegger-Studien*, see Jacques Taminiaux, "The Origin of 'The Origin of the Work of Art,'" in *Reading Heidegger: Commem-*

orations, ed. John Sallis (Bloomington: Indiana University Press, 1993), 392–404.

17. Martin Heidegger, "Die Frage nach der Technik," in *Vorträge und Aufsätze* (Stuttgart: Neske, 1954; 9th ed., 2000), 9–40, here 38. [Martin Heidegger, "The Question Concerning Technology," in *Basic Writings*, 283–317, here 316.]

18. See Marc Froment-Meurice, *That Is to Say: Heidegger's Poetics*, trans. Jan Plug (Stanford, Calif.: Stanford University Press, 1998), 164.

19. This wording at the close of the afterword also indicates a latent reorientation. In the essay itself, Heidegger had written that with art, a new and essential world opened each time, that it opened with each change in the essence of truth. In the afterword, the essential transformation of art is apparently given priority over that of truth: "The history of the essence of western art corresponds to the changes in the essence of truth" (*UK* 67).

20. This reading in terms of the history of Being is supported as well by the initially enigmatic last sentence of the afterword. Art "can be understood as little through Beauty in itself as through its experience, given that the metaphysical concept of art reaches its essence" (*UK* 67). The sentence only makes sense if one assumes that "metaphysical" is here used in the same way as in the *Introduction to Metaphysics* of 1935—that is, as synonymous with Being-historical, because later it is above all aesthetics that is metaphysics, and its insufficiency is in thinking that art would here only be possible on the basis of a metaphysical concept of art. The use of the word *metaphysics* places the text in the immediate neighborhood of the introduction—that is, in the 1930s. Its meaning, on the other hand, points in the opposite direction, toward a later composition.

21. Jacques Taminiaux, *Poetics, Speculation, and Judgment.*

22. Bernstein, who positions Heidegger in the project of a "memorial aesthetics," writes: "Heidegger's end of great art thesis allows for and makes the work of remembrance integral to our engagement with works of art. In the recuperation of the essence of art we become, through remembrance, preservers of art once removed. Preservers of a possibility." *Fate of Art*, 153.

23. In the *Contributions to Philosophy*, Heidegger is even less ambiguous in this regard: "When truth occurs, then, must art be—or only under certain conditions?"

24. Already in the artwork essay there are indications that the dissolution of the concept of art in the concept of poetry is possible not least of all because with the primacy of language, the problem of the relation of Being to Dasein as well as the problem of intersubjectivity can be better addressed.

25. Peter Fenves has pointed out to me that possibility and necessity in *Being and Time* are not to be understood as categories but as existential modalities that do not exclude one another but imply one another and in the death of each Dasein come together as "certain possibility." Martin Heidegger, *Sein und Zeit* (Tübingen: Max Niemeyer, 1984), 258. [Heidegger, *Being and Time*, trans. John

Macquarrie and Edward Robinson (New York: Harper & Row, 1962), 303.] Still, it seems to me that their opposition in the context of the later artwork essay remains plausible for the purposes of the current argument.

26. The artwork essay begins with the mutual implication of art and artwork. See *UK* 1.

27. Compare Christopher Fynsk's interpretation of the concept of the work as "address" in the chapter "The Work of Art and the Question of Man," in *Heidegger: Thought and Historicity*, 131–73.

28. On this, see the discussion between Jacques Derrida and the art historian Meyer-Shapiro in *La Vérité en Peinture* (Paris: Flammarion, 1978). [Derrida, *The Truth in Painting*, trans. Ian McLeod and Geoff Bennington (Chicago: University of Chicago Press, 1987).]

29. Michel Foucault, "What Is an Author?," 116. [Translation altered].

30. Ibid., 120.

31. Ibid., 135.

32. Ibid., 115.

33. Compare Foucault's concept of "heterotopia" in "Different Spaces," *Aesthetics, Method, and Epistemology: Essential Works*, ed. James D. Faubion (New York: The New Press, 1998), 2:175–85; and Marc Auge, *Non-Lieux: Introduction Sur Une Anthropologie De La Surmodernité* (Paris: Editions de Seuil, 1992).

34. Bruno Latour, "We Have Never Been Modern," trans. Catherine Porter (Cambridge, Mass.: Harvard University Press), 76.

35. Martin Heidegger, "Hölderlins Hymne 'Der Ister,'" ed. von Walter Biemel, in *Gesamtausgabe*, vol. 55. Citations from this text are marked in the text as "Ister" and page number. The translation is by the present translator. Here, Ister, 66.

36. We can mention two here: Beda Alleman, *Hölderlin und Heidegger* (Zürich: Atlantis Verlag, 1954); and Dieter Henrich's intense efforts to illuminate Hölderlin's place in idealism in *Der Grund im Bewußtsein: Untersuchungen zu Hölderlins Denken* (Stuttgart: Klett-Cotta, 1992).

37. We quote from the second version as it appears in Friedrich Hölderlin, *Werke und Briefe*, ed. Friedrich Beißner and Jochen Schmidt (Frankfurt a. M.: Insel Verlag, 1969), 1:86ff. [English translation by Michael Hamburger in Friedrich Hölderlin, *Hyperion and Selected Poems*, ed. Eric L. Santner, German Library Volume 22 (New York: Continuum, 1990), 157–61. The translation has been slightly amended.]

CHAPTER 7

1. Friedrich Hölderlin, *Werke und Briefe*, 1:86–88. References in the text give stanza and verse. Here, 5.1. [English translation by Michael Hamburger in Friedrich Hölderlin, *Hyperion and Selected Poems*, 157–61. The translation has been

slightly amended.] Interpretations include Wolfgang Kayser, "Stimme des Volks," in *Die deutsche Lyrik: Interpretationen vom Mittelalter bis zur Romantik*, ed. Benno von Wiese (Düsseldorf: August Babel Verlag, 1967), 381–93. From a psychoanalytic perspective and with direct reference to Freud's theory of repetition, see Rainer Nägele, "Der Diskurs des Anderen: Hölderlins Ode Stimme des Volks und die Dialektik der Aufklärung," *Le Pauvre Holterling* 4/5 (1980): 61–76; Eric Santner, *Friedrich Hölderlin: Narrative Vigilance and Poetic Imagination* (New Brunswick, N.J.: Rutgers University Press, 1986), 60–62.

2. Peter Szondi, *Einführung in die literarische Hermeneutik*, ed. Jean Bollack et al. (Frankfurt a. M.: Suhrkamp, 1975), 217–323.

3. Hölderlin, *Werke und Briefe*, 1:86.

4. Hölderlin, "Der Gesichtspunkt, aus dem wir das Altertum anzusehen haben," in *Werke und Briefe*, 2:594.

5. Peter Szondi's interpretation, "Hölderlins Überwindung des Klassizismus," can be found in *Schriften I*, ed. Jean Bollack et al. (Frankfurt a. M.: Suhrkamp, 1978). Andrezej Warminski's chapter "Endpapers: Hölderlin's Textual History," in *Readings in Interpretation*, 3–22, esp. 17–22.

6. See Reinhard Koselleck's article on "Volk" und "Nation" in *Geschichtliche Grundbegriffe: Historisches Lexikon zur politisch-nationalen Sprache in Deutschland*, ed. Reinhard Koselleck et al. (Stuttgart: Klett-Cotta, 1972f.), 7:320–48.

7. See George Boas, *Vox Populi: Essays in the History of an Idea* (Baltimore, Md.: Johns Hopkins University Press, 1969).

8. Thus for instance David Constantine in *Hölderlin* (Oxford: Clarendon Press, 1990), 228. Lawrence Ryan, as well, who is so interested in fitting Hölderlin's ode into his poetological schema of alteration of tones (*Wechsel der Töne*) that he overlooks the possibility that rivers and people may not be identical. Lawrence Ryan, *Hölderlins Lehre vom Wechsel der Töne* (Stuttgart: Kohlhammer, 1960), 169–76. By contrast, Martin Heidegger, who is usually so ready to discover a *Volk*, writes: "What about rivers? They are not Gods. They are not human beings. They are not products of nature or components of the landscape. They are also not 'images' of the human 'path through life.' To say what rivers are not is hardly helpful, but aids us at least to this extent. It shows us that every determination of the essence of rivers must strike us as odd." Martin Heidegger, "Hölderlins Hymne 'Der Ister,'" *Gesamtausgabe*, 30.

9. In spite of the admittedly overdetermined semantic field of flowing and rivers, Hölderlin's work contains a series of indications that language and rivers are connected. In "Brot und Wein" (Bread and Wine) there is the reference to "das strömende Wort" (the on-rushing word) that the Gods have left behind (Hölderlin, *Werke und Briefe*, 1:115; in Hölderlin, *Hyperion and Selected Poems*, 181.) In the thematically related poem "Germanien," words and rivers are compared: "Doch Fülle der goldenen Worte sandtest du auch, / Glückselige! mit den Strömen und

sie quillen unerschöpflich / In die Gegenden all" ("Yet you, the greatly blessed, with the rivers too / Dispatched a wealth of golden words, and they well unceasing / Into all regions now"). Friedrich Hölderlin, *Werke und Briefe*, 1:155; Hölderlin, *Hyperion and Selected Poems*, 213.

10. Translated by Michael Hamburger in Hölderlin, *Hyperion and Selected Poems*, 201.

11. Ibid., 211.

12. "Der Herbst," in Friedrich Hölderlin, *Turmgedichte*, with a foreword by D. E. Sattler (Munich: Schirmer/Mosel, 1991), 33.

13. For philologically obscure but hermeneutically plausible reasons, Ryan's interpretation is based on a textual variant that has "mine" here instead of "our." That is all the more puzzling, because the interpretation Kayser published three years earlier reads "our," and according to the Frankfurt Edition, this is in agreement with almost all versions. See Friedrich Hölderlin, *Historisch-Kritische Ausgabe*, ed. D. E. Sattler (Frankfurt a. M: Roter Stern, 1984), 4:214–22.

14. See "The Proverb's Annals," in Boas, *Vox Populi*, 8–38.

15. This citation occurs, ironically enough, in just that place where the bourgeoisie gathers its rumored apercus in Büchmann's *Lexikon geflügelter Worte* (Munich: Droemer Knaur, 1959).

Bibliography

PRIMARY LITERATURE

Adorno, Theodor W. *Aesthetic Theory*. Translated by Robert Hullot-Kentor. Minneapolis: University of Minnesota Press, 1997.

———, *Gesammelte Schriften*. Edited by Rolf Tiedemann. Frankfurt a. M.: Suhrkamp, 1997.

———, *Kierkegaard: Construction of the Aesthetic*. Translated by Robert Hullot-Kentor. Minneapolis: University of Minnesota Press, 1989.

———, *Minima Moralia: Reflections from Damaged Life*. Translated by E. F. N. Jephcott. London: Verso, 1985.

———, *Negative Dialectics*. Translated by E. B. Ashton. New York: Continuum, 1973.

———, *Notes to Literature*. 2 vols. Translated by Shierry Weber Nicholsen. New York: Columbia University Press, 1991.

———, *Prisms*. Translated by Samuel and Shierry Weber. Cambridge, Mass.: MIT Press, 1982.

Benjamin, Walter. *Gesammelte Schriften in 7 Bänden*. Edited by Rolf Tiedemann et al. Frankfurt a. M.: Suhrkamp, 1991.

———, *Illuminations*. Edited by Hannah Arendt. New York: Schocken, 1969.

———, *Origin of German Tragic Drama*. Translated by John Osborne. London: Verso, 1977.

———, *Reflections*. Edited by Peter Demetz. Translated by Edmund Jephcott. New York: Harcourt Brace Jovanovich, 1978.

———, *Selected Writings 1: 1913–1926*. Edited by Marcus Bullock and Michael W. Jennings. Cambridge, Mass.: Harvard University Press, 2000.

Hegel, Georg Wilhelm Friedrich. *Aesthetics: Lectures on Fine Art*. 2 vols. Translated by T. M. Knox. Oxford: Clarendon Press, 1975.

———, *Phenomenology of Spirit*. Translated by A. V. Miller. Oxford: Oxford University Press, 1977.

Heidegger, Martin. *Being and Time*. Translated by John Macquarrie and Edward Robinson. New York: Harper & Row, 1962.

————, *Contributions to Philosophy (From En-owning)*. Translated by Parvis Emad and Kenneth Maly. Bloomington: Indiana University Press, 1998.

————, *Gesamtausgabe*. Frankfurt a. M.: Vittorio Klostermann, 1983.

————, *Holzwege*. 7th ed. Frankfurt a. M.: Vittorio Klostermann, 1994.

————, *Nietzsche*. Pfullingen: Neske, 1961.

————, *Nietzsche*. Translated by David Farrell Krell. New York: Harper & Row, 1979.

————, "The Origin of the Work of Art." In *Basic Writings*, edited by David Farrell Krell. New York: Harper & Row, 1977.

————, *Sein und Zeit*. Tübingen: Max Niemeyer, 1984.

————, "Die Unmöglichkeit des Da-seins (<Die Not>) und die Kunst in der Notwendigkeit (<Die Bewinkende Be-Sinnung>)." *Heidegger-Studien* 8 (1992).

————, *Der Ursprung des Kunstwerkes*. Edited by Hans Georg Gadamer, 1960; Stuttgart: Reclam Verlag, 1997.

————, *Vorträge und Aufsätze*. Stuttgart: Neske, 1954; 9th ed., 2000.

————, *Zur Sache des Denkens*. Tübingen: Niemeyer, 1969.

Hölderlin, Friedrich. *Historisch-Kritische Ausgabe*. Edited by D. E. Sattler. Frankfurt a. M: Roter Stern, 1984.

————, *Hyperion and Selected Poems*. Translated by Michael Hamburger. Edited by Eric L. Santner. German Library Volume 22. New York: Continuum, 1990.

————, *Turmgedichte*. Foreword by D. E. Sattler. Munich: Schirmer/Mosel, 1991.

————, *Werke und Briefe*. Edited by Friedrich Beißner and Jochen Schmidt. Frankfurt a. M.: Insel Verlag, 1969.

Horkheimer, Max, and Theodor W. Adorno. *The Dialectic of Enlightenment*. Translated by John Cumming. New York: Continuum, 1972.

Lang, Berel, and Christine Ebel, trans. "A 1951 Dialogue on Interpretation: Emil Staiger, Martin Heidegger, Leo Spitzer." *PMLA* 105 (1990).

Nietzsche, Friedrich. *The Birth of Tragedy and The Case of Wagner*. Translated by Walter Kaufmann. New York: Vintage, 1967.

————, *Ecce Homo*. In *On the Genealogy of Morals and Ecce Homo*. Translated by Walter Kaufmann. New York: Vintage, 1989.

————, *The Gay Science*. Translated by Walter Kaufmann. New York: Vintage, 1974.

————, *Human, All Too Human*. Translated by R. J. Hollingdale. Cambridge: Cambridge University Press, 1986.

————, *Kritische Studienausgabe*. Edited by Giorgio Colli and Mazzino Montinari. 15 vols. Berlin: Walter de Gruyter, 1988.

————, *Unfashionable Observations*. Translated by Richard T. Gray. Stanford, Calif.: Stanford University Press, 1995.

OTHER WORKS

Agamben, Giorgio. *Homo Sacer: Sovereignty and Bare Life*. Translated by Daniel Heller-Roazen. Stanford, Calif.: Stanford University Press, 1998.

————, *The Man Without Content*. Stanford, Calif.: Stanford University Press, 1994.

————, *Remnants of Auschwitz: The Witness and the Archive*. Translated by Daniel Heller-Roazen. New York: Zone Books, 1999.

Alleman, Beda. *Hölderlin und Heidegger*. Zürich: Atlantis Verlag, 1954.

Allison, David B., ed. *The New Nietzsche: Contemporary Styles of Interpretation*. New York: Dell, 1977.

Anderson, Benedict. *Imagined Communities: Reflections on the Origin and Spread of Nationalism*. London: Verso, 1991.

Auge, Marc. *Non-Lieux: Introduction sur une Anthropologie de la Surmodernité*. Paris: Editions de Seuil, 1992.

Baer, Ulrich, ed. *"Niemand zeugt für den Zeugen": Erinnerungskultur nach der Shoah*. Frankfurt a. M.: Suhrkamp, 2000.

Bahti, Timothy. "Mournful Anthropomorphism and Its Passing: Hegel's *Aesthetics*." In *Allegories of History: Literary Historiography After Hegel*. Baltimore, Md.: Johns Hopkins University Press, 1992.

Baumgart, Reinhard. *Addio: Abschied von der Literatur: Variationen über ein altes Thema*. Munich: Carl Hanser Verlag, 1995.

Belting, Hans. "Das unsichtbare Meisterwerk." *DU* 12 (1997).

Benn, Gottfried. *Gedichte in der Fassung der Erstdrucke*. Edited by Bruno Hillebrand. Frankfurt a. M.: Fischer, 1982.

Bernstein, J. M. *The Fate of Art: Aesthetic Alienation from Kant to Derrida and Adorno*. Cambridge: Polity Press, 1992.

Blanchot, Maurice. *Der Gesang der Sirenen: Essays zur modernen Literatur*. Munich: Carl Hanser Verlag, 1962.

Blasche, Siegfried. "Hegelianismen im Umfeld von Nietzsches Geburt der Tragödie." *Nietzsche-Studien: Internationales Jahrbuch für die Nietzscheforschung* 15 (1986).

Blondel, Eric. "Nietzsche: Life as Metaphor." In *The New Nietzsche: Contemporary Styles of Interpretation*, edited by David B. Allison. New York: Dell, 1977.

Boas, George. *Vox Populi: Essays in the History of an Idea*, Baltimore, Md.: Johns Hopkins University Press, 1969.

Bohrer, Karl Heinz. *Der Abschied: Theorie der Trauer*. Frankfurt a. M.: Suhrkamp, 1996.

————, *Plötzlichkeit: Zum Augenblick des ästhetischen Scheins.* Frankfurt a. M.: Suhrkamp, 1981.

Bohrer, Karl Heinz, ed. *Sprachen der Ironie—Sprachen des Ernstes.* Frankfurt a. M.: Suhrkamp, 1999.

Borchmeyer, Dieter, ed. *Vom Nutzen und Nachteil der Historie für das Leben: Nietzsche und die Erinnerung in der Moderne.* Frankfurt a. M.: Suhrkamp, 1996.

Bräutigam, Bernd. *Reflexion des Schönen—Schöne Reflexion: Überlegungen zur Prosa ästhetischer Theorie—Hamann, Nietzsche, Adorno.* Bonn: Bouvier, 1975.

Brunkhorst, Hauke. *Theodor W. Adorno: Dialektik der Moderne.* Munich: Piper, 1990.

Buck-Morss, Susan. "Benjamin's Passagenwerk: Redeeming Mass Culture." *New German Critique* 29 (1983).

Bürger, Peter. *Theorie der Avantgarde.* Frankfurt a. M.: Suhrkamp, 1974.

————, *Theory of the Avant-Garde.* Minneapolis: University of Minnesota Press, 1984.

Calinescu, Matei. *Five Faces of Modernity: Modernism, Avantgarde, Decadence, Kitsch, Postmodernism*, Durham: Duke University Press, 1987.

Constantine, David. *Hölderlin.* Oxford: Clarendon Press, 1990.

Danto, Arthur. *The Philosophical Disenfranchisement of Art.* New York: Columbia University Press, 1986.

Deleuze, Gilles. *Nietzsche and Philosophy.* Translated by Hugh Tomlinson. New York: Columbia University Press, 1983.

Derrida, Jacques. *Margins of Philosophy.* Translated by Alan Bass. Chicago: University of Chicago Press, 1982.

————, "On a Newly Arisen Apocalyptic Tone in Philosophy." Translated by Peter Fenves. In *Raising the Tone of Philosophy.* Baltimore, Md.: Johns Hopkins University Press, 1993.

————, *Spurs: Nietzsche's Styles.* Translated by Barbara Harlow. Chicago: University of Chicago Press, 1978.

————, *The Truth in Painting.* Translated by Ian McLeod and Geoff Bennington. Chicago: University Chicago Press, 1987.

————, *La Vérité en Peinture.* Paris: Flammarion, 1978.

————, *Writing and Difference.* Translated by Alan Bass. Chicago: University of Chicago Press, 1978.

Djuriac, Mihailo, and Josef Simon, eds. *Kunst und Wissenschaft bei Nietzsche.* Würzburg: Königshausen & Neumann, 1986.

Düttmann, Alexander García. "Entkunstung." In *L'esprit createur* 35 (Fall 1995). Special issue, "Beyond Aesthetics?," edited by Rodolphe Gasché.

————, *Das Gedächtnis des Denkens: Versuch über Heidegger und Adorno*. Frankfurt a. M.: Suhrkamp, 1991.

————, *Kunstende: Drei ästhetische Studien*. Frankfurt a. M.: Suhrkamp, 2000.

————, "Tradition and Destruction: Benjamin's Politics of Language." *Modern Language Notes* 106 (April 1991).

Duve, Thierry de. *Kant After Duchamp*. Cambridge, Mass.: MIT Press, 1999.

Einstein, Carl. *Die Fabrikation der Fiktionen*. Edited by Sybille Penkert. Reinbek b. Hamburg: Rowohlt, 1972.

Enzensberger, Hans Magnus. "Gemeinplätze, die neueste Literatur betreffend." *Kursbuch* 15 (1968).

Fenves, Peter. "Marx, Mourning, Messianicity." In *Violence, Identity and Self-Determination*, edited by Hent de Vries and Samuel Weber. Stanford, Calif.: Stanford University Press, 1997.

————, *Raising the Tone of Philosophy*. Baltimore, Md.: Johns Hopkins University Press, 1993.

————, "Tragedy and Prophecy in Benjamin's *Origin of the German Mourning Play*." In *Arresting Language: From Leibniz to Benjamin*. Stanford, Calif.: Stanford University Press, 2000.

Foucault, Michel. *Aesthetics, Method, and Epistemology: Essential Works*. Vol. 2. Edited by James D. Faubion. New York: The New Press, 1998.

————, *The Archeology of Knowledge*. Translated by A. M. Sheridan Smith. New York: Pantheon Books, 1972.

————, *Language, Counter-Memory, Practice: Selected Essays and Interviews*. Edited by Donald F. Bouchard. Ithaca, N.Y.: Cornell University Press, 1977.

————, "Nietzsche, Genealogy, History." In *Language, Counter-Memory, Practice: Selected Essays and Interviews*. Edited by Donald F. Bouchard. Ithaca, N.Y.: Cornell University Press, 1977.

————, *Wahnsinn und Gesellschaft*. Frankfurt a. M.: Suhrkamp, 1969. Translated by Richard Howard as *Madness and Civilization: A History of Insanity in the Age of Reason*. New York: Vintage, 1973.

————, "What Is an Author?" In *Language, Counter-Memory, Practice: Selected Essays and Interviews*. Edited by Donald F. Bouchard. Ithaca, N.Y.: Cornell University Press, 1977.

Fresco, Marcel F., et al., eds. *Heideggers These vom Ende der Philosophie: Verhandlungen des Leidener Heidegger-Symposions im April 1984*. Bonn: Bouvier, 1989.

Frey, Jost. *Der unendliche Text*. Frankfurt a M.: Suhrkamp, 1990.

Friedeburg, Ludger von, and Jürgen Habermas, eds. *Adorno-Konferenz 1983*. Frankfurt a. M.: Suhrkamp, 1983.

Friedlander, Saul, ed. *Probing the Limits of Representation: Nazism and the Final*

Solution. Cambridge, Mass.: Harvard University Press, 1992.

Fries, Hent de, and Samuel Weber. *Violence, Identity, and Self-Determination.* Stanford, Calif.: Stanford University Press, 1997.

Froment-Meurice, Marc. *That Is to Say: Heidegger's Poetics.* Translated by Jan Plug. Stanford, Calif.: Stanford University Press, 1998.

Fynsk, Christopher. *Heidegger: Thought and Historicity.* Ithaca, N.Y.: Cornell University Press, 1986.

Gadamer, Hans-Georg. "Ende der Kunst? Von Hegels Lehre vom Vergangenheitscharakter der Kunst bis zur Anti-Kunst von heute." In *Ende der Kunst— Zukunft der Kunst.* Munich: Deutscher Kunstverlag, 1985.

———, "Nachwort." In *Der Ursprung des Kunstwerks*, by Martin Heidegger. Edited by Hans Georg Gadamer. 1960; Stuttgart: Reclam, 1997.

———, *Wahrheit und Methode.* Tübingen: Mohr, 1984.

Gasché, Rodolpe. *Inventions of Difference: On Jacques Derrida.* Cambridge, Mass.: Harvard University Press, 1994.

Gehlen, Arnold. *Zeit-Bilder zur Soziologie und Ästhetik der modernen Malerei.* Frankfurt: Athenäum, 1965.

Gerhardt, Volker. "Artistenmetaphysik: Zu Nietzsches frühem Programm einer ästhetischen Rechtfertigung der Welt." In *Pathos und Distanz: Studien zur Philososophie Nietzsches.* Stuttgart: Reclam, 1988.

Gethmann-Siefert, Annemarie, and Otto Pöggeler, eds. *Welt und Wirkung von Hegels Ästhetik.* Bonn: Bouvier, 1986. *Hegel-Studien*, supplemental issue 27.

Geulen, Eva. "Adorno macht's möglich: Neue Lektüren." *Monatshefte* 94 (2002). Special issue on Theodor W. Adorno, edited by Gerhard Richter.

———, "Mega Melancholia: Adorno's *Minima Moralia.*" In *Critical Theory: Current State and Future Prospects*, edited by Peter Uwe Hohendahl and Jaimey Fisher. New York: Berghahn Books, 2001.

———, "'Wiederholte Spiegelungen': Formgeschichte und Moderne bei Kommerell und Preisendanz." *Deutsche Vierteljahresschrift* 2 (June 2002).

Gross, David. *The Past in Ruins: Tradition and the Critique of Modernity.* Amherst: University of Massachussetts Press, 1992.

Groys, Boris. *Logik der Sammlung: Am Ende des musealen Zeitalters.* Munich: Carl Hanser Verlag, 1997.

———, *Über das Neue: Versuch einer Kulturökonomie.* Munich: Carl Hanser Verlag, 1992.

Gumbrecht, Hans Ulrich, and Michael Marrinan, eds. *Mapping Benjamin: The Work of Art in the Digital Age.* Stanford, Calif.: Stanford University Press, 2003.

Habermas, Jürgen. "Bewußt-machende oder rettende Kritik." In *Kultur und Kri-*

tik: Verstreute Aufsätze. Frankfurt a. M.: Suhrkamp, 1977.

————, "Die Moderne—Ein unvollendetes Projekt." In *Kleine philosophische Schriften 1–4.* Frankfurt a. M.: Suhrkamp, 1981.

————, "Introduction to Postmodernity: Nietzsche as Turning Point." In *The Philosophical Discourse of Modernity.* Translated by Frederick G. Lawrence. Cambridge, Mass.: MIT Press, 1987.

————, "Die Verschlingung von Mythos und Aufklärung: Horkheimer und Adorno." In *Der philosophische Diskurs der Moderne.* Frankfurt a. M.: Suhrkamp, 2001.

————, "Walter Benjamin: Consciousness-Raising or Rescuing Critique." In *On Walter Benjamin: Critical Essays and Recollections.* Edited by Gary Smith. Cambridge, Mass.: MIT Press, 1988.

Haftmann, Werner. *Malerei im 20: Jahrhundert.* Munich: Prestel-Verlag, 1954.

Hamacher, Werner. "Affirmative, Strike: Benjamin's 'Critique of Violence.'" In *Walter Benjamin's Philosophy: Destruction and Experience.* Edited by Andrew Benjamin and Peter Osborne. London: Routledge, 1994.

————, "Echolos." In *Nietzsche aus Frankreich.* Edited by Werner Hamacher. Berlin: Ullstein, 1985.

————, "Das Ende der Kunst mit der Maske." In *Sprachen der Ironie—Sprachen des Ernstes*, edited by Karl Heinz Bohrer. Frankfurt a. M.: Suhrkamp, 1999.

————, "Pleroma—zu Genesis und Strukur einer dialektischen Hermeneutik bei Hegel." In *Georg Wilhelm Friedrich Hegel, "Der Geist des Christentums": Schriften, 1796–1800.* Edited by Werner Hamacher. Frankfurt a. M.: Ullstein Verlag, 1978.

————, *Pleroma—Reading in Hegel.* Translated by Nicholas Walker and Simon Jarvis. Stanford: Stanford University Press, 1998.

————, *Premises: Essays on Philosophy and Literature from Kant to Celan.* Translated by Peter Fenves. Stanford: Stanford University Press, 1996.

————, "Über einige Unterschiede zwischen der Geschichte literarischer und der Geschichte phänomenaler Ereignisse." In *Kontroversen, alte und neue, IX: Historische und aktuelle Konzepte der Literaturgeschichtsschreibung; Zwei Königskinder? Zum Verhältnis von Literatur und Literaturwissenschaft*, edited by Albrecht Schöne et al. Tübingen: Niemeyer, 1985.

Hart Nibbrig, Christiaan. *Ästhetik der letzten Dinge.* Frankfurt a. M.: Suhrkamp, 1989.

Hart Nibbrig, Christiaan, ed. *Was heißt darstellen.* Frankfurt a. M.: Suhrkamp, 1994.

Hartmann, Geoffrey. "The Book of Destruction." In *Probing the Limits of Representation: Nazism and the Final Solution*, edited by Saul Friedlander. Cambridge, Mass.: Harvard University Press, 1992.

Haverkamp, Anselm, ed. *Deconstruction is/in America: A New Sense of the Political.* New York: New York University Press, 1995.

———, *Figura Cryptica.* Frankfurt a. M.: Suhrkamp, 2003.

———, *Hamlet: Hypothek der Macht.* Berlin: Kadmos, 2000.

Henrich, Dieter. *Der Grund im Bewußtsein: Untersuchungen zu Hölderlins Denken,* Stuttgart: Klett-Cotta, 1992.

———, "Kunst und Kunstphilosophie der Gegenwart (Überlegungen mit Rücksicht auf Hegel)." In *Immanente Ästhetik und Ästhetische Reflexion.* Edited by Wolfgang Iser. Munich: Wilhelm Fink Verlag, 1966.

Herzog, Reinhart. "Vom Aufhören: Darstellungsformen menschlicher Dauer im Ende." In *Das Ende: Figuren einer Denkform.* Edited by Karlheinz Stierle and Rainer Warning. Munich: Wilhelm Fink Verlag, 1996.

Hilmer, Brigitte. *Das Scheinen des Begriffs: Hegels Logik der Kunst.* Hegel-Deutungen, vol. 3. Hamburg: Felix Meiner Verlag, 1998.

Hobsbawm, Eric, and Terence Ranger, eds. *The Invention of Tradition.* Cambridge: Cambridge University Press, 1992.

Hoesterey, Ingeborg, ed. *Zeitgeist in Babylon: The Postmodernist Controversy.* Bloomington: University of Indiana Press, 1991.

Hohendahl, Peter Uwe, and Jaimey Fisher, eds. *Critical Theory: Current State and Future Prospects.* New York: Berghahn Books, 2001.

Hoy, David Couzens. "The Owl and the Poet: Heidegger's Critique of Hegel." In Spanos, *Martin Heidegger and the Question of Literature.*

Iser, Wolgang, ed. *Immanente Ästhetik und Ästhetische Reflexion.* Munich: Wilhelm Fink Verlag, 1966.

Jameson, Fredric. *Late Marxism: Adorno, or The Persistence of the Dialectic.* London: Verso, 1990.

Jamme, Christoph, and Karsten Harries, eds. *Martin Heidegger: Kunst—Politik—Technik.* Munich: Wilhelm Fink Verlag, 1992.

Jauß, Hans Robert. "Das Ende der Kunstperiode—Aspekte der literarischen Revolution bei Heine, Hugo und Stendhal." In *Literaturgeschichte als Provokation.* Frankfurt a. M.: Suhrkamp, 1979.

———, *Die nicht mehr schönen Künste.* Munich: Fink, 1968.

Jencks, Charles. "Postmodern vs. Late-Modern." In *Zeitgeist in Babylon: The Postmodernist Controversy,* edited by Ingeborg Hoesterey. Bloomington: University of Indiana Press, 1991.

Jeudy, Henri Pierre. *Die Welt als Museum.* Berlin: Merve Verlag, 1987.

Kalckenbrock-Netz, Jutta. *Fabrikation, Experiment, Schöpfung: Strategien ästhetischer Legitimation im Naturalismus.* Heidelberg: Winter, 1981.

Kayser, Wolfgang. "Stimme des Volks." In *Die deutsche Lyrik: Interpretationen vom*

Mittelalter bis zur Romantik, edited by Benno von Wiese. Düsseldorf: August Babel Verlag, 1967.

Kermode, Frank. *The Sense of an Ending: Studies in the Theory of Fiction*. New York: Oxford University Press, 1967.

Knox, Thomas M. "The Puzzle of Hegel's Aesthetics." In *Selected Essays on G. W. F. Hegel*, edited by Lawrence S. Stepelevich. Atlantic Highlands, N.J.: Humanities Press International, 1993.

Kockelmann, Joseph J. *Heidegger on Art and Artworks*. Dordrecht: Martinus Nijhoff, 1985.

König, Hans-Dieter, ed. *Neue Versuche, Becketts Endspiel zu verstehen: Sozialwissenschaftliches Interpretieren nach Adorno*. Frankfurt a. M.: Suhrkamp, 1998.

Koselleck, Reinhard, et al., eds. *Geschichtliche Grundbegriffe: Historisches Lexikon zur politisch-nationalen Sprache in Deutschland*. Stuttgart: Klett-Cotta, 1972f.

Krakauer, Eric. *The Disposition of the Subject: Reading Adorno's Dialectic of Technology*. Evanston, Ill.: Northwestern University Press, 1998.

Kramer, Sven. "'Wahr sind Sätze als Impuls . . . ': Begriffsarbeit und sprachliche Darstellung in Adornos Reflexion auf Auschwitz." *Deutsche Vierteljaturesschrift* 2 (1996).

Krauss, Rosalind E. *The Originality of the Avant-Garde and Other Modernist Myths*. Cambridge, Mass.: MIT Press, 1985.

Krell, David Farell. "Art and Truth in Raging Discord: Heidegger and Nietzsche on the Will to Power." In Spanos, *Martin Heidegger and the Question of Literature*.

Lacoue-Labarthe, Philippe. "The Detour." In *The Subject of Philosophy*. Translated by Thomas Trezise et al. Minneapolis: University of Minnesota Press, 1993.

———, *La fiction du politique*. Paris: Christian Bourgois, 1987.

Latour, Bruno. *Wir sind nie modern gewesen: Versuch einer symmetrischen Anthropologie*. Frankfurt a. M.: Fischer, 1998.

Lehmann, Hans-Thies. "Das Erhabene ist das Unheimliche: Zur Theorie einer Kunst des Ereignisses." *Merkur* 487–88 (September–October 1989).

Lepenies, Wolf. "Das Ende der Kunst und das Ende der Geschichte." In *Aufstieg und Fall der Intellektuellen in Europa*. Frankfurt a. M.: Campus Verlag, 1992.

Lewis, Wyndham. *The Demon of Progress in the Arts*. London: Methuen, 1954.

Lindner, Burkhardt. "Il faut être absolument moderne: Adornos Ästhetik: Ihr Konstruktionsprinzip und ihre Historizität." In *Materialien zur Ästhetischen Theorie: Theodor W. Adornos Konstruktion der Moderne*, edited by Burkhardt Lindner and W. Martin Lüdke. Frankfurt a. M.: Suhrkamp, 1979.

———, "Technische Reproduzierbarkeit und Kulturindustrie, Benjamins 'positives Barbarentum' im Kontext." In *Walter Benjamin im Kontext*, 2nd ed. Edited by Burkhardt Lindner. Königstein/Ts: Athenäum, 1985.

Löwith, Karl. *From Hegel to Nietzsche: the Revolution in Nineteenth Century Thought.* Translated by David E. Green. London: Constable, 1965.

Luhmann, Niklas. *Die Kunst der Gesellschaft.* Frankfurt a. M.: Suhrkamp, 1995.

Lyotard, Jean-François. "Das Erhabene und die Avantgarde." *Merkur* 424 (1984).

Man, Paul de. *Aesthetic Ideology.* Edited by Andrezej Warminski. Minnesota: University of Minnesota Press, 1996.

————, *Allegories of Reading: Figural Language in Rousseau, Nietzsche, Rilke and Proust.* New Haven, Conn.: Yale University Press, 1979.

————, *Blindness and Insight: Essays in the Rhetoric of Contemporary Criticism.* Minneapolis: University of Minnesota Press, 1983.

Maresch, Rudolf, ed. *Zukunft oder Ende: Standpunkte, Analysen, Entwürfe.* Munich: Klaus Boer Verlag, 1993.

Marquard, Odo. *Aesthetica und Anaesthetica: Philosophische Überlegungen.* Paderborn: Ferdinand Schöningh, 1989.

Marx, Karl. *Selected Writings.* ed. David McLellan. Oxford: Oxford University Press, 1977.

Marx, Karl, and Friedrich Engels. *Historisch-Kritische Gesamtausgabe.* 1960. Vol. 8.

Menke, Bettine. *Sprachfiguren: Name, Allegorie, Bild nach Benjamin.* Munich: Fink Verlag, 1991.

Menke, Christoph. "Distanz und Experiment: Zu zwei Aspekten ästhetischer Freiheit bei Nietzsche." *Deutsche Zeitschrift für Philosophie* 41 (1993).

————, *Die Souveränität der Kunst: Ästhetische Erfahrung nach Adorno und Derrida.* Frankfurt a. M.: Suhrkamp, 1991.

————, *Tragödie im Sittlichen: Gerechtigkeit und Freiheit nach Hegel.* Frankfurt a. M.: Suhrkamp, 1996.

Menninghaus, Winfried. *Schwellenkunde: Walter Benjamins Passage des Mythos.* Frankfurt a. M.: Suhrkamp, 1986.

Menthen, Erich. "Pathos der Distanz: Zur Struktur der ironischen Rede bei Nietzsche." In *Nietzsche oder "Die Sprache ist Rhetorik."* Edited by Josef Kopperschmidt and Helmut Schanze. Munich: Fink Verlag, 1994.

Michel, Karl Markus. "Ein Kranz für die Literatur." *Kursbuch* 15 (1968).

Mörike, Eduard. *Sämtliche Werke.* Edited by Herbert G. Göpfert. Munich: Carl Hanser Verlag, 1964.

Nägele, Rainer. "Der Diskurs des Anderen: Hölderlins Ode Stimme des Volks und die Dialektik der Aufklärung." *Le Pauvre Holterling* 4/5 (1980).

Nancy, Jean-Luc. *The Muses.* Translated by Peggy Kamuf. Stanford: Stanford University Press, 1996.

————, *La Remarque Speculative.* Paris: Galilée, 1973.

Nauman, Francis M. *Marcel Duchamp: The Art of Making Art in the Age of Mechanical Reproduction.* Ghent: Ludion Press, 1999.

Nehamas, Alexander. *Nietzsche: Life as Literature.* Cambridge, Mass.: Harvard University Press, 1985.

Oelmüller, Willi. "Hegels Satz vom Ende der Kunst und das Problem der Philosophie der Kunst nach Hegel." *Philosophisches Jahrbuch* 73 (1965).

Paz, Octavio. "Baudelaire als Kunstkritiker." In *Essays II.* Frankfurt a. M.: Suhrkamp, 1984.

Pfotenhauer, Helmut. *Die Kunst als Physiologie: Nietzsches ästhetische Theorie und literarische Produktion.* Stuttgart: Metzler, 1985.

Plumpe, Gerhard. *Ästhetische Kommunikation der Moderne.* Vol. 1, *Von Kant zu Hegel.* Opladen: Westdeutscher Verlag, 1993.

Pöggeler, Otto. *Die Frage nach der Kunst: Von Hegel zu Heidegger.* Freiburg i. Brsg.: Alber, 1984.

———, "Kunst und Politik im Zeitalter der Technik." In *Heideggers These vom Ende der Philosophie: Verhandlungen des Leidener Heidegger-Symposions im April 1984.* Edited by Marcel F. Fresco et al. Bonn: Bouvier, 1989.

———, *Neue Wege mit Heidegger.* Freiburg i. Brsg.: Alber, 1992.

Pöggeler, Otto, and Annemarie Gethmann-Siefert, eds. *Welt und Wirkung von Hegels Ästhetik.* Bonn: Bouvier, 1986. *Hegel-Studien*, supplemental issue 27.

Pornschlegel, Clemens. *Der literarische Souverän: Zur politischen Funktion der deutschen Dichtung bei Goethe, Heidegger, Kafka und im George-Kreis.* Freiburg i. Brsg.: Rombach, 1994.

Preisendanz, Wolfgang. *Humor als dichterische Einbildungskraft: Studien zur Erzählkunst des Poetischen Realismus.* Munich: Fink, 1976.

Pries, Christine, ed. *Das Erhabene: Zwischen Grenzerfahrung und Größenwahn.* Weinheim: VCH Humaniora, 1989.

Reijen, Wilhelm van, and Gunzelin Schmid-Noerr, eds. *Vierzig Jahre Flaschenpost.* Frankfurt a. M.: Fischer Verlag, 1987.

Ritter, Henning. "Immergleiches Spiel der Überraschungen: Die erschöpfte Freiheit der Kunst." In *Frankfurter Allgemeine Zeitung,* 17 January 1998.

Ritter, Joachim, et al. *Historisches Wörterbuch der Philosophie.* Basel: Schwabe, 1971.

Roberts, David. *Art and Enlightenment: Aesthetic Theory after Adorno.* Lincoln: University of Nebraska Press, 1988.

Ronell, Avital. *Finitude's Score: Essays for the End of the Millennium.* Lincoln: University of Nebraska Press, 1994.

Rosenberg, Harold. *The Tradition of the New.* New York: Horizon Press, 1959.

Ryan, Lawrence. *Hölderlins Lehre vom Wechsel der Töne.* Stuttgart: Kohlhammer, 1960.

Santner, Eric. In *Friedrich Hölderlin: Narrative Vigilance and Poetic Imagination*. New Brunswick, N.J.: Rutgers University Press, 1986.

Scarry, Elaine. *On Beauty and Being Just*. Princeton, N.J.: Princeton University Press, 1999.

Schnädelbach, Herbert. "Dialektik als Vernunftkritik: Zur Konstruktion des Rationalen bei Adorno." In von Friedeburg and Habermas, *Adorno-Konferenz 1983*.

Scholze, Britta. *Kunst als Kritik: Adornos Weg aus der Dialektik*. Würzburg: Könighausen & Neumann, 2000.

Schuller, Marianne. "Versuch zum Abschied." In *Moderne: Verluste*. Frankfurt a. M.: Stroemfeld, 1997.

Sedlmayer, Hans. *Verlust der Mitte: Die bildende Kunst des 19. und 20. Jahrhunderts als Symptom und Symbol der Zeit*. Salzburg: Otto Müller Verlag, 1948.

Seel, Martin. "Dialektik des Erhabenen. Kommentare zur 'ästhetischen Barbarei von heute.'" In Van Reijen and Schmid-Noerr, *Vierzig Jahre Flaschenpost*.

Seubold, Günther. *Das Ende der Kunst und der Paradigmenwechsel in der Ästhetik: Philosophische Untersuchungen zu Adorno, Heidegger und Gehlen in systematischer Absicht*. Freiburg: Verlag Karl Alber, 1997.

————, *Kunst als Enteignis: Heideggers Weg zu einer nicht mehr metaphysischen Kunst*. Bonn: Bouvier, 1992.

Spanos, William V., ed. *Martin Heidegger and the Question of Literature: Towards a Postmodern Literary Hermeneutics*. Bloomington: Indiana University Press, 1979.

Staiger, Emil. *Die Kunst der Interpretation: Studien zur deutschen Literaturgeschichte*. Zürich: Atlantis, 1955.

Steiner, Uwe. *Die Geburt der Kritik aus dem Geist der Kunst: Untersuchungen zum Begriff der Kunstkritik in den frühen Schriften Walter Benjamins*. Würzburg: Könighausen & Neumann, 1989.

Stierle, Karlheinz. "Die Wiederkehr des Endes: Zur Anthropologie der Anschauungsformen." In *Das Ende: Figuren einer Denkform*, edited by Karlheinz Stierle and Rainer Warning. Munich: Wilhelm Fink Verlag, 1996.

Szondi, Peter. *Einführung in die literarische Hermeneutik*. Edited by Jean Bollack et al. Frankfurt a. M.: Suhrkamp, 1975.

————, "Hegels Lehre von der Dichtung." In *Poetik und Geschichtsphilosophie I*. Edited by Jean Bollack et al. Frankfurt a. M.: Suhrkamp Verlag, 1974.

————, "Hölderlins Überwindung des Klassizismus." In *Schriften I*, edited by Jean Bollack et al. Frankfurt a. M.: Suhrkamp, 1978.

Taminiaux, Jacques. "The Origin of 'The Origin of the Work of Art.'" In *Reading Heidegger: Commemorations*. Edited by John Sallis. Bloomington: Indiana University Press, 1993.

—, *Poetics, Speculation, and Judgment: The Shadow of the Work of Art from Kant to Phenomenology*. Stony Brook, N.Y.: SUNY Press, 1995.

Theunissen, Michael. "Negativität bei Adorno." In von Friedeburg and Habermas, *Adorno-Konferenz 1983*.

Thomä, Dieter. *Erzähle dich selbst: Lebensgeschichte als philosophisches Problem*. Munich: C. H. Beck Verlag, 1998.

—, *Die Zeit des Selbst und die Zeit danach: Zur Kritik der Textgeschichte Martin Heideggers, 1910–1976*. Frankfurt a. M.: Suhrkamp, 1990.

Tiedemann, Rolf. *Dialektik im Stillstand: Versuche zum Spätwerk Walter Benjamins*. Frankfurt a. M.: Suhrkamp, 1983.

Trawny, Peter. "Über die ontologische Differenz in der Kunst: Ein Rekonstruktionsversuch der Überwindung der Ästhetik bei Martin Heidegger." *Heidegger-Studien* 10 (1994).

Valéry, Paul. *Gesammelte Schriften*. Frankfurt a. M.: Insel Verlag, 1971.

Vattimo, Gianni. "Tod oder Untergang der Kunst." In *Das Ende der Moderne*. Translated and edited by Rafael Capurro. Stuttgart: Reclam, 1990.

Viëtor, Karl. *Goethe—Dichtung. Wissenschaft. Weltbild*. Bern: Francke, 1975.

Warminski, Andrezej. *Readings in Interpretation: Hölderlin, Hegel, Heidegger*. Minneapolis: University of Minnesota Press, 1987.

Weber, Samuel. "Genealogy of Modernity: History, Myth and Allegory in Benjamin's *Origin of the German Mourning Play*." *Modern Language Notes* 106 (April 1991).

—, "Upping the Ante: Deconstruction as Parodic Practice." In *Deconstruction is/in America: A New Sense of the Political*. Edited by Anselm Haverkamp. New York: New York University Press, 1995.

Weidlé, Wladimir. *Die Sterblichkeit der Musen: Betrachtungen über Dichtung und Kunst in unserer Zeit*. Stuttgart: Deutsche Verlagsanstalt, 1958.

Welsch, Wolfgang. "Ach, unsere Finaldiskurse . . . Wider die endlosen Reden vom Ende." In *Zukunft oder Ende: Standpunkte, Analysen, Entwürfe*, edited by Rudolf Maresch. Munich: Klaus Boer Verlag, 1993.

Wyss, Beat. "Klassizismus und Geschichtsphilosophie im Konflikt." In *Kunsterfahrung und Kunstpraxis im Berlin Hegels*, edited by Annemarie Gethmann-Siefert and Otto Pöggeler. *Hegel-Studien*, supplement 22. Bonn: Bouvier, 1983.

Yale French Studies 67 (1984). Special issue, "Concepts of Closure," edited by David Hult.

Index